"Phil Moore's new commentaries are outstanding: biblical and passionate, clear and well-illustrated, simple and profound. God's Word comes to life as you read them, and the wonder of God shines through every page."

– **Andrew Wilson**, Author of Incomparable and If God Then What?

"Want to understand the Bible better? Don't have the time or energy to read complicated commentaries? The book you have in your hand could be the answer. Allow Phil Moore to explain and then apply God's message to your life. Think of this book as the Bible's message distilled for everyone."

– **Adrian Warnock**, Christian blogger

"Phil Moore presents Scripture in a dynamic, accessible and relevant way. The bite-size chunks – set in context and grounded in contemporary life – really make the Word become flesh and dwell among us."

– **Dr David Landrum**, The Bible Society

"Through a relevant, very readable, up-to-date storying approach, Phil Moore sets the big picture, relates God's Word to today and gives us fresh insights to increase our vision, deepen our worship, know our identity and fire our imagination. Highly recommended!"

– **Geoff Knott**, former CEO of Wycliffe Bible Translators UK

"What an exciting project Phil has embarked upon! These accessible and insightful books will ignite the hearts of believers, inspire the minds of preachers and help shape a new generation of men and women who are seeking to learn from God's Word."

– **David Stroud**, Leader of ChristChurch London and author of Planting Churches, Changing Communities

For more information about the Straight to the Heart series, please go to **www.philmoorebooks.com**.
You can also receive daily messages from Phil Moore on Twitter by following **@PhilMooreLondon**.

STRAIGHT TO
THE HEART OF

Isaiah

60 BITE-SIZED INSIGHTS
Phil Moore

MONARCH
BOOKS

Oxford, UK & Grand Rapids, Michigan, USA

Published by Monarch Books
an imprint of
Lion Hudson plc
Wilkinson House, Jordan Hill
Road, Oxford OX2 8DR, England
Email: monarch@lionhudson.com
www.lionhudson.com/monarch

ISBN 978 0 85721 754 7
e-ISBN 978 0 85721 755 4

First edition 2016

Acknowledgments

Unless otherwise marked,
scripture quotations are taken
from the *Holy Bible, New
International Version* Anglicised.
Copyright © 1979, 1984, 2011
Biblica, formerly International
Bible Society. Used by permission
of Hodder & Stoughton Ltd, an
Hachette UK company. All rights
reserved. "NIV" is a registered
trademark of Biblica. UK
trademark number 1448790.
Both 1984 and 2011 versions are
quoted in this commentary.
Scripture quotations marked
"New English Translation" are
from the NET Bible copyright ©
1996–2006 by Biblical Studies
Press, L.L.C. All rights reserved.
Scripture quotations marked
"King James Version" taken from
The Authorized (King James)
Version. Rights in the Authorized
Version are vested in the Crown.
Reproduced by permission of
the Crown's patentee, Cambridge
University Press.

pp. 97, 250, 262: Extracts from
The Knowledge of the Holy by A.
W. Tozer, copyright © 1961 by
Aiden Wilson Tozer. Reprinted
by permission of HarperCollins
Publishers.
pp. 133, 134–35: Extracts from
Sit, Walk, Stand by Watchman
Nee, copyright © Watchman Nee,
1957. Used by permission of
Gospel Literature Service.
p. 215: Extract from *What's So
Amazing About Grace?* by Philip
Yancey, copyright © Philip Yancey,
1997. Used by permission of
Zondervan.
p. 258: Extract from *What Shall
This Man Do?* by Watchman Nee,
copyright © Watchman Nee,
1961. Used by permission of
Christian Literature Crusade.

A catalogue record for this book is
available from the British Library.

This book is for the Church in the West.
Arise, shine, for your light has come.

CONTENTS

PART THREE: HALF-TIME SUBSTITUTION (ISAIAH 36–39)

PART FOUR: GOD IS STRONGER THAN YOU THINK (ISAIAH 40–55)

PART FIVE: GOD IS CLOSER THAN YOU THINK (ISAIAH 56–66)

About the *"Straight to the Heart"* Series

On his eightieth birthday, Sir Winston Churchill dismissed the compliment that he was the "lion" who had defeated Nazi Germany in World War Two. He told the Houses of Parliament that *"It was a nation and race dwelling all around the globe that had the lion's heart. I had the luck to be called upon to give the roar."*

I hope that God speaks to you very powerfully through the "roar" of the books in the *Straight to the Heart* series. I hope they help you to understand the books of the Bible and the message which the Holy Spirit inspired their authors to write. I hope that they help you to hear God's voice challenging you, and that they provide you with a springboard for further journeys into each book of Scripture for yourself.

But when you hear my "roar", I want you to know that it comes from the heart of a much bigger "lion" than me. I have been shaped by a whole host of great Christian thinkers and preachers from around the world, and I want to give due credit to at least some of them here:

Terry Virgo, Dave Holden, Guy Miller, John Hosier, Adrian Holloway, Greg Haslam, Lex Loizides and all those who lead the Newfrontiers family of churches; friends and encouragers, such as Stef Liston, Joel Virgo, Stuart Gibbs, Scott Taylor, Nick Sharp, Nick Derbridge, Phil Whittall and Kevin and Sarah Aires; Tony Collins, Margaret Milton, Jenny Ward, Jessica Scott and Simon Cox at Monarch books; Malcolm Kayes and all the elders of The

Coign Church, Woking; my fellow elders and church members here at Everyday Church in London; my great friend Andrew Wilson – without your friendship, encouragement and example, this series would never have happened.

I would like to thank my parents, my brother Jonathan and my in-laws, Clive and Sue Jackson. Dad – your example birthed in my heart the passion which brought this series into being. I didn't listen to all you said when I was a child, but I couldn't ignore the way you got up at five o' clock every morning to pray, read the Bible and worship, because of your radical love for God and for his Word. I'd like to thank my children – Isaac, Noah, Esther and Ethan – for keeping me sane when publishing deadlines were looming. But most of all, I'm grateful to my incredible wife, Ruth – my friend, encourager, corrector and helper.

You all have the lion's heart, and you have all developed the lion's heart in me. I count it an enormous privilege to be the one who was chosen to sound the lion's roar.

So welcome to the *Straight to the Heart* series. My prayer is that you will let this roar grip your own heart too – for the glory of the great Lion of the Tribe of Judah, the Lord Jesus Christ!

Introduction: God is Bigger Than You Think

*With whom will you compare me or count me
equal?… I am God, and there is none like me.*

(Isaiah 46:5, 9)

If the book of Isaiah doesn't make your head hurt, you are not reading it properly. It was designed to stretch your mind and blow your senses with the greatness of God. Jesus of Nazareth understood this. It's why he quoted more from Isaiah in his teaching than from any other book in the Old Testament except for Psalms. The apostle Paul understood this too. It's why he quoted more from Isaiah in his letters than from any other book in the Old Testament. Those who know God best have always understood that the book of Isaiah gives unrivalled insight into his character. It tests our understanding to the limit as it explains to us that God is far bigger than any of us thinks.

Isaiah has a special name for God which underlines this truth. Twenty-six times Isaiah calls him *"the Holy One of Israel"*. The Hebrew word *qādōsh* is difficult to translate. The closest English words are "holy" or "sacred", but it carries the concept of "completely set apart" or "entirely in a league of its own". God is only called by this name six times in the rest of the Bible, but Isaiah makes it the very heart of his message to the Jewish nation. He wants to persuade them that all their problems stem from dragging God down to their own base level, and that their only hope lies in getting back a bigger view of God. *"'To whom will you compare me? Or who is my equal?' says the Holy One...*

'I am God, and there is no other; I am God, and there is none like me'" (40:25 and 46:9).

The first thirty-nine chapters of Isaiah are known as the "Book of Judgment". They confront the Jewish nation with God's perfect character and spell out what he will do to them unless they turn from their sinful behaviour and become like him. The final twenty-seven chapters are known as the "Book of Comfort". They console the Jewish nation with God's love and mercy, wooing them with promise after promise of what he will do for them if they turn to him and embrace him as their Saviour. Many readers see a parallel here between the thirty-nine books of the Old Testament and the twenty-seven books of the New, because the "Book of Judgment" and the "Book of Comfort" summarize the message of the entire Bible. In Isaiah, we have the Bible in miniature.

More than any other book in the Old Testament, Isaiah reveals *the depth of God's character*. In addition to God's supremacy, majesty, sovereignty and stunning generosity, Isaiah also reveals God clearly as Trinity. He tells us that God is the Father of all those who love and serve him (63:16 and 64:8), that he saves them through his Son (7:14 and 9:6) and that he promises to fill them with his Holy Spirit (32:14–15 and 44:3). Isaiah has such profound insight into God's character that he is almost single-handedly responsible for the fact that Christians call the third Person of the Trinity the Holy Spirit. When the angel Gabriel announced to Mary that she would give birth to Jesus, he used terminology from the book of Isaiah to inform her that *"The Holy Spirit will come on you... so the child to be born will be called the Holy One, the Son of God."*[1]

More than any other book in the Old Testament, Isaiah also reveals *the depth of the Gospel*. In his "Book of Judgment", Isaiah describes the vast gulf between God's character and our own,

---

[1] This is a literal translation of Luke 1:35. Isaiah 63:10 and 63:11 are the only two places in the Old Testament, except for Psalm 51:11, where the third Person of the Trinity is referred to as the *"Holy Spirit"*.

using the compelling logic of a gifted barrister to pass a guilty verdict on every man, woman and child. In his "Book of Comfort", Isaiah explains the only way in which that guilty verdict can be overturned. God will himself become a man and sacrifice his own sinless body and soul so that justice can be satisfied, even as the guilty are declared innocent of any crime. That's why Isaiah has been dubbed "the evangelist of the Old Testament" and his prophecies have been hailed as "the Romans of the Old Testament". The great fourth-century theologian Gregory of Nyssa urged the early Christians to give the book of Isaiah their avid attention because *"This great prophet knew the mystery of the religion of the gospel more perfectly than anyone else."*[2]

Consequently, more than any other book in the Old Testament, Isaiah reveals *the depth of God's great plan for world history*. Unlike most of his Jewish contemporaries, Isaiah knew that God wanted to save people from every nation of the world. He spends long chapters warning the pagan nations around Israel that God will judge them, but he also includes them in God's astonishingly merciful offer of salvation. When God the Father speaks to God the Son in Isaiah 49:6, he declares that *"It is too small a thing for you to be my servant to restore the tribes of Jacob and bring back those of Israel I have kept. I will also make you a light for the Gentiles, that my salvation may reach to the ends of the earth."* Jerome was so surprised by Isaiah's insight into this when he translated his book into Latin that he marvelled, *"All the mysteries of the Church of Christ are described so clearly that you would assume he was not prophesying about the future, but was composing a history of things past!"*[3]

We still need Isaiah's insights far more than we know. We are like my ten-year-old son, convinced that he is the greatest goalkeeper in the world because he has been playing in the

---

[2] Gregory of Nyssa, writing in c.380 AD in *Against Eunomius* (5.1).

[3] Jerome in the preface to his translation of Isaiah in c.405 AD. Some modern scholars respond by arguing that Isaiah did not write the "Book of Comfort" at all. More about this in the chapter "Isaiah Sawn in Two".

school playground far too long. We have too high a view of ourselves and too low a view of God. Reading the book of Isaiah is like stepping into goal against Manchester United in the FA Cup Final. All of our school playground assumptions evaporate in a moment – about God, about ourselves and about what is truly going on in the world.

Isaiah wants to bring you to your senses. He wants to convince you that **God is holier than you think** (Isaiah 1–12) and to warn you that **God is sterner than you think** (Isaiah 13–35). After a quick **half-time substitution** (Isaiah 36–39), he wants to change his tone with you. He wants to reassure you that **God is stronger than you think** (Isaiah 40–55) and to call you to action because **God is closer than you think** (Isaiah 56–66).

Isaiah wants his prophecies to kill off all your little-league ideas about God. He wants to free you from the naïve self-confidence which you have picked up in the playground of this world. He wants to open your eyes to the Holy One of Israel. He wants to stretch your mind and blow your senses with the reality of God.

Whoever you are and whatever your background, Isaiah has good news for you. God is far bigger than you think.

Part One:

God is Holier Than You Think

(Isaiah 1–12)

Out-of-Court Settlement
(1:1–31)

"Come now, let us settle the matter," says the Lord.
"Though your sins are like scarlet, they shall be as
white as snow."

(Isaiah 1:18)

There is a reason why the New Testament emphasizes Isaiah's boldness in Romans 10:20. The prophet doesn't mince his words. He begins his book with a single verse of introduction, simply stating his father's name and dating his prophecies between 740 and 686 BC. Then he rushes straight into words of confrontation.[1] He has no time for small talk. God has commanded him to put the nation of Judah on trial, urging it to accept an out-of-court settlement while it still can.

Even Isaiah's brief words of introduction serve a legal purpose. They name the plaintiff and the defendant in a trial. Isaiah claims to have been given divine authority to prosecute the nation of Judah and its capital city Jerusalem.[2] Its people believe that God is pleased with them, since they are enjoying a period of greater prosperity than at any time since the death of King Solomon in 930 BC and the breakaway of the ten northern tribes of Israel, but Isaiah testifies in the courtroom of chapter

---

[1] Isaiah 6:1 tells us he began to prophesy in the final year of King Uzziah of Judah (792–740 BC). He prophesied throughout the reigns of Jotham (750–732 BC), Ahaz (735–715 BC) and Hezekiah (715–686 BC).

[2] The Hebrew word *hāzōn* in 1:1 is only ever used in the Old Testament to describe a prophetic *vision*.

1 that they are deluded.[3] God has seen their sinfulness and he is about to bring down the full force of the Jewish Law upon them.

In 1:2–4, Isaiah calls two witnesses into God's courtroom. He calls the earth and sky to testify about the sins of Judah. The ox and the donkey are smart enough to submit to their masters, but the people of Judah are too dumb to submit to the one who feeds them by making rain fall down from the sky and crops grow up from the ground. They have the Holy One of Israel as their Father, yet they despise him. They prefer to act like the children of corrupt evildoers rather than the children of God.[4]

In 1:5–9, Isaiah begs his fellow countrymen to repent. They are stupider than a donkey if they choose to feel God's whip instead of eating from his hand. The prophet appeals to them tenderly, addressing the mountain on which Jerusalem is built as *"Daughter Zion"*.[5] Since the Jewish Law dictates that those who rebel against their parents must die (Deuteronomy 21:18–21), he begs them to turn back to their Father before their sin completely destroys them. God has already disciplined them through the Aramean invasion of 734–732 BC.[6] They have been surrounded and outnumbered by their enemies, like a tiny shed in the middle of a field of cucumbers. God has been merciful and has preserved for them a remnant of survivors, but

---

[3] The Lord never fully recognized the schism between the ten northern and two southern tribes of Israel. That's why he still refers to the southern kingdom of Judah as "Israel" throughout Isaiah.

[4] Isaiah presents their choice as a satanic parody of their calling. He says that Abraham's *seed* has become the *seed* of evildoers (*zera'*) and has exchanged God's *heavyweight* glory for *heavyweight* guilt (*kābēd*).

[5] Isaiah refers to Jerusalem as *Zion* 47 times, more than any other book in the Bible. As the book progresses, this affectionate personification of Jerusalem expands to include all of God's New Covenant people.

[6] Isaiah's prophecies do not always appear in chronological order. Isaiah 1–5 dates from the 730s BC and Isaiah 6 from 740 BC. Chapter 1 appears where it does to serve as a helpful summary of the book as a whole.

their time is running out.[7] God's courtroom is about to pass a clear verdict on them: They are guilty.

In 1:10–17, Isaiah invokes a legal precedent. Everybody in Jerusalem knew what God had done to the sinful cities of Sodom and Gomorrah in Genesis 19, so Isaiah accuses Jerusalem of being no better.[8] God is not impressed with their many sacrifices at the Temple, because blood sacrifice is worthless unless it is accompanied by hearts that turn away from sin.[9] Nor is God impressed with their religious festivals, their incense or their prayers. Without heartfelt repentance, these acts of hypocrisy actually make their conduct even more repulsive to God.[10] Isaiah's legal precedent should make Judah tremble. It warns them that they cannot pull the wool over God's eyes.

That's why what Isaiah says in 1:18–20 is so astonishing. If you find the start to this book of prophecies harsh, read these verses slowly. Everything about God's courtroom cries out that the people of Judah are guilty and need to be punished. Reliable witnesses, the Jewish Law and legal precedent all bear united testimony against them. The people of Judah have no excuse for their prosperous complacency, allowing God's blessing to make them neglect God's Word and, as a result, oppress the poor.[11] Their hands are not merely black with sin; they are scarlet and crimson with the blood of the workers and widows and orphans

---

[7] One of the big themes of Isaiah is that God will always save a *remnant* of the Jewish nation (37:32; 46:3). Paul quotes this verse in Romans 9:29 to restate the promise even after the Jews crucified their Messiah.

[8] Ezekiel 16:46–48 goes one step further and tells the people of Judah that they are even worse than Sodom.

[9] Repentance cannot save us without God's blood sacrifice (Hebrews 9:22), but nor can God's blood sacrifice save us without our repentance (Matthew 3:8; Acts 26:20). Both elements are required.

[10] The Bible warns us repeatedly that the Lord hates hypocritical prayer. See Proverbs 15:8; 28:9; Zechariah 7:13; Hebrews 5:7; James 5:16; 1 Peter 3:7, 12.

[11] Isaiah warns us in 1:17 that we need to *"learn to do right"*. Neglecting Bible study isn't just foolish. It is fatal.

that they have failed to deliver from harm.[12] Justice demands that their bloodguilt be atoned for by swift execution – when suddenly God offers them an out-of-court settlement: *"Come now, let us settle the matter. Though your sins are like scarlet, they shall be as white as snow; though they are red as crimson, they shall be like wool."*

Suddenly we see why Isaiah refuses to mince his words in God's courtroom. He does not want to condemn his nation, but to startle it into accepting God's gracious offer of salvation. He does not explain yet how God can be at the same time both just and merciful towards the guilty. We will have to wait until chapter 53 for a full explanation. For now, he simply tells enough for the people of Judah to see that they ought to grab hold of his offer with both hands.

That's why, in 1:21–31, Isaiah warns them that they are standing in the same place as did their ancestors in the final chapters of Deuteronomy. God is offering them a stark choice between his blessing and his curse, between devouring food from his hand and being devoured by his sword,[13] between worshipping idols under sacred trees and becoming trees of righteousness themselves,[14] between pouring out their lives as God's choice wine and forcing God to pour out his anger upon them, between spiritual prostitution and a rediscovery of their calling to be God's Faithful City.[15] Will they choose to be God's

---

[12] One of the most sobering aspects of the warning in Isaiah 1 is that God treats our sins of passivity as seriously as our sins of active evil. See also Micah 6:8; James 1:27; 4:17.

[13] The same Hebrew word *'ākal* is used for both types of *devouring* in 1:19 and 1:20.

[14] God promises to punish them for worshipping fertility gods in this way by making them utterly infertile, but if they turn back to him he promises to turn them into *"oaks of righteousness"* themselves (61:3).

[15] The Hebrew words are the same for *Faithful City* in 1:21 and 1:26. James 1:27 looks back to Isaiah 1 and to a similar prophecy in Micah 6:8 when it tells us that this is the kind of religion that the holy God demands.

children or God's enemies? Will they accept God's merciful out-of-court settlement?

Isaiah still prophesies these words to you and me. He still asks us if we will join the ranks of those who complain that God has been unfair towards them, or if we will recognize that our great need from God isn't justice but mercy. To help us make our decision, in 1:24, Isaiah uses one of the fullest names for God in the entire Bible. He calls him *"the Lord, the Lord Almighty, the Mighty One of Israel"*.

God is far holier and far more powerful in judging sin than most people think. So don't be a fool. Accept his generous offer of an out-of-court settlement today.

What Unites the Nations
(2:1–22)

In the last days the mountain of the Lord's temple will be established as the highest of the mountains; it will be exalted above the hills, and all nations will stream to it.

(Isaiah 2:2)

When I was last in New York City, I decided to visit the headquarters of the United Nations. On the wall outside was an enormous inscription from Isaiah 2: *"They shall beat their swords into ploughshares and their spears into pruning hooks. Nation shall not lift up sword against nation, neither shall they learn war any more."*

Now I don't want to be unfair to the United Nations. It has accomplished a remarkable amount since the end of World War Two. But whoever chiselled that inscription didn't understand what Isaiah is saying. He isn't promising that we will live in peace with one another if we discuss our differences instead of rushing to take up arms. He is warning us that we will never live in peace with one another unless we allow God to deal with the sin that divides us, deep down in our hearts.

In 2:2, Isaiah tells us that true peace is always a miracle from God. Zion was a puny mountain. It wasn't even the highest mountain in the region. At only 765 metres high, it was 55 metres smaller than the Mount of Olives, let alone Mount Everest, towering twelve times taller. Nevertheless, Isaiah prophesies that the Lord will make it *"the highest of the mountains"* by making its message the key to world peace. The United Nations encourages self-centred nations to butt their heads against one another in boardrooms instead of on battlefields, but the Lord promises to give the world true peace by going to the heart of the problem and dealing a killer blow to the self-centredness that divides us. Isaiah uses the Hebrew word *nāhar*, which means *to flow like a river*, to underline that this will be a miracle. Rivers always flow downhill, never uphill, yet God will cause the nations to stream up the slopes of Mount Zion together.

In 2:3–4, Isaiah tells us that true peace will only come when the nations confess their rebellion and respond to God's generous offer of an out-of-court settlement. That's what the sculptor at the United Nations headquarters failed to grasp. The second half of 2:4 makes no sense without the rest of the verse and the wider passage. Isaiah is saying that a day is coming when people from every nation will respond to God's command in 1:17 to *"Learn to do right"* and will ask him to *"teach us his ways, so that we may walk in his paths"*. They will unlearn war with one another when they learn to side with God against sin. Only then will true peace come, when the holy God turns people from every nation into his new holy city, a New Jerusalem on a New Mount Zion, a missionary city holding out his message of peace to the world.[1]

In 2:6–9, we discover how much we need God to work this miracle within us. The people of Judah resolved to follow him but have failed. They have become entirely infected with sin. Isaiah addresses these four verses to the Lord, confessing that Jerusalem's merchants have traded away their national calling to be holy. Instead of exporting the Word of God, they have imported superstitions from the east, witchcraft from the west and idols from the north and south. Instead of demonstrating the greatness of their God to the world, they have come to rely on their stockpiles of silver and gold. Their ever-growing army

---

[1] The word for teach in 2:3 is the Hebrew verb *yārāh* and the word for *law* in 2:3 is its Hebrew noun *tōrāh*, meaning *teaching*. Peace can only come through people learning God's Word and teaching it to others.

of warhorses and chariots testifies that they are nothing like the peaceful missionary city which Isaiah has just described.[2] When Isaiah cries out to the Lord, *"Do not forgive them!"*, it is the cry of justice. Isaiah passes sentence on them in God's courtroom. By rejecting his out-of-court settlement, they have chosen to experience the full force of the Law.[3]

In 2:10–21, Isaiah describes their day of judgment. Before God can make the New Jerusalem flourish in humility, he must first demolish the Old Jerusalem in its pride. God will not find this difficult. One tiny glimpse of *"the fearful presence of the Lord and the splendour of his majesty"* will be enough to flatten every tall tree, every towering mountain, every lofty castle and every mighty galleon.[4] As soon as they see God as he really is, they will throw away their puny idols to where only underground moles and cave-dwelling bats will be able to see them. Isaiah warns the people of Jerusalem that their true enemy is not the Aramean soldiers who have invaded Judah, but the sinful pride that has invaded their hearts.[5] It is at work inside them like a deadly cancer.

In 2:22, Isaiah gives us the punchline: *"Stop trusting in mere humans, who have but a breath in their nostrils. Why hold them in esteem?"* Those first four Hebrew words could just as easily be translated, *"Give up on man!"* They form a deliberate contrast with the phrase he used three times in 2:10, 2:19 and 2:21, because human schemes to unite the nations are no match for *"the fearful presence of the Lord and the splendour of*

---

[2] Deuteronomy 17:16–17 expressly forbade this because it would foster fatal self-reliance (2:22; 31:1).

[3] Even as he passes sentence on his countrymen, Isaiah still identifies with them and pleads with them, *"Let **us** walk in the light of the Lord."*

[4] Isaiah refers literally in 2:16 to *every ship of Tarshish*, meaning ships as great as those which sailed the great Mediterranean trade route from the Lebanese port of Tyre to the Spanish port of Tarshish.

[5] The Bible repeatedly warns us that God hates human pride so intensely that he does not simply refuse to bless the proud; he actively opposes them (2 Samuel 22:28; Proverbs 3:34; James 4:6; 1 Peter 5:5).

his majesty". True peace will only come to the world when God founds his New Jerusalem – a community of people who admit their weak reliance upon God for their next breath, let alone for their peaceful dealings with one another.

While Isaiah was prophesying to the southern kingdom of Judah, another prophet named Micah was prophesying to the northern kingdom of Israel. His words in Micah 4:1–3 are almost identical to Isaiah 2:2–4, so scholars debate whether Isaiah copied Micah or Micah copied Isaiah. They are missing the point. The same God inspired two different prophets in two different nations to proclaim the same message because it is the only true path to peace in the world. The Lord has a plan to unite people from every nation through faith in his Word, turning them into a better Temple in a better Jerusalem on a better Mount Zion.[6] He promises to do it *"in the last days"* – the period between the ascension of Jesus to heaven and his triumphant return at the end of world history – through the work of his coming Messiah.[7] God alone can unite the nations.

A month ago I visited the Peace Palace in The Hague. It opened in August 1913 as a way of helping rulers to talk to one another instead of waging war. Eleven months after it opened, the madness of World War One began. The day after I visited the Peace Palace, I had the privilege of preaching in one of the largest churches in The Hague and proclaiming the words of Isaiah: Human attempts to unite the nations always fail because sin is too great an enemy for us. But God has defeated our enemy and he promises to unite us together, if we will let him, in love for him and in holy hatred of sin.

---

[6] Ephesians 2:14–22; Hebrews 12:22–24. See also 1 Corinthians 3:16–17; 6:19; 2 Corinthians 6:16.

[7] Peter announced in May 30 AD that *"the last days"* have begun (Acts 2:14–17). Hebrews 1:2, James 5:3 and the rest of the New Testament echo this. We are now living in these days prophesied by Isaiah.

Heaven's Branch in Jerusalem (3:1–4:6)

In that day the Branch of the Lord will be beautiful and glorious.

(Isaiah 4:2)

The people of Judah prided themselves that they were a branch of heaven on the earth. Nobody disputed that God's head office was in heaven. King Solomon had admitted as much when he dedicated his Temple in 1 Kings 8. But the people of Judah were so convinced that his Temple had made Jerusalem the earthly branch of heaven that they refused to take Isaiah seriously when he threatened their city with destruction.[1] Hadn't he ever read the words of Psalm 132: *"The Lord has chosen Zion, he has desired it for his dwelling, saying, 'This is my resting place for ever and ever; here I will sit enthroned, for I have desired it'"*? Isaiah 3–4 therefore continues the vision which the prophet began to share in chapter 2. He is determined to demolish the misplaced confidence of the people of Judah.

Isaiah's book groups his prophecies by theme rather than by strict chronology. The prophecy in chapter 1 dates from 732 BC, after the Arameans had ravaged the land of Judah. The prophecy in chapters 2 to 5 dates from a few years earlier and predicts what will happen when the Arameans invade in 734 BC. In order to follow Isaiah's argument, we therefore need to know a little of what was happening at the time.

---

[1] The Temple was actually on Mount Moriah, but since Mount Zion was the greatest of the five mountains on which Jerusalem was built the prophets always use *Zion* as shorthand for "Jerusalem and its Temple".

Judah had a problem and its name was Assyria. In 745 BC, a general named Pul had murdered the royal family of Assyria and had himself crowned the new King Tiglath-Pileser III. He immediately began militarizing his new kingdom, conquering Babylon to the south and Armenia to the north, before turning west to expand the Assyrian Empire still further. When he captured the Aramean city of Arpad in 740 BC, the kings of Aram and Israel bought themselves a temporary reprieve by sending him costly tributes of silver, then set about forming an alliance of local rulers to resist Tiglath-Pileser.[2] When the king of Judah refused to join them, they invaded his kingdom in order to replace him with a puppet ruler who would.

It helps to understand this when Isaiah warns in 3:1–12 that God is about to close down his branch of heaven in Jerusalem. He prophesies that God will use the Arameans to remove everything on which the people of Judah have mistakenly relied. Their prosperity will end and their stockpiles of gold and silver will fail to buy them even basic supplies of food and water. So many of their leaders will die on the battlefield and in the besieged cities that they will run out of heroes, rulers, prophets, officers, soldiers, craftsmen and wise counsellors. They will face such a leadership crisis that any man who owns a cloak will be pounced upon as a potential saviour: *"You have a cloak, you be our leader; take charge of this heap of ruins!"* But he will reply, *"I have no remedy... Do not make me the leader of the people."*[3] Judah will be therefore ruled by women and teenagers and children as phase one in the closure of heaven's local branch in Jerusalem.[4]

[2] 2 Kings 15:19–20 tells us that Israel's share of this tribute was a massive 34 tons of silver. The alternative name for Aram was *Syria*, but I refer to it as Aram in this commentary to avoid confusion with Assyria.

[3] This could just as easily describe the low bar of leadership which is set in many Western churches today. Isaiah's prophecies are just as relevant today as they were when he spoke them to the people of Judah.

[4] This is a pronouncement of judgment on the men of Judah rather than a general critique of women as leaders. However, we are about to discover in

A fresh comparison with Sodom in 3:9 unleashes phase two of the closure, which we read about in 3:13 to 4:1. It takes us back to the courtroom scene of chapter 1, as Isaiah warns that *"the Lord takes his place in court; he rises to judge the people."* Since the rulers of Judah have oppressed the poor and needy, their vacant leadership positions will be filled by their pampered wives and daughters.[5] The Lord will judge those women in turn for trying so hard to look good on the outside and so little to be good on the inside. The Arameans will take away their perfumes and will make them stink. They will replace the sashes round their waists with the ropes of a slave trader.[6] They will plunder their fine clothing and make them mourn their dead in sackcloth. They will disfigure their beautiful faces by branding them as slaves, and they will not lift a finger to help them when their diseased scalps start shedding hair. They will kill so many of the men for whom they preened themselves that seven women will fight to marry the same man and will allow him to state his own terms for marriage, just as long as he accepts them in their ugliness and fruitlessness.[7]

Isaiah's language here is graphic because he wants to terrify us with the deadly consequences of rejecting the Lord. In 3:1 and 3:15, he uses one of his favourite compound names for God – *"The Lord, the Lord Almighty"* – a name he uses thirteen times throughout this "Book of Judgment".[8] God is far bigger and far holier than we think. Isaiah warns in 3:26 that if the

---

3:13–4:1 that the women of Judah were no better than the men.

[5] Note that in 3:10 Isaiah expects those who love the Lord to welcome his promise of judgment as good news. He will vindicate the oppressed and do whatever it takes to open a true Branch of Heaven.

[6] The *crescent necklaces* mentioned in 3:18 may well have been symbols of the Canaanite moon-god Yarikh.

[7] God wants churches that lack gifted leadership and regular conversions to recognize the disgrace of their condition. As we will discover in the next chapter, he wants them to rediscover the promise of John 15:1–16.

[8] In Hebrew this is *'adōnai yahweh tsebāōth*. Isaiah uses the shorter name *"the Lord Almighty"* a further 49 times.

people of Jerusalem fail to weep over their sin, the gates of their city will weep over their sudden slaughter.[9] The prophet leaves us in no doubt: God is about to close down his branch of heaven in Jerusalem.

We have to grasp this before we are ready to hear the good news in 4:2–6. These words of judgment form the pitch-black backdrop against which Isaiah suddenly reveals the bright light of the Gospel. *"In that day the Branch of the Lord will be beautiful and glorious,"* he reassures us. Having closed down the old branch of heaven in Jerusalem, the Lord will establish a new and better Branch – the one who is described in more detail in 11:1 and in 53:2.[10] A new and better King will step into the leadership vacuum in Judah and he will gather the survivors of God's people into a New Jerusalem on a New Mount Zion. He will purify them through his Holy Spirit and will restore to them the intimate friendship with God which the Israelites enjoyed when they followed the pillar of cloud and fire in the desert.[11] He will become the pride of his humbled people. He will make Jerusalem *qādōsh* – a city that is as *holy*, as *set apart* and as *in a league of its own* as the God it claims to worship. God will reopen a new and better Branch of heaven on the earth.

Isaiah has not finished prophesying, but let's pause for a moment to worship. We know the name of this Branch is Jesus. We know the name of this city is the Church. We know that God has called us to become part of this new earthly outpost of heaven. The gates of Zion are waiting to see how we will respond to God's Word to us today.

---

[9] Isaiah loves to capture our attention by personifying inanimate objects (1:2, 8; 3:26; 5:14; 24:23; 35:1–2; 44:23; 55:12). Jesus is perhaps inspired by Isaiah when he does something similar in Luke 19:40.

[10] Although Isaiah uses three different Hebrew words in these three verses, they all mean a sprouting twig or branch. The Messiah is also described as a *branch* in Jeremiah 23:5 and 33:15, and in Zechariah 3:8 and 6:12.

[11] Exodus 13:21. The Hebrew word which is used for the *Spirit* of judgment and fire is *rūach*. The New Testament refers back to this prophecy in Matthew 3:11, Romans 15:16 and 1 Corinthians 6:11.

Vineyard Music (5:1–30)

I will sing for the one I love a song about his vineyard.

(Isaiah 5:1)

Prophets tend to be creative. They have to be in order to get a hearing for their message. Isaiah could tell that the people of Judah were not warming to his words of judgment, so he began to serenade them with a love song. Isaiah 2–5 forms a single prophecy, but chapter 5 is different. Isaiah knows that the people of Judah like nothing better than singing about love and drinking wine. Having compared Judah to a vineyard in 3:14, he therefore sings them a very beautiful prophetic song.

In 5:1–7, we can tell he is inspired by another great songwriter from Jerusalem. One of King David's worship leaders, a man named Asaph, had already likened Israel to a vine in Psalm 80:8–15. He had taught the nation of Judah to sing to God, *"You transplanted a vine from Egypt; you drove out the nations and planted it. You cleared the ground for it, and it took root and filled the land... God Almighty! Look down from heaven and see! Watch over this vine, the root your right hand has planted, the branch you have raised up for yourself."*[1]

Isaiah is a very clever songwriter. He knows that the Hebrew word *bēn* in Psalm 80:15 can mean either a father's *son* or a fresh *branch* on a vine. He therefore continues to prophesy about God's plan to establish a fresh Branch of heaven in Jerusalem through his Son. He may have changed his method

---

[1] Isaiah was not the only prophet to draw inspiration from Asaph's song about Israel as a vine. See also Hosea 10:1; 14:7; Micah 7:1; Jeremiah 2:21; 12:10; Ezekiel 17:6–8; 19:10–14.

of prophesying by deciding to sing a song about God's vineyard, but he hasn't changed his tune. He is still confronting the people of Judah with the fruitless failure of their branch of heaven. Instead of red wine, their vine has yielded bloodshed. Instead of providing God's mouth with a sweet taste, they have furnished his ears with cries of injustice and oppression.[2] Isaiah's song describes a deep but thoroughly unrequited love. The people of Jerusalem cannot be surprised that God is about to come and close down their disgraceful branch of heaven.[3]

In 5:8–30, Isaiah's song suddenly changes its key. He exchanges major chords for minor ones as he speaks six woes over the people of Judah, the passage which inspired Jesus when he spoke seven similar woes over the leaders of Jerusalem in Matthew 23.[4] Isaiah's sweet song suddenly turns sour. God will not endure his people's fruitlessness any longer. He is about to clear the ground so that a better Branch can grow.

The first woe, in 5:8–10, confronts Jerusalem for its materialism and for the way in which its wealthy citizens have broken God's Law by forcing their poorer neighbours to sell their family inheritances.[5] The Lord promises to strike back so severely at their homes and fields through the Aramean invasion that their vineyards will only yield three bottles of wine per acre and their fields will only yield a harvest worth a tenth of what was sown. These verses would be terrible enough if they were only addressed to Judah, but it also sounds far too much like the experience of many fruitless churches today.

---

[2] Isaiah uses a clever play on words in the Hebrew lyrics of 5:7. The Hebrew words for justice and bloodshed are *mishpāt* and *mispāh*. The Hebrew words for righteousness and distress are *tsedāqāh* and *tsa'aqāh*.

[3] The vineyard in 1:8 had only a flimsy shelter for those who tended it. The prosperity which the Lord gave to the people of Judah is depicted by his provision of a luxurious watchtower and winepress.

[4] It came hot on the heels of the Parables of the Workers in the Vineyard and of the Tenants in Matthew 20:1–16 and 21:33–46. The second of these particularly echoes the words of Isaiah 5:1–7.

[5] Contrast 1 Kings 21:1–16 with Ezekiel 46:18.

The second woe, in 5:11–17, confronts Jerusalem for abusing the wine that God has given them. They are only interested in Isaiah's song because it reminds them of the minstrels at their drinking feasts, for they think less of God than they do of where their next drink is coming from. Because they have failed to respond to God's command in 1:17 to *"Learn to do right"*, their lack of learning will destroy them.[6] They will only grasp that God is bigger than they think when he proves himself to be the Holy One by pouring out his fierce judgment on their drunken city.

The third woe, in 5:18–19, confronts Jerusalem for imagining that God is blind to their sinfulness. They think that their deceitfulness has masked the sin which follows them wherever their go, and they are about to discover that God sees far more than they think.

The fourth woe, in 5:20, confronts Jerusalem for seeking to redefine sinfulness as virtue and virtue as sin. It is linked to the fifth woe, in 5:21, which challenges the wise men of Jerusalem for thinking that they know better than the plain teaching of God's Word. We can only imagine the specifics here. Were they promoting multi-faith worship services, same-sex relationships or doubt over the authority of certain passages of Scripture? Whatever the specifics, it sounds far too much like what is happening in many churches today for us to enjoy listening to the distant melody of Isaiah's song.

The sixth woe, in 5:22–25, confronts Jerusalem for forgetting the holy calling which God has given them. They are better at drinking wine than at devouring the Scriptures, better at mixing drinks than at comparing Bible passages and better at accepting bribes to pervert the cause of justice than at accepting their calling to be a branch of heaven on the earth. Since they are not interested in stepping into the shoes of David

---

[6] God also says something similar in Hosea 4:6. Ignorance is not bliss. It spells disaster.

and his mighty men of valour, God will bring a horde of Aramean warriors against them.[7]

This leads Isaiah into the final stanza of his song and the final words of this four-chapter-long prophecy. The Lord will lift up a banner for the nations to come and ravage the land of Judah – initially the Arameans in 734–732 BC, but later on the Assyrians and Babylonians too.[8] Isaiah's song appears to end with judgment rather than hope but, in fact, it ends with a magnificent promise for anyone who is listening to his lyrics carefully. The Hebrew word which Isaiah uses for the *banner* that will rally troops to Mount Zion is *nēs*, the same word which he will use later to describe his new and better Branch in 11:10 and 11:12: *"In that day the Root of Jesse will stand as a banner for the peoples; the nations will rally to him... He will raise a banner for the nations and gather the exiles of Israel; he will assemble the scattered people of Judah."*

This is important, so don't miss it. Isaiah's vineyard music is a song of hope. It prophesies that God is calling time on fruitless Judah in order to clear the way to plant a new and better vine on the slopes of Mount Zion. It predicts the coming of Jesus, the Son of God, the true Branch of heaven who taught his disciples in John 15:1–16 that *"I am the true vine... You are the branches. If you remain in me and I in you, you will bear much fruit... I chose you and appointed you so that you might go and bear fruit – fruit that will last."*

---

[7] Isaiah chooses his words carefully for dramatic effect. The Hebrew words he uses in 5:22 for *heroes* and *champions* at drinking are the same words which are used in 2 Samuel 23 and 1 Chronicles 11–12.

[8] God will prophesy judgment on those nations too in Isaiah 13–23. He will even use a very similar format to Isaiah 5 when he pronounces five woes over the Babylonians in Habakkuk 2:6–20.

The Beatles and the Angels
(6:1–13)

Holy, holy, holy is the Lord Almighty; the whole earth is full of his glory.

(Isaiah 6:3)

The year 740 BC spelled disaster for Isaiah and the people of Judah. After three years of siege, the Aramean city of Arpad finally fell to King Tiglath-Pileser of Assyria. After the bloodbath that followed, he turned his greedy eyes south towards Jerusalem and at that moment, just when his people needed him most, the king of Judah suddenly died. King Uzziah was a military genius who had won wars against the Philistines, the Arabs and the Ammonites. When he succumbed to the leprosy with which he had been stricken for underestimating the greatness of God and barging into the sacred inner room of the Temple, King Uzziah left his throne to a far lesser man. The year 740 BC was therefore a year of great trouble abroad and great disaster at home for Judah.[1]

Isaiah responded by going to worship in the Temple courtyard. There he saw a vision of God which turned him into the answer to his own prayers. King Uzziah had just been replaced by the weak King Jotham, but Isaiah *saw the Lord, high and exalted, seated on a throne* as the real King of Judah, a King so magnificent that even the hem of his royal robe completely

---

[1] King Uzziah was also known as Azariah. You can read about his reign in 2 Chronicles 26:1–23.

filled Solomon's Temple.[2] In contrast to Tiglath-Pileser's burning ambition, the Lord was surrounded by fiery angels who proclaimed that *"the whole earth is full of his glory."*[3] Standing in the Temple courtyard, Isaiah could see that their voices were powerful enough to shake the 10-metre-high bronze pillars that held up the Temple portico, and yet they did not dare to gaze upon the Lord.[4] As the Temple filled with smoke, Isaiah suddenly realized that Uzziah had never been the real king of Judah. He gasped in wonder, *"My eyes have seen the King, the Lord Almighty."*[5]

Isaiah never actually describes what the Lord looked like in his vision. He describes God's throne, God's robe and God's angels, but he does not dare describe God himself. He simply tells us that the angels cried out to one another in Hebrew that he is *qādōsh qādōsh qādōsh*, meaning *"holy, holy, holy"*. There is a hint here that God exists in three Persons, since he asks in 6:8 *"Who will go for us?"* and since the New Testament tells us that Isaiah saw, not just the Father, but also the Son and the Holy Spirit in his vision (John 12:37–41 and Acts 28:25–27). Nevertheless, the angelic song also means more than this. When 2 Kings 25:15 seeks to describe pure gold and pure silver in Hebrew, it says *"gold, gold"* and *"silver, silver"*. When the angels look for a way to describe God's pure holiness, they therefore have to invent an even stronger superlative in Hebrew. God isn't just *qādōsh* and

---

[2] The Hebrew word *shūl* in 6:1 is used for the hem of the high priest's robe in Exodus 28:33–34 and 39:24–26.

[3] *Seraph* is Hebrew for *one burning with fire*. Glorious though these angels are, they use their wings to cover their own imperfections from the Lord and to shield their eyes from his utter perfection. They even sing their song to each other rather than to the Lord, for fear that they might catch too powerful a glimpse of him.

[4] These two massive bronze pillars had Hebrew names which meant *Stability* and *Strength*, yet even they could not stand still before the majesty of the Lord (1 Kings 7:15–22).

[5] Smoke speaks of God's glorious presence in 1 Kings 8:10–12 and Revelation 15:8.

he isn't even *qādōsh qādōsh*. He is *qādōsh qādōsh qādōsh*. He is far holier than any human language can ever properly describe.[6]

That's why Isaiah's initial reaction to his vision of the Lord is not encouragement but despair. He is immediately convicted of his own sinfulness and of that of Judah: *"Woe to me! I am ruined! For I am a man of unclean lips, and I live among a people of unclean lips, and my eyes have seen the King, the Lord Almighty."* Whatever self-confidence he may have had on his way to the Temple, his reaction shows us how we will all feel when we finally see the Lord on the Day of Judgment. Isaiah is in such distress that one of the angels flies to the altar in the middle of the Temple courtyard and retrieves one of the coals that burns with fire sent down from heaven.[7] When Isaiah's neighbours ask him later how his lips came to be scarred, he will be able to share with them the angel's promise of forgiveness: *"See, this has touched your lips; your guilt is taken away and your sin atoned for."*[8]

Isaiah does not resent this facial wound at the hands of the angel. He immediately volunteers to use his wounded lips to speak God's message of forgiveness to the people of Judah. He wants to tell his countrymen what he has seen, that God is far bigger than they think, and to use his scarred face to convince them that the Holy One wants to make us holy too. He begs God for the privilege of telling his nation about the one whose death is prophesied by the bronze altar of blood sacrifice in the Temple courtyard. Those who have truly seen the Lord always want to tell the world about him.

The Lord grants Isaiah's wish but warns that, like

---

[6] The only other place in the whole of the Bible where such a superlative is used again is in Revelation 4:8, where the angels in heaven fall back on the same language, worshipping the Lord as *"Holy, holy, holy"*.

[7] 2 Chronicles 7:1–3; Leviticus 6:9–13; 16:12.

[8] The Lord also touches Jeremiah's mouth in 1:9. If we are to speak the words of God, we need to be very careful what else comes out of our mouths (James 3:9–12). It is a serious thing to speak for God.

Cassandra of Troy, he will speak the truth without being believed. The Gospel never leaves those who hear it unchanged – it always softens or hardens their hearts towards God – but in Isaiah's case it will generally make people hard-hearted, deaf and blind.[9] Martin Luther emphasizes this in the preface to his German translation of Isaiah:

> *You should not think of Isaiah except as a man who was despised among the Jews and considered a fool and madman. For they did not regard him as we now regard him, but, as he himself testifies in chapter 58, they shot out their tongues and pointed their fingers at him and held his preaching as foolishness, all except a few godly children in the crowd, such as King Hezekiah. For it was the habit of the people to mock the prophets and hold them madmen; and this has happened to all servants of God and preachers; it happens every day and will continue.*

We need to be prepared for this. The theme tune of our culture is "Love, love, love" by The Beatles. It is a very different theme tune from the one the angels teach us to sing: *"Holy, holy, holy"*. It takes courage to speak of God's holiness to a world which opposes his standards as old-fashioned bigotry and intolerance. Each of the four gospels quotes the words of 6:9–10 to remind us that the world hated Jesus' message, and Acts quotes them to warn that it will often hate our own words too.[10] Nevertheless, the Lord still asks, *"Whom shall I send? And who will go for us?"* He still calls us to reply with the same courage as Isaiah, *"Here am I. Send me!"*

The Lord promises that, if Isaiah faithfully prophesies in the face of opposition, his words will clear the ground for *"the*

---

[9] Isaiah will emphasize this feature of his ministry again in 28:11–13, 29:9–14 and 42:18–25.

[10] Matthew 13:14–15; Mark 4:12; Luke 8:10; John 12:37–41; Acts 28:25–27.

holy seed" to grow. If we faithfully proclaim Jesus as the holy seed of Israel, we can trust the Lord to use our message, even if it seems to fall on deaf ears much of the time. Isaiah invites us to gain the same perspective which he gained when he *"saw the Lord, high and exalted, seated on a throne"*. Isaiah wants us to join him in telling the world the good news that God is far bigger than we think.

Read the Signs (7:1–8:18)

We are signs and symbols in Israel from the Lord Almighty, who dwells on Mount Zion.

(Isaiah 8:18)

There is a brilliant scene in the movie *Bruce Almighty*. As Jim Carrey hurtles down the road at high speed, he prays for God to give him a sign to show him what to do. Suddenly a neon sign lights up in the darkness – *"Caution ahead"* – but he is too busy speeding past to notice. Again he prays: *Lord, I need your help. Please send me a sign what to do.* A truck pulls out in front of him filled with road signs which read "wrong way" and "stop". Complaining that God never speaks to him, he increases his speed, loses control of his car and crashes into a lamppost. The truck full of road signs overtakes him as he examines the damage and shouts angrily to God that none of this would have happened if he had given him a sign.[1]

That scene is truer to life than most of us know. It certainly was for King Ahaz of Judah. He stubbornly ignored every warning sign which the Lord tried to give him after he became king of Judah in 735 BC. Even though his godly father was still alive for the first three years of his reign, we are told in 2 Chronicles 27:2 that King Jotham was too weak to control his subjects, let alone his stubborn son. When Isaiah came to him at the start of his reign and delivered the urgent warnings of chapters 2 to 5, Ahaz ignored the sign that God had given him through the burn marks on the prophet's face. As a result, in 734 BC, the Aramean and Israelite armies crossed over the border into Judah.

---

[1] *Bruce Almighty* (Universal Pictures, 2003).

At the start of chapter 7, Isaiah tells us that when King Ahaz and his subjects heard this news they *"were shaken, as the trees of the forest are shaken by the wind"*. The Lord therefore gave him a second sign by sending Isaiah to meet him outside the walls of Jerusalem with his strangely named son.[2] Shear-Jashub meant *A Remnant Will Return*, so his name was meant to encourage Ahaz after hearing that 120,000 of his soldiers had been killed in a single battle and the Edomites and Philistines had also joined in the invasion.[3] Isaiah did more than simply promise that King Rezin of Aram and King Pekah of Israel were *"two smouldering stubs of firewood"*, whose plan to replace Ahaz with an Aramean puppet ruler was doomed to fail.[4] He also offered to give him a sign of his own choosing that the northern kingdom of Israel would be completely destroyed within sixty-five years.[5] Ahaz sounds very pious as he turns down this offer in 7:12 – *"I will not ask; I will not put the Lord to the test"* – but the Lord is angry. He sees straight through this false veneer of faith and recognizes that Ahaz is afraid that a sign might force him to believe and to repent of his sin. Ahaz actually wants to remain blind to all that God is doing in his land.

Isaiah therefore offers him a sign of his own. A virgin birth will take place within Judah. We are told in Matthew 1:22–23 that this prefigured the even greater Virgin Birth of Jesus, but it also described some kind of genuine miracle in Isaiah's own day. A Jewish virgin would name her miracle baby Immanuel, meaning *God Is With Us*, as a sign to King Ahaz that his nation still had God on its side. Before the boy was old enough to celebrate

---

[2] Hezekiah's envoys would meet with the commander of the Assyrian army in this exact same spot in 36:2.

[3] 2 Chronicles 28:5–8, 17–18. For perspective, less than half as many died on the first day of the Battle of the Somme.

[4] *Tabeel* in 7:6 is an Aramaic rather than a Hebrew name (Ezra 4:7). Pekah had usurped the throne by force, so by calling him *"Remaliah's son"* the Lord emphasized that he was an illegal commoner.

[5] The northern kingdom would be destroyed in 722 BC. Fifty-five years later there would be no Israelite survivors.

his bar mitzvah, both Aram and Israel would be conquered. However, there would be a price tag for the king's refusal to read the signs. Because he preferred to steal treasures from God's Temple and to send them as tribute to Tiglath-Pileser, his nation would endure an Assyrian invasion far more violent than the present one.

God is merciful. Even after King Ahaz plundered his Temple, he continued to furnish him with further warning signs in chapter 8. Isaiah's wife had to be a prophetess in order to accept the idea of giving their second son the unwieldy name Maher-Shalal-Hash-Baz, meaning *Quick to the Plunder and Swift to the Prey*, but it enabled Isaiah to use him as a prophetic symbol for King Ahaz, just as he used his older brother in 7:3. His name prophesied that God was about to destroy Aram and Israel.[6]

When King Ahaz refuses to take note of these final signs, Isaiah launches into a prophecy which is quoted five times in the New Testament. Because King Ahaz has treated God as something tiny, like the Pool of Siloam outside the walls of Jerusalem, his nation is about to feel the full force of the great Assyrian river, the Euphrates. The boy Immanuel will suffer during this new invasion, but his name will remain a sign of God's mercy towards anyone who is listening. Judah will know that *God Is With Us* on the day that the power of Assyria is broken at the Pool of Siloam outside the walls of Jerusalem.[7]

Isaiah therefore ends this prophecy by proclaiming that he and his children remain signs and symbols for the people of Israel and Judah. When Hebrews 2:13 quotes the proclamation of 8:18, it says that Jesus now declares the same thing about his followers. God does not simply perform signs and wonders

---

[6] Assyria would destroy Aram in 732 BC and Israel in 722 BC (2 Kings 16:7–9; 17:1–6), but because of the stubbornness of King Ahaz, it would then turn against Judah (2 Chronicles 28:16–27).

[7] The Hebrew for *God Is With Us* in 8:10 is exactly the same as for *Immanuel* in 7:14 and 8:8.

through his people. He turns them into walking, talking signs and wonders through the holy way in which they live their lives.[8]

First Peter 3:14 quotes from 8:12 to remind us that our steady faith in God is a powerful sign to a world which quickly panics when it reads the news.[9] Hebrews 2:13 quotes from 8:17 in order to remind us that our patient endurance also sends a powerful signal that the Gospel is true. Romans 9:33 and 1 Peter 2:8 both quote from 8:14 to set our expectations that many people will refuse to read the signs, just like King Ahaz with Isaiah.

But if we hold our ground as disciples of Jesus and as children of God, many people will eventually read the signs. When they look at the way we live our lives, they will confess – just like Jim Carrey at the end of *Bruce Almighty* – that God is bigger than they think.

Jesus is looking for better disciples than the ones that Isaiah gathered around him in 8:16. He is looking for better children than Shear-Jashub and Maher-Shalal-Hash-Baz in 8:18. He is looking for people about whom he can say to the world, *"Here am I, and the children the Lord has given me. We are signs and symbols in Israel from the Lord Almighty, who dwells on Mount Zion."*

---

[8] The Lord repeats this in Isaiah 20:3. See also Philippians 1:27–28; Ephesians 3:10.

[9] Isaiah tells us that when we *qādash* the Lord, recognizing that he is *qādōsh* or *holy*, then our fear of God drives out any other fear. 1 Peter 3:15 refers back to this verse to re-emphasize the same thing.

Dawn Chorus (8:19–9:7)

The people walking in darkness have seen a great light; on those living in the land of deep darkness a light has dawned.

(Isaiah 9:2)

Isaiah was right. The Arameans and the Israelites failed in their attempt to place a new king on the throne of Judah so that it would join them in their alliance against Assyria. Tiglath-Pileser conquered Aram, destroyed its capital city of Damascus, executed King Rezin and took his subjects into captivity. Aram had been a major force in the region for over 500 years, but it was destroyed forever in 732 BC.

Next, Tiglath-Pileser marched his army south across the Israelite border. He conquered the territory around Lake Galilee and took the Israelites who lived there into slavery. He would have conquered and enslaved the whole of Israel by the end of 732 BC, had it not been for a treacherous court official named Hoshea. When Hoshea murdered King Pekah and proved his loyalty to Tiglath-Pileser by sending him a third of a ton of gold and thirty-seven tons of silver, the Assyrians decided to accept him as their new puppet ruler of Israel. The northern kingdom had survived to live another day, but at a very heavy price. The nation was in shock and in mourning.[1]

During Israel's darkest hour, Isaiah prophesied the

---

[1] You can read about this in 2 Kings 15:27–30 and 16:7–9. The size of Hoshea's tribute is recorded among the writings of the Assyrians, in the annals of King Tiglath-Pileser III.

breaking of a bright new dawn.[2] In 8:19–22, he warned them not to turn to the mediums who promised to consult the dead on their behalf. If they sought counsel from dead men instead of from the living God, they would never see the light of dawn, but *"only distress and darkness and fearful gloom"*. If they treated their sorrow as a reason to cry out against the Lord, they would rob themselves of a share in the bright new start which God had planned.

The first seven verses of chapter 9 contain such a magnificent prophecy about Jesus that they are still read at many Christmas carol services today. They are prominent in Handel's *Messiah* and they have inspired countless worship songs throughout Church history. This isn't speculative. Matthew 4:13–16 confirms that they are a prophecy about Jesus. Isaiah is about to reveal a wealth of detail about the one that he has so far only described mysteriously as *"the Branch of the Lord"*. Let's slow down to take in fully what he says. God has not forgotten Israel. He is already singing them a dawn chorus.

In 9:1–2, Isaiah prophesies that God will initially open his new Branch of heaven in Galilee, not in Jerusalem. If we find this confusing, then our confusion is nothing compared to that of the people of Israel. Everybody knew that the Messiah would be born to the dynasty of David – in other words, in David's hometown of Bethlehem in Judah, as predicted by one of Isaiah's contemporaries in Micah 5:2. He would not be born to the northern tribes of Zebulun and Naphtali, nor would he come from the despised region of Galilee. It had been known as *"Galilee of the Gentiles"* even before it was annexed by the Assyrians, since its mixed population reflected the fact that it lay on the "Way of the Sea", the trade route from Damascus to the Mediterranean. The Arameans had even annexed it for a time, so it was a place for foreigners and merchants and fishermen,

---

[2] As we will see later, the prophecy in 8:19–9:7 was probably given at the same time as 7:1–8:18. Isaiah therefore prophesied these words before Assyria even conquered Galilee.

not for royalty. Nevertheless, Isaiah prophesies good news to the north of Israel. The Messiah will not just come to the land of Judah. He will be a Galilean.

In 9:3-5, Isaiah explains what this promise of a new dawn means for the northern kingdom. He praises God that *"You have enlarged the nation."* King Tiglath-Pileser may have reduced the size of Israel by annexing Galilee, but the Lord is committed to saving Israel in its entirety. Isaiah promises that, just as in Judges 7 Gideon defeated a vast Midianite army in one night on the northern hills of Israel, so too the Lord will also work a massive and sudden victory in those same northern lands. When the Messiah comes to Galilee, he will turn darkness into light, night into dawn, distress into joy, defeat into plunder, oppression into liberty and soldiers' clothing into fuel for the fire.

In 9:6, Isaiah reveals the identity of God's new Branch of heaven on the earth. He will be the true Immanuel, the true fulfilment of God's promise in 7:14 to give his people a son born to a virgin. He will be the true King, smashing the yoke of oppression and taking the burden of government onto his own shoulders. He will also be something more than human. He will be the *"Mighty God"* and he will show the world the glory of all three Persons of the Trinity: the *"Everlasting Father"*,[3] the *"Prince of Peace"* and the *"Wonderful Counsellor"*.[4] The Branch will be far greater than Israel could ever have imagined. The holy God will come and live among his people.

In 9:7, it gets even better. God's new Branch will move south from Galilee to Jerusalem and he will reign on David's

---

[3] This same name *"Mighty God"* is used for the Lord in 10:21, so this is a clear statement of Jesus' divinity. The Jews found this idea so outrageous that they downgraded *"Wonderful Counsellor, Mighty God, Everlasting Father"* in the Greek Septuagint so that it merely reads, *"Messenger of the Mighty Counsellor... Health to him!"*

[4] Technically, the Hebrew can also be translated with a comma: *"Wonderful, Counsellor"*. See Judges 13:18.

throne like the kings of Judah at their very best.[5] He will reign over the entire kingdom of David (not just over Judah, but also over Galilee and the ten northern tribes) and his rule will not end at the borders of Israel. He will fulfil the promise which the Lord made to David's dynasty in Psalm 2:8 by expanding his Kingdom to every nation of the earth forever: *"Of the increase of his government and peace there will be no end... The zeal of the Lord Almighty will accomplish this."*

As a church leader, I find these verses revolutionary. People tell me that God has finished with Europe and that our spiritual fruitlessness is deserved, but Isaiah tells me that God does not give up on rebellious territories like Galilee or Europe. People tell me that church planting is difficult, but Isaiah tells me that God wants to enlarge his Kingdom and to create a people who reflect his holy character. People tell me that the obstacles are too difficult, but Isaiah reassures me that the responsibility for fulfilling God's plans for the world lies on his shoulders, and not on mine.[6]

Whatever your own situation, you should find these verses revolutionary too. People may see no hope for you, but God does. People may see no way out of your situation, but God does. People may be resigned to the darkness of this world, but God is bigger than they think. Right now, he is singing this dawn chorus over you.

---

[5] The prophecy that he will reign *"with justice and righteousness"* links back to 2 Samuel 8:15, 1 Chronicles 18:14 and 2 Chronicles 9:8.

[6] Jesus may well be referring to this prophecy when he promises us an easy burden in Matthew 11:28–30.

God's Toolbox (9:8–10:34)

Does the axe raise itself above the person who swings it, or the saw boast against the one who uses it?

The grandfather of Charlemagne carried the proud nickname "The Sledgehammer". He had led his Frankish army to such a comprehensive victory over the Muslims at the Battle of Tours that thereafter he became known as Charles Martel, or Charles the Sledgehammer. That was in 732 AD, but in 732 BC the Lord had already named another great general The Sledgehammer. He had declared that Tiglath-Pileser and his officers were the hammer, the rod, the club, the axe and the saw in his toolbox of judgment.

One of the key statements in these two chapters of prophecy is found in 10:5 – *"Woe to the Assyrian, the rod of my anger, in whose hand is the club of my wrath!"* Another key verse is 10:15 – *"Does the axe raise itself above the person who swings it, or the saw boast against the one who uses it? As if a rod were to wield the person who lifts it up, or a club brandish the one who is not wood!"* We need to understand this as the major metaphor which God uses throughout these two chapters to describe what is happening in the eighth century BC. Although these words are ancient, they still provide God's commentary on the rise and fall of nations. He wants to open up his toolbox and let us take a look inside.

In 9:8–10:4, Isaiah continues his prophecy to the northern

kingdom of Israel.[1] He warns its capital city Samaria and its two largest tribes Ephraim and Manasseh that they will never enjoy the new dawn that he has promised unless they repent of their persistent sin. They will never repent until they grasp that the disaster that has befallen them did not initiate with the Assyrians or with any of the other nations who have taken advantage of their momentary weakness.[2] Instead of picking themselves up off the ground and rebuilding their shattered nation, they need to heed the prophet's repeated warning in 9:12, 9:17, 9:21 and 10:4: *"Yet for all this, his anger is not turned away, his hand is still upraised."* The true demolisher of Israel was the Lord himself. The hostile nations were simply items which he took out of his toolbox for the job. The Lord Almighty had begun to punish them for their sinfulness and he would continue to punish them unless they saw what had happened to their nation as loving discipline from the Holy One of Israel.[3]

In 10:5–19, Isaiah prophesies against the nation of Assyria. Tiglath-Pileser has let his victories go to his head. He believes that his conquests are due to his military genius and that, like a man stealing eggs from an unguarded bird's nest, he will conquer Israel as easily as he has conquered pagan nations.[4] He fails to realize that he is merely a useful item in God's toolbox (10:5) and that he cannot boast as if his axing and sawing and smashing reflects the greatness of his own strength instead of

[1] The prophecy of 9:8–10:34 is part of the same prophecy as 8:19–9:7. Note the choice which the Lord gives Israel – either the uniforms of their enemies can become fuel for the fire (9:5) or they themselves can (9:19)!

[2] King Rezin's was not the only kingdom within Aram, so 9:12 tells us that both Arameans and Philistines had taken advantage of Israel's struggle with Assyria to launch raids of their own.

[3] Isaiah's prophecy is still very relevant today. Whenever church leaders view each other as rivals (9:21) and rely on programmes instead of prayer (9:10), it means that God has opened up his toolbox against them.

[4] Tiglath-Pileser had already conquered the Aramean cities of Arpad and Damascus, as well as the Hittite city of Carchemish. He boasts in 10:9 that this means he will conquer Samaria just as easily.

the greatness of the Lord (10:15). God promises to judge his pride by destroying the might of the Assyrian army in a single day (10:16-19). We will read about this astonishing turnaround in chapter 37.

In 10:20-23, Isaiah prophesies that God will use the people of Israel to show the nations that the rise and fall of empires is always caused by the items he chooses to take out of his toolbox. When the people of Israel stop relying on Arameans and Assyrians and Egyptians – on all the nations that have struck them down over the years – and start to look beyond the might of foreign armies to the one who wields them like a club, they will demonstrate that world history is an edifice planned and built by God alone. We can tell that these verses form a single prophecy with chapters 7 and 8, because the Hebrew words in 10:21 and 10:22 which are translated *"a remnant will return"* are the same as the name of Isaiah's firstborn son, Shear-Jashub. When Samaria falls to the Assyrians in 722 BC, the surviving Israelites will become as humble as their conquerors are proud. They will place their trust in the Lord as the "Holy One" and as the "Mighty God" about whom Isaiah prophesied in 9:6.[5] As Paul reminds us when he quotes from 10:22-23 in Romans 9:27-28, God still uses his toolbox to humble and to bless Israel.

In 10:24-34, Isaiah therefore prophesies to the people of the southern kingdom of Judah. He tells them not to fear the imminent Assyrian invasion of their land, for God has already determined that it will fail.[6] He has decided to take his whip out of his toolbox as he did when he used Gideon to defeat the Midianites.[7] He has decided to take his rod out of his toolbox as he did when he used Moses to drown the Egyptian army in the

---

[5] This link is yet another indication that Isaiah probably delivered 7:1–12:6 as a single prophecy.

[6] Isaiah tells us in 10:12 that God will also use the Assyrian invasion as a tool with which to discipline his disobedient children.

[7] Gideon killed the Midianite general at the rock of Oreb in Judges 7:25, linking back yet again to 9:4.

Red Sea. They need not panic when the Assyrian army makes its way south to Jerusalem past the towns mentioned in 10:28–32. They need not even fear when the army reaches the walls of Jerusalem. The Assyrians may shake their fist at the Jewish capital, but God will intervene like a protective Father on behalf of Daughter Zion. Assyria is merely an axe in his toolbox and he has many more axes to use against it. The king who thought himself a *"mighty one"* in 10:13 will soon discover that the Lord is the true *"Mighty One"*. Assyria may briefly be the tallest tree in the forest, but the Lord is about to chop it down.[8]

It seemed incredible to Isaiah's listeners that the superpower Assyria could ever be defeated by little Judah. It seemed equally unthinkable to the British in 1940 that the sudden fall of tiny Singapore would result in the rapid destruction of their global empire. It seemed ludicrous in 1965 that America could ever lose a war to the North Vietnamese. It seemed impossible in 1979 that the Soviet Union might lose a war with Afghanistan and then suddenly self-implode.

But it did not seem impossible to God. What we call America and Russia and China and Britain and North Korea, God calls his axe and his hammer and his club and his saw. Isaiah wants you to remember this the next time you watch the news. God is in a completely different league from the nations of the world. He opens up his toolbox every evening on the TV news as a daily reminder that he is far greater than you think.

---

[8] Although the Hebrew text of 10:27 can be translated as a promise to break the yoke off Judah's shoulders *"because you have grown so fat"*, it is better translated *"because of the anointing"*. See 61:1–3.

David's New Psalm
(11:1–12:6)

A shoot will come up from the stump of Jesse; from his roots a Branch will bear fruit.

(Isaiah 11:1)

David was the great psalmist of Israel. He had begun to write his first psalms while tending sheep for his father Jesse in the fields surrounding Bethlehem. When the jealous King Saul made him an outlaw, he continued to write psalms in caves while on the run. When he finally became king, he expanded his collection of psalms and taught the nation of Israel how to sing them. But David had been dead for almost 250 years. King Ahaz was no more interested in singing than he was in signs.

That's why Isaiah is excited. His talk at the end of chapter 10 about lopping off boughs and felling trees inspires him to prophesy once more about God's new Branch in Jerusalem. The Branch will be David's son and he will inspire great new psalms of his own. Therefore Isaiah starts strumming a tune, as he did in chapter 5, to capture the attention of Israel and Judah as he brings this first section of his book to an end.

In 11:1–2, Isaiah prophesies that the Branch will be filled with the Holy Spirit. He will be born to David's fallen dynasty (the reference to *"the stump of Jesse"* warns us that this prophecy will only be fulfilled after the exile of Judah) and he will live out the words of 1 Samuel 16:13 when it tells us that *"the Spirit of the Lord came powerfully upon David"*. Isaiah describes the third Person of the Trinity variously as the Spirit of the Lord, the Spirit of wisdom, the Spirit of counsel and of might, and the

Spirit of the knowledge and fear of the Lord. David was known in Hebrew as the *messiah*, meaning *the anointed one*, because he received the Holy Spirit when the prophet Samuel anointed him with oil. Jesus will be all this and more. He will be the true Messiah, the true Anointed One, the man who shows the world what it truly means to be full of the Spirit's power.

In 11:3–5, Isaiah prophesies that the Branch will judge the world with justice and righteousness. The Holy Spirit within him will make him live and breathe the holy standards of heaven.[1] He will not judge based on his own human senses but based on what God's Spirit says to him. Unlike King David, who often knew what he ought to do but was too weak to do it, the Branch will have the power to enforce justice with a mere command.[2] Since the world came into being through his powerful word, it will instantly submit to him as soon as it recognizes its Master's voice.[3]

In 11:6–9, Isaiah prophesies that the Branch will bring peace to a troubled world. He paints a vivid picture of sweet harmony between wolves and lambs and leopards and goats and lions and cows and bears and calves and cobras and children. There is no reason why we should view the rest of this prophecy as a description of Jesus' rule today and yet postpone this particular promise until after his Second Coming. Isaiah tells us that the Branch will bring about the fulfilment of 2:1–4. He will create a new community, a New Mount Zion, in which God will reconcile both Jew and Gentile, black and white, man and woman, child and parent, slave and master. This

---

[1] The Hebrew word in 11:3 for his *delighting* in the fear of the Lord is *rūach*, the same word used repeatedly for God's *Spirit* in 11:2. His holy passion will stem from his having been filled with the Holy Spirit.

[2] Contrast 2 Samuel 3:39 with Psalm 2:9, Matthew 8:16 and 21:19, Mark 4:39 and 2 Thessalonians 2:8. The Lord did not use Assyria as his rod in 10:5 because he needed help. His own words are rod enough.

[3] Once again the Hebrew word which is used in 11:4 to describe the Messiah's *breath* is *rūach*. Jesus is both the *Branch* (11:1) and the *Root* (11:10) of Jesse because he is both Jesse's Son and Jesse's Creator.

new community will begin in Jerusalem but it will soon fill the entire earth. The Branch will open up little branches of heaven in every nation of the world.[4]

In 11:10–16, Isaiah spells out what this means. The sea isn't merely full of water, it is water, so 11:9 means that the Branch will take the statement in 6:3 that the whole earth is full of God's glory and he will make that glory fully known. He will demolish any idea that there are parts of the earth which do not belong to God when he becomes a better banner than the one that was raised in 5:26 to bring the Aramean and Israelite armies against Jerusalem. He will raise a banner which will bring back the scattered remnant of Israel and Judah from the pagan nations. The talk of doing this *"a second time"* in 11:11 depicts this as a second Exodus for Israel, as the Lord dries up the Red Sea and the River Euphrates to make a highway home. Later on in his book of prophecies, Isaiah will explore further this idea of a holy highway connecting the pagan nations to Mount Zion, but the apostle Paul explains that the salvation of the Gentiles is already in view here when he quotes from 11:10 in Romans 15:12.[5] Jesus had these verses in mind when he revealed in John 12:32 on the eve of his crucifixion that Isaiah's banner was a prophecy about his cross: *"When I am lifted up from the earth, I will draw all people to myself."*

Isaiah has almost finished the first section of his book of prophecies, so he breaks into song in the final six verses. He is so excited about this new Son of Jesse that, in 12:1–6, he pens a new psalm of David for his countrymen to sing. Note how he echoes the song of Moses by the Red Sea in Exodus 15 when he tells us to rejoice that *"the Lord is my strength and my song; he has become my salvation."* He urges us in the first three verses of his song to shake off our passivity and to rejoice over his mercy,

---

[4] Habakkuk 2:14 repeats the promise of 11:9, insisting that nothing can prevent God's plan from succeeding.

[5] Isaiah will describe this holy highway in more detail in 19:23, 35:8, 40:3–4, 57:14 and 62:10.

like the Israelites in the desert, as we actively *"draw water from the wells of salvation".*[6]

Isaiah switches focus in the final three verses of his song. Worshipping is not enough. Witnessing must follow. Singing about the Branch is not enough. We are to go as little branches to every nation of the world. Isaiah calls us to respond to this first section of his book by proclaiming to the nations that our God is the Holy One of Israel. He calls us to declare to the peoples of the earth that the Holy One has decided to dwell among sinners. He calls us to explain to the world that this is only possible because the Lord has promised to come to us in person as our flesh-and-blood Saviour.[7]

God is far holier than we think, but he has found a way to save sinners through his new Branch of heaven on the earth. He has found a way to rebuild Mount Zion and to fill the whole earth with the sound of his Messiah's great salvation song.

One of the famous phrases in David's psalms is *"Oh, magnify the Lord with me."* That's what Isaiah has tried to help us do in these first twelve chapters of his book. He has given us a more exalted view of the Holy One of Israel. So let's sing this new psalm of David along with him. Let's celebrate the fact that God is far bigger than people think.

---

[6] The New Testament also issues us with similar warnings not to be passive in our response to the Gospel. See John 7:37–39; 1 Timothy 4:7–8; 2 Peter 3:14; Jude 20–21.

[7] Isaiah has not yet fully explained the mystery of 12:6, how God can be the Holy One and yet live among sinners. We need to continue reading his book of prophecy in order to find out the answer.

Part Two:

God is Sterner Than You Think

(Isaiah 13–35)

Foreign Policy Predictions
(13:1–23:18)

This is the plan determined for the whole world; this is the hand stretched out over all nations.

(Isaiah 14:26)

Making predictions about foreign affairs is fraught with danger. Think of all the generals who went off to war in the summer of 1914, confidently predicting that they would bring their soldiers home before Christmas. Think of Neville Chamberlain, the British prime minister, who returned from a meeting with Adolf Hitler in 1938 declaring that he had secured *"peace for our time"*. Think of Saddam Hussein, boasting that the First Gulf War would be *"the mother of all battles"* before his army crumbled so quickly that they barely fought a battle at all. Only a fool would make confident predictions about the state of foreign affairs next week, let alone across the next 200 years.

Only a fool, that is, unless the person talking happens to be God. If you have the nations of the earth in your toolbox, making predictions about foreign affairs isn't a risky thing at all. In fact, it is one of the easiest ways to prove to the world that you are in a league entirely of your own. So don't lose interest when the "Book of Judgment" descends into eleven straight chapters of foreign policy predictions. The Lord is proving to us that he is the Lord of history by predicting the rise and fall of nations.

In 13:1–14:27, the Lord predicts the downfall of Assyria. Don't be confused when Isaiah refers to Assyria as *Babylon*. The city was Tiglath-Pileser's greatest prize and he was so proud of his conquest that he styled himself "King Pul of Babylon". Everyone predicted that the invincible walls of Babylon would stand forever, so the Lord proves his control of history by predicting that the Medes and Persians will destroy them. Where walls once stood there will be only marshland and it will be easier to find gold among the ruins than a Babylonian survivor. These words of prophecy sounded far-fetched when Isaiah spoke them but, sure enough, they were fulfilled in 539 and 516 BC.[1]

In 14:28–32, the Lord predicts the downfall of the Philistines. Although Isaiah is speaking in 740 BC, he predicts that the Philistines will want to celebrate the death of King Sargon II of Assyria in 705 BC. He warns them not to rejoice over the demise of the man who would sack their city of Ashdod in 711 BC, because his death will pave the way for kings even more violent than himself. The Lord will judge the sins of the Philistines so sternly that, unlike Israel and Judah, there will be no remnant of survivors left for him to save.[2]

In 15:1–16:14, the Lord predicts the destruction of Moab at the hands of King Sargon in 715 BC. Isaiah weeps that the Moabites have shown such lack of interest in his promise about a new king who will sit on David's throne, even though David's great-grandmother came from Moab. Prophesying in 718 BC, Isaiah warns that in three years only a tiny remnant of Moabites will be spared to witness the coming of the Messiah.

In 17:1–3, the Lord predicts the destruction of Aram and its capital Damascus in 732 BC. In 17:4–11, he also predicts that their Israelite allies will feel the heat of Aram's judgment. Isaiah's description of Israel as a beaten olive tree in 17:6 would later inspire the apostle Paul when he wrote Romans 11. The Lord promises to preserve a remnant of survivors from the northern kingdom who will repent and turn back to him.

---

[1] Jesus quotes from 13:10 in Matthew 24:29 and Mark 13:24 in order to liken the suddenness of his second coming to the sudden fall of Babylon.

[2] The Hebrew word which Isaiah uses in 14:29 is *seraph*, the same word he used in 6:2 and 6:6. King Sargon's successors will be venomous snakes, whose bite will make people feel as though their body is on fire.

In 18:1-20:6, the Lord predicts the destruction of Egypt and Cush, two nations on the River Nile which were both ruled by the same pharaoh. Speaking in 711 BC, Isaiah warns them that the coalition of nations that their ambassadors are trying so hard to forge against Assyria is doomed to fail. The Lord will judge them for their idolatry by afflicting them with civil war (19:2), foreign invasion (19:3-4), drought (19:5-10), foolish politicians (19:11-15) and eventually captivity (20:1-6). This took place in 670 BC when King Esarhaddon of Assyria conquered them, abruptly ending Egypt's many centuries as a superpower.[3] Nevertheless, the Lord holds out hope to the people of Egypt. He reminds them of his promise in 11:16 to create a holy highway on which the pagan nations can travel to Zion. Egypt's political downfall will lead to its spiritual revival. Many will turn from the sun-god Ra to the one who sings a great dawn chorus over their darkness. By God's grace, the former oppressors of Israel will be saved alongside their former enemies and slaves (19:18-25).[4]

In 21:1-10, the Lord predicts the rise of the Babylonian empire and its sudden fall to the Medes and Persians in 539 BC. In 21:11-12, the Lord predicts the fall of Edom and the way in which the nomadic Arabs will suffer at the hands of both the Assyrians and the Babylonians (21:13-17), leaving only a tiny handful of Arab survivors to worship the Lord alongside the people of Judah. The Lord is unconcerned about the dangers of making such definite predictions about foreign affairs. The nations are his toolbox, so he can simply declare in 21:17, *"The Lord, the God of Israel, has spoken."*[5]

---

[3] It was costly for Isaiah to serve as God's prophet. 20:2-4 tells us that he went about semi-naked for much of 711 to 708 BC in order to illustrate this prophecy. Being God's signs and wonders to the world isn't easy.

[4] Israel hated Egypt, which hated Assyria, which hated Israel. The ending of this triangle of hatred in 19:23-25 reflects the promises in 2:2-4 and 11:1-16. The Gospel turns bitter enemies into friends.

[5] The Lord also states this as the final word on the matter in 1:20, 21:17, 22:25, 24:3, 25:8, 40:5, 48:15 and 58:14.

In 22:1–25, the Lord predicts the destruction of Jerusalem. Knowing that its citizens will be rubbing their hands in glee over his stern words to their enemies, he refers to their region obliquely as *"the Valley of Vision"* so that he can suddenly shock them by revealing that he means Jerusalem. Since they have ignored Isaiah's prophecies, preferring drunken parties to tearful repentance, he will destroy their nation at the hands of the Babylonians in 586 BC.

In 23:1–18, the Lord ends this long series of prophecies with a prediction that he will also destroy the great Phoenician port city of Tyre. For centuries it had dominated trade across the Mediterranean along with Tarshish, its sister city in far-off Spain. The idea that its hegemony was about to come to an abrupt end seemed unthinkable when Isaiah spoke these words but, sure enough, the Assyrians sacked Sidon in 677 BC and the Babylonians reduced Tyre to poverty during the siege of 586–573 BC.[6]

So what? That's the question most modern readers ask when they wade through these eleven chapters of foreign policy prediction. What does all this ancient history have to do with us today? Well, absolutely everything. God uses it to demonstrate his complete control of the events of world history, proving to us that he is far bigger than we think. These chapters form a prelude to the Lord's boast in Isaiah 48:5 and 45:21:

> *I told you these things long ago; before they happened I announced them to you so that you could not say, "My images brought them about; my wooden image and metal god ordained them." "Who foretold this long ago, who declared it from the distant past? Was it not I, the Lord? And there is no God apart from me."*

---

[6] Assyria was the greatest power on land; Tyre was the greatest power at sea. This probably explains why the prophecies against them are at either end of this series of prophecies against the nations.

Look Who's Talking
(14:12–17)

How you have fallen from heaven, morning star, son of the dawn!

(Isaiah 14:12)

Many people find these eleven chapters of judgment very offensive. That's because they do not know the Lord as Isaiah knew him. They have grown far too comfortable singing *"Love, love, love"* with The Beatles and they have never truly learned what it means to sing *"Holy, holy, holy"* with the angels. The Gospel is radically inclusive yet holiness is radically exclusive. When people complain that God appears too strict and intolerant in these chapters, it reveals that they have not yet grasped how serious sin is.

From the earliest times, Christians have detected the voice of the Devil in Isaiah 14:12–17. The great third-century theologian Tertullian was among them: *"The prophet makes him say, 'I will raise my throne above the stars... I will ascend above the tops of the clouds; I will make myself like the Most High' – this can only mean the Devil."*[1] When Dante wrote his *Inferno* and John Milton wrote his *Paradise Lost*, they reinforced this by referring to the Devil by the Latin word for *"morning star"* in 14:12 – we still use this name today whenever we refer to him as *"Lucifer"*. None of this is to deny that these words are spoken by the human ruler who liked to be known as "King Pul

---

[1] Tertullian in *Against Marcion* (5.11 and 5.17).

of Babylon". It is simply to recognize that he was inspired by another, far more sinister power on the inside.

Along with a similar passage in Ezekiel 28:12–19, these six verses explain how the Devil came to be in the world. He was originally a beautiful angel, one of those the Lord had created to help him sing his great dawn chorus to the world. At first he enjoyed his calling to be one of God's mighty guardian angels, but eventually he started to want more. We do not know whether he was jealous of the divine relationship between the Father and the Son, or whether he was jealous of God's plan to create humans in his own likeness to enjoy this relationship with him, but Lucifer decided that it was time to make his own bid for divinity. He rebelled against the Lord and was cast down to earth along with the angels who rebelled with him. Jesus refers to this when he tells us in Luke 10:18 that *"I saw Satan fall like lightning from heaven."* Revelation 12:8–9 refers to it when it tells us that *"He was not strong enough, and they lost their place in heaven. The great dragon was hurled down – that ancient serpent called the devil, or Satan, who leads the whole world astray. He was hurled to the earth, and his angels with him."* The Devil is a fallen angel who infects the world with his sin. He fights dirty because he knows he is on the losing team.

If you find these chapters a bit too stern and judgmental for your liking, it is probably a sign that you have failed to grasp that there is a war on. God is holy, Satan is evil and each of us has to choose a side. Tiglath-Pileser chose the side of arrogance, violent self-assertion and rebellion against God.[2] Hosea 10:13–14 tells us that his army was even willing to murder children to achieve its goals, which is why the Lord promises to return their own actions back upon them in 13:16, 13:18 and 14:21. Isaiah shows us that God is sterner than we think. He will not ignore it when people choose to side with the Devil.

---

[2] Tiglath-Pileser wanted to become one of the gods which were said to dwell together on Mount Zaphon (14:13). He also wanted to supplant God's true Branch as the central figure of world history (14:19).

Isaiah expects us to hear the Devil talking in the rest of these prophecies too. The Moabites have sold their souls to Satan, sacrificing their own children to the demon-god Chemosh in return for his promise of prosperity and success. The Israelites have sided with Asherah, the demon-goddess of fertility. The Egyptians have placed their trust in idols and in witchcraft. The scorching heat and drought which the Lord promises to send against them are the direct result of their decision to worship the sun and the River Nile. The economic prosperity of the people of Tyre has made them behave as if they are little gods.[3] The Lord makes it clear in 19:1 and 21:9 that he is declaring war on the idols of the nations and not just on their worshippers. If we side with the Devil, we will share in his fate. We really need to stop and look who's talking.

Tolerance is therefore not necessarily a virtue. God sees it as a terrible vice in the people of Judah. The Lord refers to Mount Zion as the *Valley* of Vision in chapter 22, because King Ahaz had taken to worshipping the idol Molech in the valley outside Jerusalem. He had sacrificed his own children in the fire to the demon-god in the hope of working his own way to glory.[4] Instead of trusting in the Lord, the Israelites looked to their weapons, their ramparts and their moats for safety. They were acting just like the Devil when he launched his failed bid for power and lost his place in heaven.

In 13:3, the Lord therefore refers to the Persian army which will destroy Babylon as his *qādōshim* – his *holy ones*, who have been set apart to side with him against the Devil's havoc in the world. In the same way, the Lord is calling us to side with him in his stern determination to deal decisively with sin, instead of complaining that he judges so severely. Through these chapters he invites us to become his holy people, alert to the subtle voice of the Devil in our world. What Christians call tolerance is often

---

[3] Isaiah 16:6, 12; 17:8; 19:3; 23:8–9. See also 1 Kings 11:7; 2 Kings 3:26–27.
[4] 2 Kings 16:2–4; 2 Chronicles 28:1–4.

naivety. The Lord calls us to open our eyes and ears to see who is talking.

A few years ago, one of my friends was pregnant and went to the hospital for her twelve-week scan. The sonographer took the nuchal measurements of her baby and then broke the bad news to her. There was a high risk that her baby had Down's syndrome. Did she want to terminate the pregnancy and start again? Immediately she panicked. How could she cope with a baby with special needs? How could she foist such a problem on her husband, on her parents, on the state or on herself? I sat in her kitchen a few weeks ago having lunch with her and her child – born without any disability – and she marvelled out loud at how close she had come to believing the Devil's lie that the life of her perfectly healthy son was a problem which had to be eliminated.

It made me wonder what other lies we may be listening to, unawares. The lie there is no harm in lusting after another person's body? The lie that alcohol or drugs or popularity can ever truly satisfy us? Take a look at who is talking and take a look at what God says will happen on the Day of Judgment to the Devil and to anyone who listens to his lies:

> *Those who see you stare at you, they ponder your fate...*
> *All the nations who knew you are appalled at you; you*
> *have come to a horrible end and will be no more.*[5]

---

[5] Isaiah 14:16–17; Ezekiel 28:18–19; Revelation 12:12.

David's House Key
(22:15–25)

*I will place on his shoulder the key to the house of
David; what he opens no one can shut, and what he
shuts no one can open.*

(Isaiah 22:22)

There's a lullaby that I sing to my little daughter before she goes
to sleep at night. It goes like this: *"They call me a poor man, they
call me a poor man. But it simply isn't true. 'Cause I could never be
a poor man as long as I've got a daughter like you."* The people of
Judah were about to get poor fast. The years of prosperity would
evaporate in an instant when the Assyrian army captured their
fields, their vineyards and their olive groves. They would lose
everything, which is why the Lord gave them some good news in
the midst of these prophecies of judgment. They had something
that no foreign army could ever steal. Like the lullaby I sing to
my daughter, the Lord had given them something that ensured
they could never truly be poor.

One of the richest men in Jerusalem was named Shebna.
As both royal treasurer and palace administrator, he was the
most senior royal official in the early years of King Hezekiah.
However, he had succumbed to the same sin as Tiglath-Pileser
and the other foreign rulers who provoked these eleven chapters
of judgment. The Lord has to single him out at the end of his
prophecy against Judah and accuse him of being an imposter in
the palace. He is not part of the solution to Judah having chosen
sinfulness over holiness. He is part of the problem. He boasts in
his own strength by racing through the streets in a chariot, he

abuses his position and he has just commissioned for himself a splendid tomb. Because he has ordered craftsmen to chisel for him a mausoleum in the rock face, the Lord decrees that the Assyrians will drag him away to die in exile, far away.[1]

Sinful Shebna would be replaced as palace administrator by a godly man named Eliakim. We can read about his service to King Hezekiah in 36:3. The name Eliakim means *God Will Raise Up* and it dropped a hint to the people of Judah that he was a prophetic picture of a greater servant in the future. His palace duties pointed to the day when God would open up his new Branch of heaven in Jerusalem. Eliakim's daily schedule proclaimed to the people of Judah that they could never be poor when God had promised them his Messiah.

On his first day at work, Eliakim was dressed in fine clothes and given a sash which proclaimed his royal authority. He was given *"the key to the house of David"* – in other words, the master key that opened every royal treasure room in Hezekiah's palace. Later on in 39:2, Isaiah will tell us in quite some detail what Hezekiah kept in these storehouses: silver, gold, spices, olive oil, armour and state-of-the-art weaponry. Eliakim had been granted access to all areas. There was nothing King Hezekiah owned that Eliakim's key could not secure. Imagine him on his first day at work, wide-eyed at all these treasures. Now listen to what Jesus says in Revelation 3:7–10 about what these verses mean for us today.

Jesus appeared to the apostle John in a vision on the island of Patmos during a very difficult moment for the early Christians. The Roman Emperor Domitian had imprisoned and exiled many of them. Some of them had even been executed. They felt as poor as the people of Judah during the Assyrian invasion, so Jesus pointed them back to this amazing promise in Isaiah.

---

[1] We are told in 36:3 that God was very merciful to Shebna. His downfall began with mere demotion to court secretary. Even in his judgment, God gave Shebna time to come to his senses and repent.

In John's vision, Jesus tells us that he is the true and better Eliakim.[2] He is the Holy One who speaks God's truth to the world, and he has been given the true key to David's treasure rooms. Jesus quotes from 22:22 when he promises us that *"What he opens no one can shut, and what he shuts no one can open."* But he also goes one step further. He promises us, *"See, I have placed before* **you** *an open door that no one can shut."* Jesus does not merely hold David's house key in his own hand, even though that would be encouraging enough, but he has given David's house key to us! That's what he meant when he promised, *"I will give you the keys of the kingdom of heaven; whatever you bind on earth will be bound in heaven, and whatever you loose on earth will be loosed in heaven."*[3]

Are you poor and in need? Then you have heaven's riches laid before you. You have something better than silver and gold, since God has made us *"heirs of God and co-heirs with Christ"* of all the riches of his grace and mercy and kindness and glory.[4] You have something better than spices, since the New Testament tells us that this is a symbol of God answering our prayers.[5] You have something better than fine oil, since the New Testament tells us that this is a symbol of God anointing us with his Holy Spirit.[6] We have something better than metal armour and royal weaponry, since we have been given the armour of God and have been armed against our enemies with holy character, with the Word of God, with the gifts of the Spirit and with the same

---

[2] Isaiah hints at this by saying in 22:20 that this prophecy will be fulfilled *"in that day"* – a phrase he has just used in 19:16, 18, 19, 21, 23 and 24 to refer to the coming of the Messiah.

[3] Jesus initially said this only to Peter but later broadened it to include everyone (Matthew 16:19; 18:18).

[4] Romans 2:4; 8:17; 9:23; 11:33; Ephesians 1:7, 18; 2:7; 3:8, 16; Philippians 4:19; Colossians 1:27; 2:2.

[5] Revelation 5:8; 8:3–4. Jesus promises us seven times in John 14–16 alone that, if we dwell in him and let him dwell in us, we will receive whatever we ask for in prayer.

[6] Mark 6:13; James 5:14–15. See also 1 Samuel 16:13.

faith that knocked down the walls of Jericho. As Christians, we can no longer behave like paupers. Jesus has given us a treasure trove which reflects his glory as our Risen King.[7]

Of course there is a price tag. Jesus paid it himself. Isaiah likens Eliakim to a nail which is driven into a piece of wood, using the same Hebrew word that the prophet Zechariah uses to describe the Messiah shortly before predicting that *"they will look on me, the one they have pierced."*[8] Isaiah is upfront with the people of Judah that Eliakim will eventually let them down, and that it will appear for a while as if their Messiah has failed too. But he promises that the new and better Eliakim will arise to let them share in the glory of his Father and to sing to them a better father's lullaby:

> *You're not a poor man, poor man,*
> *So don't be lonesome and don't be blue*
> *'Cause you can never be a poor man.*
> *David's house key is given to you.*

----

[7] Ephesians 6:13–18; Romans 13:12–14.

[8] Zechariah 10:4; 12:10.

Perspective (24:1–23)

See, the Lord is going to lay waste the earth and
devastate it.

(Isaiah 24:1)

Every tourist does it when they visit the Taj Mahal. I have even done it myself. If you position your body at a certain angle and stretch your hand out in the right way, you can fool a camera that you are picking up the Taj Mahal by the spire on its dome. Perspective is a funny thing and it can make our eyes play tricks on us. You should try it if you ever visit the Taj Mahal or St Paul's Cathedral or the Capitol.

Playing games with perspective helps us to understand Isaiah's prophecies of judgment. It is never very clear whether his long chapters of prophecy against the nations of the ancient world are all about the little judgment days that befell them or whether they point towards a greater Judgment Day that is yet to come. The truth is that these chapters do both. They speak about the fate of ancient nations (why else be so specific?) but they also speak about the end of time (why else bother to include so much detail in the Bible?). We need to get a true perspective when we read these chapters, because they are talking about two events, not just one. They are both microscopic (talking about events close at hand) and telescopic (talking about events many centuries away).

The New Testament emphasizes this strongly. Jesus quotes from 13:10 in Matthew 24:29 and Mark 13:24 in order to warn us that the little judgment days predicted in chapters 13–23 all point towards a greater Judgment Day that will end world history.[1] He quotes the words, *"The sun will be darkened, and the moon will not give its light; the stars will fall from the sky, and the heavenly bodies will be shaken,"* and then he adds some further commentary of his own: *"Then will appear the sign of the Son of Man in heaven. And then all the peoples of the earth will mourn when they see the Son of Man coming on the clouds of heaven, with power and great glory."* Jesus therefore likens the sudden fall of Babylon to his own sudden return from heaven. He warns that God has set a Judgment Day (13:6) when he will pour out his stern anger on the wicked (13:9). He will root out all sinfulness from the world in order to create new heavens and a new earth for his people (14:7).

The apostle Paul also quotes from these chapters in order to teach us that they speak about a greater Judgment Day. He uses the words of 22:13 in 1 Corinthians 15:32 to describe what will happen to people who sneer at the idea that Jesus is coming back from heaven to judge the world. The people of Jerusalem in Isaiah's day were not the only ones to reassure themselves that life is all about having fun – *"Let us eat and drink for tomorrow we die!"* It is precisely what the complacent King Belshazzar of Babylon said to his courtiers when he invited them to a drinking party on the night that their city fell to the Persians (21:5). People in every generation have shared this complacency. Even in the fearful Middle Ages one poet wrote that *"Some there are who tell of one who threatens he will toss to hell the luckless pots he marred in making – pish! He's a good fellow and 'twill all be well."*[2] Paul warns us that these chapters ought to change our perspective. All will not be well for sinners, because God is far sterner than most of us think.

The apostle John also quotes from these chapters in order

---

[1] Jesus' teaching in Matthew 24 and Mark 13 is itself both microscopic (predicting the Fall of Jerusalem in 70 AD) and telescopic (predicting the Final Judgment). This is very common for biblical prophecy.

[2] The eleventh-century Persian poet Omar Khayyám wrote this in his *Rubaiyat* (number 88).

to teach us that they warn about the Final Judgment Day. Picking up on the way that Isaiah identifies the Devil's voice with that of Babylon in 14:12–17, John describes the work of demons throughout history as the reign of *"Babylon the Great, the mother of prostitutes and of the abominations of the earth"*. He takes Isaiah's coyness in naming Jerusalem and Babylon to mean that they are primarily spiritual rather than urban entities.[3] He tells us that the whole of world history is a tale of two cities: Babylon against Jerusalem, the Prostitute against the Bride. When he rejoices over God's Final Judgment, he echoes the words of 21:9: *"Fallen! Fallen is Babylon the Great, which made all the nations drink the maddening wine of her adulteries."*[4]

Armed with this proper New Testament perspective on Isaiah 13–23, we are now ready to read the words of Isaiah 24. The prophet explains what Jesus and Paul and John have already taught us – that each little prediction of judgment also prophesies a far greater Judgment Day to come. *"See, the Lord is going to lay waste the earth and devastate it,"* he warns us. *"The earth will be completely laid waste and totally plundered. The Lord has spoken this word... A curse consumes the earth; its people must bear their guilt... From the ends of the earth we hear singing: 'Glory to the Righteous One.'"*

Chapters 24–27 are known collectively as "Isaiah's Little Apocalypse" or as "Isaiah's Mini-Revelation". It is easy to see why. God made his detailed foreign policy predictions, not just to prove his control of ancient history, but also to prove his utter control of the events that will lead up to the end of time. Having used the phrase *"in that day"* eight times in 19:16–25 and 22:15–25 to refer to the first coming of his Messiah, he now uses that same phrase seven times in chapters 24–27 to refer to the Messiah's Second Coming. Make no mistake about it. Isaiah

---

[3] Isaiah refers to Babylon as *"the Desert by the Sea"* (21:1) and to Jerusalem as *"the Valley of Vision"* (22:1).

[4] Revelation 14:8; 16:19; 17:1–18:24. Babylon must fall for the New Jerusalem to be revealed in 21:1–27.

is calling us to get a proper perspective. God's judgment on these ancient nations proves that there is a greater Judgment Day to come.

The same medieval poet that I quoted earlier laughed at this idea: *"Would ever a peevish boy break the bowl from which he drank in joy? Then would he that made a vessel in pure love, in an after rage destroy?"*[5] Isaiah warns us not to laugh along with him. No matter what our social background (24:2), no matter what our level of understanding (24:5),[6] no matter what man-made precautions we have taken (24:18) and no matter how highly other people think of us (24:21–23) – unless we have surrendered to the Lord and received his forgiveness, we will find ourselves in hell (24:22). God is determined to re-create this sinful world to make it home to his New Jerusalem on his New Mount Zion.

So don't fool yourself. Get a proper perspective. Get ready for the Judgment Day which is to come.

---

[5] Omar Khayyám in his *Rubaiyat* (number 85).

[6] Isaiah talks in Hebrew about the people of the earth disobeying their own *torahs*, or *laws*. Everybody has an understanding of God's standards, however limited, and each person will be judged for breaking it.

Thank God He Judges
(25:1–12)

Lord, you are my God; I will exalt you and praise your name, for... you have made the city a heap of rubble.

(Isaiah 25:1–2)

It is easy to tell whether or not you have grasped what it means for God to be the Holy One of Israel. When you read his stern words of judgment in Isaiah, instead of feeling offended you feel like worshipping. So, how do you feel so far? To help you process your feelings, Isaiah steps forward to act as our worship leader.

Don't misunderstand me. There is nothing trite and unthinking about Isaiah's positive reaction to God's judgment. He is so horrified that he has already burst into tears twice, in 15:5 and 16:9: *"My heart cries out over Moab... I weep, as Jazer weeps... Heshbon and Elealeh, I drench you with tears!"* Isaiah does not lead us into worship because he fails to feel proper emotion for those against whom he has prophesied. He leads us into worship because he feels proper emotion towards the Lord. He has not forgotten his glorious vision of the Lord in the Temple courtyard. He has grasped that God is far bigger than we think. He has learned to sing the same song as the angels: *"Holy, holy, holy"*.

In 25:1, Isaiah begins his song of worship: *"Lord, you are my God; I will exalt you and praise your name."* He does not see the last fourteen chapters of judgment as a blot on God's character. He sees them as the natural outworking of it. If the Lord is truly holy, he cannot turn a blind eye to all the sin that is in the world. If he did so, he would not be holy at all. Although

Isaiah weeps over the human tragedy of God's judgment, he is delighted that God judges sternly. It means that he truly is the God he says he is.

John Calvin helps us here while commenting on similar words in the Psalms:

> *The love of godliness does not thrive sufficiently in our hearts unless it generates a hatred of sin such as David speaks of here... For whoever indulges wicked deeds and encourages them through silence is a falsehearted betrayer of God's cause... Whenever a person offends our own welfare, reputation and comfort, our keen sense of self ensures we never hesitate to oppose them, yet in defending the glory of God we are most timid and cowardly... If the majesty of God is outraged, no one stirs himself. If we have a true zeal for God then it will prove itself by our resolve to declare irreconcilable war on the wicked and on all who hate God, rather than being alienated from God in order to court their favour.*[1]

In 25:1–5, Isaiah therefore celebrates the fact that the Lord's judgment demonstrates the beauty of his character. We may find it hard to stomach when Isaiah says that *"I will exalt you and praise your name, for... you have made the city a heap of rubble,"* but let's hear him out. He points out that God's judgment achieves at least four things. First, it proves his perfect faithfulness, since it means he was not lying when he warned Adam in Genesis 2:17 that the wages of sin is death. Second, it proves his perfect control of world history, since this is precisely what he said he would do. Third, it proves his perfect love, because judging the wicked is the only way to ensure that their victims are protected in the future. Fourth, it proves his commitment to righteousness, since it acts as a deterrent, ensuring that *"strong peoples will*

---

[1] Calvin in his *Commentary on the Book of Psalms*, talking about Psalm 139:21–22.

honour you; cities of ruthless nations will revere you." When we object to God's judgment, it is not a sign of our goodness and mercy. Quite the opposite. It means we are unwilling to pay the price for goodness and mercy to prevail.

In 25:6–9, Isaiah celebrates a further reason why God's judgment is such good news. His commitment to rooting out every last vestige of sin is necessary for the re-founding of a new and better Mount Zion. This should be obvious to us but often it isn't. We forget that paradise would not be paradise if it were just like our present world. Imagine waking up in heaven and finding a newspaper on your doormat that describes what is happening throughout God's celestial city. It reports a rape in one part of heaven, some petty theft elsewhere and a growing problem of road rage on the holy highway. You would be furious. You would feel you had been lied to about paradise. That's why Isaiah celebrates so loudly in these verses. He is thrilled that God has the resolve to do what it takes to make the New Mount Zion everything he hoped it would be and more. There is no more darkness, no more death, no more sadness and no more disgrace anywhere among God's people. Isaiah celebrates that God has saved the world as thoroughly as he promised: *"Surely this is our God; we trusted in him, and he saved us. This is the Lord, we trusted in him; let us rejoice and be glad in his salvation."*

In 25:10–12, Isaiah therefore rejoices in the violent destruction of the enemies of God. He chooses Moab to represent them – the very nation over which he wept so bitterly in 15:5 and 16:9 – and he praises God for making their fate as repulsive as that of a diver attempting to swim his way through a steaming lake of manure. He wants us to celebrate God's judgment with him and so does the New Testament. Paul quotes from 25:8 when he encourages us in 1 Corinthians 15:54 to rejoice with him that Jesus has done everything it takes to destroy death once and for all. John quotes twice from 25:8 when he encourages us in Revelation 7:17 and 21:4 to rejoice with him that God has done all it takes to put an end to this world's suffering, once and for all.[2]

Many of our worship songs today contain the Hebrew phrase *Hallelujah*, meaning *"Praise the Lord."* What most Christians fail to realize is that this phrase is only used four times in the New Testament and that all four of them are in the song that God's people sing in Revelation 19:1–10 after the sudden destruction of Babylon. The Hallelujah Chorus of the New Testament comes as a direct response to the blood, fire and judgment which go before. Those verses even point back to Isaiah 25:6, describing this Messianic Banquet as *"the wedding supper of the Lamb"*.

So don't be offended by all these chapters about God's judgment. Don't even be embarrassed by them in your conversations with unbelievers, squirming when they ask you how a loving God can send people to hell or why the God of the Old Testament appears so nasty and ill-tempered in their eyes, which have never seen him. Instead, be encouraged. Thank the Lord that he is far sterner than you ever thought. Thank God that he judges sin, because it is the only way in which the world can ever truly be saved.

---

[2] God's promise that he will wipe every tear from our eyes speaks of more than simply freedom from pain. It also speaks of intimacy. Even among the crowd of the redeemed, we will not be distant from the Lord.

The Voice (26:1–27:13)

In that day – "Sing about a fruitful vineyard."

(Isaiah 27:2)

It is not hard to see why the TV programme *The Voice* has become so popular with viewers all around the world. Accomplished recording artists sit as judges in swivel chairs, which face away from the stage so that they cannot see the contestants while they sing. They have to listen to the sound of their voices and to the words they sing in order to make a decision whether or not to press the button that will turn around their swivel chair and declare that they are committed to helping them.

I hope you are sitting comfortably in your swivel chair, because Isaiah tries to woo us with a beautiful song in the last two chapters of his "Little Apocalypse". We cannot see his face. We have only his words and the sound of his voice as he appeals to us to decide whether or not we are committed to the Holy One of Israel.

In 26:1–6, Isaiah appeals to us to commit to God's plan to create a New Jerusalem. We have already seen that this book of prophecies is a tale of two cities, but Isaiah begins to step up the importance of this after predicting the downfall of Babylon and the Old Jerusalem. Walter Brueggemann describes the entire book of Isaiah as *"a continued meditation upon the destiny of Jerusalem"*, since it begins in 1:1 with the sinful city of Jerusalem and ends in 66:19–24 with the New Jerusalem on God's holy mountain.[1] Isaiah therefore sings us a love song about this city, appealing for us to commit our lives to building it

---

[1] Walter Brueggemann in *An Introduction to the Old Testament* (2003).

with God. He sings about its strength, its walls, its ramparts and its gates. He wants us to be as excited as he is that every *"lofty city"* will be destroyed so that a remnant from each of them can take their place in *"the righteous nation"* which inhabits the New Jerusalem.[2]

Countless believers have been inspired by these words and by Isaiah's promise that the Lord will grant perfect peace to anyone who puts their trust in him.[3] One of the most famous hymns in the English language was inspired by the name which Isaiah uses for God in 26:4. This reference to the *"Rock of Ages"* should serve as a reminder that Isaiah wants to do more than inspire us. He wants to help us sing new songs of our own.

In 26:7–19, Isaiah appeals to us to commit to waiting patiently for God's plan to be accomplished. He reminds us in 26:8 that Christian faith is seen as much by our willingness to wait for God's timing as it is by our willingness to rush into action for him. The world cannot understand this embracing of whatever it takes to form God's character within us, because it builds fast and for only one lifetime. We are different. We serve the Upright One and we know that he is looking for straight-sided bricks with which he can build his holy city. A lot of our commitment to Christ will never be noticed by the world – studying his Word (26:8),[4] subjecting our own desires to his name and his renown (26:8), praying in the morning and in the evening (26:9)[5] and accepting the daily frustration of not being

---

[2] The new city is no longer home only to the Jews. All people groups form part of this new nation (25:6–8).

[3] Isaiah uses a play on words in 26:3, since the word *shālōm* or *peace* lies at the heart of the name Jerusalem. The city's name means *Foundation of Double Peace*, and the Hebrew for *perfect peace* is *shālōm shālōm*.

[4] When we are unsure what to do in any given situation, 26:8 tells us that we should obey the general instruction of God's Word until we receive specific guidance from the Lord.

[5] In Hebrew, Isaiah describes communion with God *at night* and *at the break of dawn*.

as spiritually fruitful as we long to be (26:18). Yet these hidden acts of patient obedience are very precious to the Lord.

To help us make a firm commitment to God's plan, Isaiah uses language that reminds us of what we have already learned so far in his book of prophecies. The Lord judges sinners sternly because he loves them and knows that they will ignore him if he blesses them with non-stop prosperity (26:9–11). He is determined to enlarge the nation of Israel, not just by reintegrating the Galileans, as he promised in 9:3, but also by including the pagan nations too (26:15). For this to happen, he has to convince his people that they can achieve nothing without him; he alone can accomplish something for them (26:12).[6] Only then will they be freed from the evangelistic infertility that afflicts self-confident churches and be enabled to breathe life into the spiritually dead (26:16–19). Can you hear Isaiah singing? Only a fool would turn down this amazing invitation from the Lord. He is asking us to push the button on our swivel chairs and to commit to the patient and unglamorous work of building the New Jerusalem with him.

In 26:20–27:1, Isaiah appeals to us to commit to the Lord's timing. He points us back to the Exodus, when the Israelites hid inside their houses during the Passover before bursting forth to destroy Pharaoh and his army in the Red Sea. Isaiah urges us to trust in God during the *"little while"* that it takes for his promised judgment to fall. Our enemies may seem stronger than Pharaoh and as mighty as the great sea monster known as the Leviathan, but the Lord will destroy them all in a single day.[7] Isaiah uses the phrase *"in that day"* four times in chapter 27 because he wants us to know that the Messiah's second coming will complete every unfulfilled promise in a moment.

---

[6] Christians can only be fruitful when they recognize: *"All that we have accomplished you have done for us."*

[7] The Hebrew word *tannîn* in 27:1 can mean a *sea monster*, but it is also used to describe the massive cobra which confronted Pharaoh in Exodus 7:9–12 and to describe Pharaoh himself in Ezekiel 29:3.

In 27:2–13, Isaiah therefore appeals to us to commit ourselves entirely to God's unfolding plan. Having sung a song against the sinful vineyard of Israel in chapter 5, he now promises that God will establish a new and better Vineyard (27:2–6). Having prophesied against the idolatrous city of Jerusalem in chapter 22, Isaiah now promises that God will deal with the treble problem of its sin, its idolatry and its spiritual ignorance (27:7–11).[8] Having promised a holy highway running from Egypt to Assyria in 19:23–25, Isaiah now prophesies that God will combine the people of Israel, Egypt and Assyria (representing every nation of the earth) into one holy city, the New Jerusalem (27:12–13). Isaiah has come back to where he started his song. He urges us to commit to calling the nations to *"come and worship the Lord on the holy mountain in Jerusalem."*

Isaiah has finished singing. He has come to the end of his "Little Apocalypse". It is time for us to respond. Will we continue our lives as they were before we started reading or will we commit the rest of our lives to building the New Jerusalem?

In the movie *Midnight In Paris*, Marion Cotillard expresses her amazement that Paris exists and anyone could choose to live anywhere else in the world. Isaiah feels the same way about the New Jerusalem. As the final echo of his voice begins to die away, he is still looking at the back of your swivel chair. He is asking you to commit your life to helping God build his holy city. It is your move.

---

[8] Isaiah is not saying in 27:9 that the Israelites managed to atone for their sins through their own suffering. Paul quotes this verse in Romans 11:27 as *"I will take away their sins."* Their sins were atoned for through the suffering of Jesus, the new and better Israel and the new and better Vine.

Downfall (28:1–29)

The Lord, the Lord Almighty, has told me of the destruction decreed against the whole land.

(Isaiah 28:22)

Early in the morning on 10th May 1940, the German army launched its invasion of Western Europe. Belgium and the Netherlands were quickly overwhelmed and fell. France was outwitted and completely outmanoeuvred. The German advance took on the nature of a rout. On 15th May, only five days after the invasion had begun, the French prime minister phoned his counterpart in London. He told Winston Churchill, *"We have been defeated; we are beaten; we have lost the battle."*[1]

Hold that thought. The scenery suddenly changes in Isaiah 28–35. In order to understand these chapters, it helps to know that Israel and Judah were about to face a moment every bit as dire as that face by the French and British in May 1940. They had not listened to Isaiah's warnings in his early chapters. They had imagined they knew better. Now the Lord was about to initiate their downfall.

In 28:1–13, the Lord confronts the stupidity of the northern kingdom of Israel. He begins with the word *"Woe!"* and he uses this same word to begin each of the six main prophecies in this section of Isaiah.[2] The Lord curses Israel for treating their capital city Samaria as their "wreath and beauty" (28:1–4). It

---

[1] Churchill quotes the French prime minister in his memoirs, *Their Finest Hour* (1949).

[2] 28:1; 29:1, 15; 30:1; 31:1; 33:1. These "six woes" may well have inspired Jesus to proclaim his own "six woes" against the Jewish leaders in Luke 11:39–52.

might well look impregnable in its magnificent hilltop location, but it will crumble in a moment when the Assyrian army draws near.[3] Because the Israelites refuse to recognize the Lord as their true "wreath and beauty", they will miss out on knowing him as *a source of strength to those who turn back the battle at the gate"* (28:5–6).[4] Imagine how it felt for the French when Paris fell to the Germans on 14th June 1940 and Adolf Hitler posed for a grinning photo in front of the Eiffel Tower. That's how these verses are meant to make us feel as we read about the downfall of Israel.

The root of Israel's problem was that its leaders were fools. They were more interested in escaping their troubles by getting drunk than they were in facing up to them (28:7–8). They refused to listen to Isaiah because they felt that he was lecturing them like children (28:9–10).[5] Very well then, the Lord warns, I will graduate you suddenly from the Hebrew kindergarten to the university of Assyria! Paul quotes from 28:11 to challenge us in 1 Corinthians 14:21 that this warning is for our day too. If we refuse to listen voluntarily to the words of Isaiah, we will be forced to listen to them the hard way.

These words were fulfilled in 722 BC. King Hoshea of Israel had grown tired of acting as Assyria's puppet ruler. When Tiglath-Pileser died and was succeeded by his son Shalmaneser, Hoshea saw it as an opportunity to renegotiate the terms of his rule. Emboldened by the promise of help from Egypt, he declared that Israel would no longer pay its annual tribute to Assyria. Shalmaneser reacted firmly, besieging Samaria and putting its inhabitants to the sword. Fewer than 30,000 Israelites survived

---

[3] Isaiah has a brilliant picture for this in 28:4. Samaria will be "plucked and eaten like a fig from a tree".

[4] The Hebrew word *'atārāh* in 28:1, 3 and 5 can be translated *crown* as well as wreath. The Hebrew word *tiph'ārāh* in 28:1, 4 and 5 can be translated *finery* as well as beauty.

[5] 28:10 and 13 really sound like kindergarten talk in Hebrew: *tsaw lātsāw tsaw lātsāw qaw lāqāw qaw lāqāw*.

to go into captivity. Most of the others died in the northern kingdom's sudden downfall.[6]

In 28:14–29, the Lord turns to confront the stupidity of the southern kingdom of Judah. They have not listened to Isaiah's warnings either. The Assyrian border is now only eight miles north of Jerusalem, yet they are still relying on idols to protect them instead of on the Lord. Their images of metal and stone are not saviours. They are *lies* and *falsehood*, and they spell *death and hell* for the southern kingdom.[7] The people of Judah need to open their eyes and *"See, I lay a stone in Zion, a tested stone, a precious cornerstone for a sure foundation; the one who relies on it will never be stricken with panic."* The New Testament quotes this verse three times to tell us that it is a prophecy about the Messiah.[8] The Lord still promises to deliver the people of Judah if they turn their eyes to Eliakim in the royal palace and trust that he is a prophetic picture of the one who holds the true key to their salvation. The Lord still promises to grant them a victory similar to the ones he gave to David over the Philistines at Mount Perazim and to Joshua over the Amorites in the Valley of Gibeon (28:17–22).[9] Although the northern kingdom fooled itself that it was too educated to need Isaiah's prophecies, the Lord still promises to save Judah if its people embrace the humble wisdom of a common farmer (28:23–29).[10]

---

[6] 2 Kings 17:1–24. We know the number of Israelites taken into captivity because it is recorded in the imperial annals of King Sargon II of Assyria (722–705 BC).

[7] The Hebrew word *she'ôl* in 28:15 occurs nine times in Isaiah. It is variously translated *the realm of the dead*, *the grave*, *hell* and *hades*. Judah's stupidity is fatal.

[8] Romans 9:33, Romans 10:11 and 1 Peter 2:6 all follow the Greek Septuagint translation, which promises *"they will never be put to shame."* However, Isaiah actually promises in Hebrew that *"they will not panic."* Placing our trust in Jesus means refusing to trust in the man-made solutions which clamour for our attention.

[9] Joshua 10:10–12; 2 Samuel 5:20; 1 Chronicles 14:11.

[10] 28:23–29 teaches "natural revelation" – that even the wisdom of unbelievers has been given them by God.

The northern kingdom of Israel had experienced a mighty downfall, yet the southern kingdom of Judah need not experience a similar downfall of its own. As we read the many ways in which the Lord promises this throughout this chapter, we need to remember what we learned earlier about having a proper perspective. He is not just making promises to the people of Isaiah's day. He makes these promises to each one of us as we read this chapter.

The Lord promises to be the true "wreath and beauty" on which we can rely (28:5). He promises to empower us to turn back the tide of trouble, even when it advances to the very gates of our lives (28:6). He promises to calm our fears and to deliver us if we fix our eyes on his Messiah (28:16). He promises to be our Wonderful Counsellor and to save us through his gift of divine wisdom (28:29).[11]

We need to remember this when the difficulties around us make us feel like the people of France and Britain in 1940 or the people of Judah in the days of Isaiah. We need to remember that the award-winning movie *Downfall* is not about Adolf Hitler's victory, but about his ultimate defeat at the hands of those he had once threatened to destroy. We need to remember his dejected admission: *All is lost. Totally lost.*[12]

So don't be like the people of Israel, who ignored Isaiah's prophecies and reaped an unnecessary downfall. Don't be like the people of Judah, who continued to listen half-heartedly. Let the words of this chapter stir you to cry out in prayer for God to forgive you and strengthen you to avert the disaster which is at the gates of your generation.

---

[11] Although the syntax is slightly different, the same two Hebrew root words are used in 28:29 to describe the Lord as *"wonderful in counsel"* as are used in 9:6 to describe him as our *"Wonderful Counsellor"*.

[12] *Downfall* (Constantin Film, 2004).

Faking It (29:1–24)

*These people come near to me with their mouth and
honour me with their lips, but their hearts are far from
me.*

(Isaiah 29:13)

Imagine the look of horror on Daniel Filipacchi's face when he
discovered that his painting was a fake. The magazine mogul
had paid $7 million for *The Forest* by the artist Max Ernst. He
enjoyed it for two years before being informed that he had been
duped by a brilliant pair of forgers. Even after getting caught,
one of the forgers continued boasting: *"The widow of Max Ernst
saw the painting and said that it was the most beautiful picture
that Max Ernst had ever painted. We're still laughing about it."*[1]

The people of Judah had been faking it too, but the Lord
wasn't laughing. He inspired Isaiah to launch into the second of
his "six woes" in order to confront the southern kingdom with its
hypocrisy. On the outside, it looked as though Judah had turned
back to the Lord. The first act of King Hezekiah's reign, in 715
BC, had been to rid the Temple courtyards of the idols which his
father Ahaz had placed there. Next, he summoned the people of
Judah to worship the Lord, attracting also some survivors from
the ruined northern kingdom and a few foreigners who were
ready to surrender their lives to the Holy One of Israel. King
Hezekiah led them in a better celebration of the Passover than
any since the devout days of David and Solomon, and then he

---

[1] This quote comes from an exposé of the forgery in *Vanity Fair* (October
2012).

sent them home to rid the land of all its idols.[2] On the surface, it looked as if his kingdom was experiencing a major spiritual revival. But the Lord sent Isaiah to warn the people of Judah that he could see their hearts. For all their outward devotion, he knew that they were faking it.

Four times in this chapter the Lord addresses Jerusalem as Ariel, which means *"the Lion of God"*. This unusual poetic name is probably meant to remind his hearers of what Jacob had prophesied over his son Judah in Genesis 49:8–12. Jerusalem needed to rediscover its calling to take a righteous lead on behalf of the twelve tribes of Israel. Gathering at the Lord's altar like King David was good, but it had to be much more than an outward show of religion. Their hypocrisy was so repulsive to the Lord that he was about to turn the Lion of God (*'arī'ēl* in Hebrew) into a charred altar hearth (also *'arī'ēl* in Hebrew). He was about to come to the city where David settled (*hānāh* in Hebrew) and encamp against it (also *hānāh* in Hebrew). This is clever wordplay in Hebrew but it isn't meant to make us laugh. It is meant to make us tremble that hypocrisy can turn God into our enemy. Even though he promises in 29:5–8 that he will perform a sudden mighty miracle to spare Jerusalem from the Assyrians, he says that they will suffer first in order to bring them to a place of genuine repentance.

These words were prophesied for us and not just for the people of Jerusalem. In case we forget this perspective, the New Testament spells it out for us clearly by quoting five times from this chapter and applying it more broadly. Jesus uses the words of 29:13 to describe the Pharisees in Matthew 15:7–9 and Mark 7:6–7, and Paul uses the words of 29:10, 29:14 and 29:16 to confront generally stubborn unbelief in Romans 9:20 and 11:8, and in 1 Corinthians 1:19. Let's therefore read these verses, not as ancient history, but as a challenge to ourselves.

In 29:9–14, the Lord warns us that he has a policy of

---

[2] 2 Kings 18:1–6; 2 Chronicles 29:1–31:1.

judging arrogant hypocrites by handing them over to their own folly.[3] In words which remind us of what he said to Isaiah when he appeared to him in the Temple courtyard in 6:9–10, the Lord tells us that he makes hypocrites believe their own propaganda. He blinds their eyes, he deafens their ears, he befuddles their brains and he makes the plain meaning of Scripture unintelligible to them. He says of those who pursue outward religion without inward surrender, *"These people come near to me with their mouth and honour me with their lips, but their hearts are far from me."* He declares over those who accord too much authority to tradition or to man-made philosophy or to the bullying dictates of the culture around them, *"Their worship of me is based on merely human rules they have been taught."* Because they boasted of their own wisdom, he judges them by handing them over to utterly foolish conclusions. There will be plenty of wise and intelligent churchgoers in hell.

The Lord begins 29:15–24 with his third *"Woe!"* He wants us to grasp just how serious this warning is. If the smiling men of Judah in King Hezekiah's day could be accused of faking it, and if the devout first-century Pharisees could be accused of faking it too, then we are fools if we believe that we are immune to hypocrisy ourselves. If we secretly pursue our own agenda with God (29:15–16), we can expect him to humble us in order to jolt us out of our deception (29:17–21). He will do whatever it takes to make our deaf ears hear, our blind eyes see and our proud eyes humble enough to delight in the beauty of the Holy One of Israel. He will teach us to fear him like the founding fathers of Israel (29:22–24).

Fear. That's a very common theme in Isaiah's "Book of Judgment". We may not like the idea of the Lord wanting us

---

[3] Isaiah talks in 29:10 about the Lord pouring out a *rūach*, or *spirit*, of spiritual sleepiness on people. He says something similar in 19:14 and 37:7. This ties in with passages such as Judges 9:23, 1 Samuel 16:14 and 2 Thessalonians 2:9–12 to warn us that God judges wilful rebels by handing their minds over to demons.

to fear him, but he insists repeatedly that it is an inalienable aspect of knowing that he is holy. Isaiah's first reaction when he saw God's holiness in the Temple courtyard was not to sing happy songs but to shout out in 6:5, *"Woe to me! I am ruined! For I am a man of unclean lips."* He spoke in 2:10 about *"the fearful presence of the Lord"*, and in 11:2 about *"the Spirit of the knowledge and fear of the Lord".*[4] He warned us sternly in 8:13 that *"The Lord Almighty is the one you are to regard as holy, he is the one you are to fear, he is the one you are to dread."* Unless we understand this, we are as ignorant as the people of Judah. A proper understanding of God's holiness will always inspire fear.

The forger who attempted to dupe Daniel Filipacchi is now in jail, for a long time. Do we really believe that we can try to fake it with the Lord and receive no punishment ourselves? That's why Isaiah ends this chapter by reminding us that Jacob knew God as *"the Fear of Isaac".*[5] It's why he ends by calling us to respond to God's holiness by walking before him in fear and reverence and awe.[6]

Fear of God serves as a great antidote to faking it in worship. Don't be a fool. Listen to Moses when he tells you in Exodus 20:20 that fear of the Lord is a good thing, because *"The fear of God will be with you to keep you from sinning."*

---

[4] The New English Translation captures what a proper fear of God accomplishes when it renders 11:2 as *"a spirit that produces absolute loyalty to the Lord"*.

[5] Genesis 31:42, 53. We are warned in Hebrews 2:1–4, 10:26–31 and 12:25–29 that God's greater revelation of himself to us through Jesus ought to result in our fearing him far more, not far less.

[6] The Lord's name is already *qādōsh*, or *holy*, but the Lord commands us twice in 29:23 to *qādash* his name – *to demonstrate that we recognize it as holy* – through the way in which we fear him.

Maginot Line (30:1–31:9)

Woe to the obstinate children... who go down to
Egypt without consulting me; who look for help to
Pharaoh's protection.

(Isaiah 30:1–2)

There is a reason why the French were so unprepared for the German invasion that came in May 1940. I can give you the reason in just three words: the Maginot Line. It was enormous, stretching all the way from Switzerland to Belgium. It was incredibly well fortified and brilliantly engineered. Unfortunately, it was also entirely useless. The Germans simply outflanked it by invading France through neutral Belgium.

The people of Judah had their own Maginot Line. Its name was Pharaoh, king of Egypt. Instead of looking to the Lord to save them from the advancing empire of Assyria, they fooled themselves that an alliance with Egypt would save them. Like the French in 1940, they would learn the hard way that feeling confident and being safe are not the same.

Egypt and Cush had recently united together as two kingdoms under one pharaoh. He set about forming a grand alliance of nations against Assyria in 713 BC. Initially King Hezekiah of Judah refused to join it, perhaps based on the influence of Isaiah. This was wise, since the Egyptians reneged on their treaty promises to help the Philistine city of Ashdod and, once it fell in 711 BC and its king fled to Egypt for protection, they even extradited him to Assyria in the hope of currying favour with King Sargon. It didn't work. The Egyptians were forced to try and salvage their grand alliance. Having already broken its promise to help Samaria in 722 BC, Egypt was fast developing a reputation for treachery, so fresh allies were hard to find. It needed the help of Judah, and a pro-Egyptian faction among King Hezekiah's courtiers was pressuring him to agree.[1]

That's why, in 30:1–5, the Lord warns the people of Judah sternly that reliance on Egypt will prove to be an unmitigated disaster. This is the fourth of Isaiah's "six woes" and it calls the people of Judah *"obstinate children"* for refusing to listen to God as their Father. If they trust in Egypt, they are declaring war on him.[2] We simply cannot trust in the Lord as our Saviour while at the same time creating backup plans of our own.[3] This prophecy was written down for our sake too. Hebrews 13:5–6 tells us that when we put our trust in money we are guilty of similar unbelief towards the Lord.[4]

In 30:6–11, the Lord inspires Isaiah to prophesy about the costly gifts which Hezekiah will need to send across the Sinai Peninsula if he decides to negotiate with Pharaoh. Dodging lions and venomous snakes will be the least of his problems. Egypt will be as dangerous to Judah as the sea monster Rahab, even if it poses no danger to Assyria on the battlefield.[5] Once again Isaiah rebukes God's people for being *"children unwilling to listen to the Lord's instruction"*. Because they are as unwilling

---

[1] 2 Kings 17:3–4; Isaiah 36:6. We know about Ashdod from one of Sargon II's inscriptions, found at the Kurdish town of Tang-i Var. An alliance would incur Assyrian anger without gaining any real Egyptian aid.

[2] The Hebrew for forming an alliance in 30:1 means literally *pouring out drink offerings*. Alliances made with Egypt always involved performing an act of reverence towards the Egyptian gods.

[3] The Egyptian city of Hanes is singled out in 30:4 for a reason: in Hebrew its name meant *Grace Has Fled*. Zoan is mentioned because it was the Egyptian capital during Israel's years of slavery (Psalm 78:12, 43). The Lord is warning his people not to turn the clock back on the Exodus.

[4] Like the hypocritical people of Judah in 30:22 and 31:7, it is a modern form of idolatry.

[5] The name Rahab means *Proud and Insolent One* in Hebrew. Job and Psalms also mention this sea monster.

as the northern kingdom to listen to God's prophets, they will reap a similar judgment from the Holy One of Israel.[6]

In 30:12–18, the Lord tells the people of Judah that he knows they will not listen to his warning. He will therefore punish them by turning Pharaoh into their Maginot Line. He will give them a false sense of security, like a high wall that suddenly topples over onto those who hide behind it. He will cause them to be massacred in battle, and anyone who attempts to escape on their Egyptian-bought horses will soon discover that they are no match for the horses of Assyria. Nevertheless, amidst this prophecy of judgment, the Lord speaks lovingly to his people. *"The Lord longs to be gracious to you,"* he reassures them. *"In repentance and rest is your salvation, in quietness and trust is your strength."* We badly need to take this promise to heart in our own stressed-out and crazy-busy generation.[7] The Lord tells us that faith in him means stopping all our striving and starting to trust in him to work for us instead.[8]

In 30:19–33, the Lord promises what he will do to the Assyrian army. As soon as the people of Judah shake off their Maginot Line mentality, believing his Word and throwing away their idols in disgust, he will heal the wounds they have received through their reliance on Egypt.[9] He will cause them to sing worship songs when they see him striking down the invading Assyrian soldiers and dealing out their just deserts.[10]

---

[6] They responded to Isaiah in exactly the same way that Micah 2:11 tells us the northern kingdom responded. We should not be surprised if we receive a similar reaction from unbelievers too.

[7] Leviticus 26:8 promises that one man or woman of faith is a match for 100 enemies. Joshua 23:10 upgrades this to 1,000 enemies. Yet Isaiah 30:17 warns that one enemy will rout 1,000 crazy-busy so-called believers.

[8] Verse 18 reminds us that faith isn't always about bold advance. More often it means waiting patiently for God.

[9] Verse 22 ties in with 64:6, where the Lord also likens sinful idolatry to a used sanitary towel. The essence of repentance is that we start to share the Holy One of Israel's sense of revulsion against our sin.

[10] Topheth was part of the valley outside Jerusalem which Jesus calls *Gehenna* and uses as a metaphor for hell. Sennacherib and his men will be thrown into Gehenna before they can ever break into Jerusalem!

In 31:1–9, Isaiah proclaims the fifth of his "six woes", continuing his call for Judah to stop trusting in Egypt. Egyptian horses and Egyptian chariots are – well – merely Egyptian. They are mortal, like the thousands of Egyptian firstborn sons that the Lord destroyed on the night before the Exodus. The Lord uses a not-too-subtle pun in order to remind the people of Judah of this event, promising in 31:5 to "pass over" Jerusalem. He wants them to read the hieroglyphics on the wall. Only the same God who saved their ancestors from Egypt can possibly save them from Assyria now. Isaiah reminds us in 31:2 that the Lord will never renege on his promises like Pharaoh. It is time for his people to return to him as their oldest friend instead of making him their newest enemy.

We will discover in a few chapters' time that King Hezekiah refused to listen to Isaiah's warning. He was emboldened by Pharaoh's flattery to tell the king of Assyria that he would no longer pay an annual tribute to him. When King Sennacherib invaded Judah as a result, he feared that the Egyptian army might come to Judah's aid. However, Pharaoh proved more interested in his pyramids than in his promises, more concerned with guarding his treasures than with keeping his treaties. It would be left to the Lord to prove himself a faithful Father to his stubborn children. Let's not learn this lesson the hard way, like Hezekiah. Let's put our trust in God alone.

We cannot put our trust in both God and money. We cannot put our trust in both God and friends. We cannot even put our trust in both God and church. Unless we trust in God alone, the Lord warns us we are not trusting in him at all.

Deliverance (32:1–33:24)

"Now will I arise," says the Lord. "Now will I be exalted; now will I be lifted up."

(Isaiah 33:10)

When Paris fell in May 1940, the French prime minister predicted that *"In three weeks England will have her neck wrung like a chicken."*[1] By the end of the following year his prediction had been proved wrong, but Winston Churchill was still very worried. Britain needed more than survival. It needed safety and it could not overcome the German threat alone. That's why Churchill greeted the news with elation when he was told that the Japanese had bombed Pearl Harbor and that the Americans had finally entered the war. He celebrated:

> *To have the United States at our side was to me the greatest joy... We had won after all! Yes, after Dunkirk; after the fall of France... We had won the war. England would live; Britain would live... We should not be wiped out. Our history would not come to an end. We might not even have to die as individuals. Hitler's fate was sealed... There was no more doubt about the end... I went to bed and slept the sleep of the saved and thankful.*

Isaiah does not celebrate in chapters 32–33 like a man who has just secured the help of an earthly superpower. He has just spent two chapters convincing us that faith in human alliances means

---

[1] Quoted by Churchill in the second volume of his World War Two memoirs, *Their Finest Hour* (1949). The next quote comes from his third volume, *The Grand Alliance* (1950).

lack of faith in the Lord. No, Isaiah's celebration in chapters 32–33 stems from the Lord's promise at the end of chapter 31 – that he will become his people's great Deliverer. Isaiah is elated. He begins to prophesy about God's amazing battle plan.

In 32:1–8, Isaiah prophesies about the Messiah. Remember our two perspectives here.[2] On one level, Isaiah is predicting that in his hour of need King Hezekiah will turn wholeheartedly to the Lord and become the type of ruler that his nation badly needs. On another level, he is using Hezekiah as a prophetic picture of his far greater descendant, even though Jesus would not be born to David's dynasty until 700 years after the defeat of the Assyrian army at the walls of Jerusalem. *"See, a king will reign in righteousness,"* Isaiah begins, for great moves of God often begin with a single person. They never stay that way. Isaiah prophesies that, inspired by their righteous king, many *"rulers will rule with justice. Each one will be like a shelter from the wind and a refuge from the storm, like streams of water in the desert and the shadow of a great rock in a thirsty land."*

King Hezekiah's wholehearted response to the Lord in his hour of crisis would spark genuine spiritual revival throughout Judah. Men like Eliakim would do more than simply help him to rebuild the ruined fields and vineyards that the Assyrians left behind. They would also help him lead the Jewish nation back to God. In doing so, they would become a prophetic picture of something greater. When Jesus finally came to a Jewish nation under the tyranny of Rome, he inspired a mighty army of apostles and prophets and evangelists and pastors to preach the good news of his Kingdom to every nation. Perhaps this is one of the Scriptures to which he is referring when he commands his followers in John 7:37–38: *"Let anyone who is thirsty come to me*

---

[2] 32:10 dates this prophecy to 702 BC. The Assyrians would invade Judah in 701 BC.

and drink. Whoever believes in me, as Scripture has said, rivers of living water will flow from within them."[3]

In 32:9–20, Isaiah continues this theme as he turns to address the women of Judah. The Lord has seen their complacency and he will judge them by striking their fields and vineyards. However, when he finally drives the Assyrian invaders from the land, he will grant it a period of unprecedented fertility and harvest. Even the deserts of Judah will bear as much fruit as a fertile field, and a fertile field will bear as much fruit as a forest. King Hezekiah and Eliakim and the other noblemen of Judah would live to celebrate the fulfilment of this promise with their wives and daughters.[4] However, let's zoom out again for a more complete perspective. What happened in the days of Hezekiah would only find its true fulfilment in 30 AD.

The weeks leading up to the Day of Pentecost were painful for the followers of Jesus. First, they saw him crucified and buried. Their world completely fell apart for a weekend until he appeared to them and convinced them that he had risen from the dead. Their jubilation was tempered by the fact that he constantly appeared and disappeared over the next forty days, before ascending back to heaven and leaving them all alone. The Day of Pentecost, ten days later, was the Jewish feast of first-fruits. It must have been a very difficult morning for the 120 followers of Jesus as they gathered together in prayer. Looking around, their motley crew made the Messiah's ministry look very unfruitful. Then suddenly Isaiah's revolution took place before their eyes: *"The Spirit is poured on us from on high, and the desert becomes a fertile field, and the fertile field seems like a forest."* Empowered by the Holy Spirit, those ordinary followers of Jesus would go on to bear miraculous Gospel fruit all over the world.

---

[3] Contrast this with false teachers in 32:6, who leave people feeling even thirstier than before.

[4] Isaiah uses the same Hebrew words in 32:18 for *secure* and *undisturbed* as he used in 32:9 for *secure* and *complacent*. The Gospel replaces our misplaced self-confidence with genuine confidence in Christ.

In 33:1–24, Isaiah therefore proclaims the last of his "six woes". In the same way that Sennacherib and his army had to be judged for Judah to be revived, sinners have to be shaken today so that the good news about Jesus can bear fruit in every nation.[5] The Lord will therefore shatter the nations before him (33:1–6) and he will discipline the Church to make her pure (33:7–16).[6] When Christian leaders start to weep over their own failure (33:7–8)[7] and fruitlessness (33:9),[8] they will finally begin to fall in love with the Lord's holy presence (33:14–16). They will finally see as God sees, rejoicing in the beauty of their Messiah (33:17) and in the New Jerusalem he is building on the New Mount Zion (33:20). They will delight in him as their mighty Deliverer (33:18–19). They will praise him for his security (33:20), for his powerful rule (33:22), for his blessings (33:23),[9] for his healing (33:24) and for his forgiveness (33:24). They will sing the song of Zion together: *"The Lord is our judge, the Lord is our lawgiver, the Lord is our king; it is he who will save us."*

What a Messiah. What a Saviour. Picture Winston Churchill dancing in his pyjamas as he celebrates the knowledge that the power of the United States is now on his side. Make sure that you celebrate far more than him as you read these two chapters. They describe what Jesus is like. Worship him as your mighty Deliverer.

---

[5] Sennacherib was a betrayer because he accepted tribute from Hezekiah, then attacked him anyway (2 Kings 18:13–17). He was betrayed because his own sons killed him after his failure to capture Jerusalem (37:37–38).

[6] Note yet another reference in 33:6 to our *fearing* the Lord. Isaiah says this is the key to all true knowledge and wisdom and experience of our salvation. See also Proverbs 9:10, Psalm 111:10 and Job 28:28.

[7] The warriors and envoys knew that they had failed when no army came from Egypt to honour their treaty.

[8] Lebanon, Sharon, Bashan and Carmel were all famously fruitful. The Arabah was a wilderness.

[9] The Church will often appear an unseaworthy vessel, but the Lord will bless her beyond all deserving.

Bittersweet Symphony
(34:1–35:10)

Those the Lord has rescued will return. They will enter Zion with singing.

(Isaiah 35:10)

When we grasp that God is sterner than we thought, it is always a bittersweet feeling. When the prophet Ezekiel, rather strangely, ate a scroll that bore God's message to the world, he noted that *"on both sides of it were written words of lament and mourning and woe,"* yet he also found to his surprise that it *"tasted as sweet as honey in my mouth"*. Similarly, when the apostle John followed suit, he *"took the little scroll from the angel's hand and ate it. It tasted as sweet as honey in my mouth, but when I had eaten it, my stomach turned sour."*[1] It is time for us to bite off a share of their strange meal ourselves. Isaiah has picked up his musical instrument again and he wants us to join him in a bittersweet symphony.

Isaiah 34–35 effectively represents the last two chapters of the "Book of Judgment", since the remaining four chapters really serve as a narrative which transitions the "Book of Judgment" into the "Book of Comfort". These two chapters therefore serve as a resounding conclusion to God's long cascade of judgment in the first half of Isaiah. As such, it should not surprise us that they taste decidedly bitter. Just read the opening verses of chapter 34: *"The Lord is angry with all nations; his wrath is on all their armies. He will totally destroy them, he will give them over*

---

[1] Ezekiel 2:9–3:3; 3:14–15; Revelation 10:8–11.

to slaughter. Their slain will be thrown out, their dead bodies will stink; the mountains will be soaked with their blood." If you don't feel like squirming in your seat as you read verses like these, there is something wrong with you. They make for very difficult reading.

In 34:1–17, the Lord gives us a bitter pill to swallow. He reminds us that these prophecies about individual nations point towards a far bigger Judgment Day at the end of time (34:1–2). His predictions about slaughter on ancient battlefields actually point to the eternal judgment of hell and to the violent destruction of the skies and earth (34:3–4). The Lord tells us that he is a King who judges the earth with a bloody sword (34:5–7). Knowing that many of us will try to dismiss passages such as these as "too Old Testament", Jesus quotes from 34:4 in Matthew 24:29 and Mark 13:25 as a prediction of his Second Coming. Make no mistake about it. Isaiah is describing the God that Christians worship. That is, if they are truly worshipping the real Christian God.

A. W. Tozer warns us that

> *It is my opinion that the Christian conception of God... is so decadent as to be utterly beneath the dignity of the Most High God... The idolatrous heart assumes that God is other than He is – in itself a monstrous sin – and substitutes for the true God one made after its own likeness... The essence of idolatry is the entertainment of thoughts about God that are unworthy of Him.*[2]

This is where the bitter pill starts to taste extremely sweet. It is why King David saw judgment passages in the Old Testament as *"sweeter than honey, than honey from the honeycomb".*[3]

---

[2] A. W. Tozer in *The Knowledge of the Holy* (1961).

[3] Psalm 19:7–10. David isn't talking about the gospels or Paul's letters. He is talking about the first few books of the Old Testament – the ones which describe God's judgment falling on the Canaanites and Midianites.

David doesn't just mean the life-transforming power of the Gospel, sweet though that is. He is talking about the sweetness of discovering the truth about God's character. He is talking about the sweetness of exchanging false images of God for an encounter with the true God, the one who is far holier and sterner than we think. These chapters are sweet because they correct our puny view of God.

The Lord does not enjoy judging people he created to know him. In 28:21, he described it as an *"alien task"* for his hands.[4] He judges sin because of his unflinching resolve to ensure that justice is done in the world (34:8 calls it *"a day of vengeance, a year of retribution"*), and because of his unflinching resolve to ensure that righteousness triumphs (34:8 says it is *"to uphold Zion's cause"*).[5] To help us understand why his bitter judgment tastes very sweet, he takes Edom, the nation which was most persistently hostile towards Israel, and he uses Edom and its capital city Bozrah as a symbol of everything unrighteous in the world.[6] He helps us understand that ridding the world of "Edom" is a necessary precursor to his creating the new heavens and new earth.[7]

Therefore, in 35:1–10, Isaiah's symphony becomes a sweet song of salvation. God's firm hand with sinful Edom enables him to reach out his hand of blessing towards Zion. Out of the wastelands which he created through his judgment, he is now

---

[4] See also Ezekiel 18:23; 33:11; 1 Timothy 2:1–4; 2 Peter 3:9.

[5] The "Book of Judgment" begins with the Old Jerusalem in 1:1 and it ends with the New Mount Zion in 35:10. True Zionism does not mean supporting the state of Israel at any cost (Isaiah says that many Israelis are "Edomites"). It means helping God to build his New Mount Zion and inviting Jews to become part of it too.

[6] See Numbers 20:18; 1 Samuel 14:47; 1 Kings 11:14; Psalm 137:7; Lamentations 4:21–22; Malachi 1:2–4. The symbolism is helped by the fact that Bozrah's economy was based on the slaughter of sheep and goats.

[7] Without the *everlasting judgment* of hell (34:10 and 17), there can be no *everlasting joy* of heaven (35:10).

able to bring forth the pasturelands of a glorious new paradise.[8] Having turned the polluted streams of the old world into an arid lair of jackals in 34:9–15, he is now able to turn those arid places into pure streams of water which grant life throughout his new world. Don't glaze over as you read this because some of Isaiah's language seems a bit obscure. Hebrews 12:12 quotes the words of 35:3 as a reason why Christians should rejoice in God's loving hand of discipline today.[9] Jesus quotes from 35:5–6 in Matthew 11:5 and Luke 7:22 as an encouragement to John the Baptist to trust in the Lord even in the midst of pain.[10] These verses are therefore still very relevant. Knowing that builders need to clear the ground ahead of them before they can construct a superhighway,[11] we ought to feel excited when the Lord tells us that he has cleared the ground to build his holy highway for us.[12]

The Gospel is bitter. It speaks of God's holiness and of his sternness. It warns us that he is totally committed to his task as Judge. Yet at the same time the Gospel is sweet, deliciously sweet. As Isaiah reminds us in 35:4, God's vengeance and God's salvation always go hand in hand. The wilderness understands this in 35:1 and it starts singing. The humble understand it in 35:6 and they start singing too. Those God has rescued

---

[8] As we noted in 33:9, Lebanon, Sharon and Carmel were very fertile regions. The Arabah was a wilderness.

[9] Hebrews 12:13–14 also appears to be a freestyle summary of the promises in 35:5–10.

[10] Isaiah refers literally to a *panicking heart* in 35:4. Faith in these promises will make us strong amidst trouble.

[11] When we complain that God promises to judge the *unclean*, *wicked fools*, *lions* and *ravenous beasts* in order to build his holy highway, we demonstrate that we have not yet understood his holiness at all.

[12] This *holy highway* is a major theme of Isaiah (11:16; 19:23; 35:8; 40:3–4; 57:14; 62:10). Isaiah tells us in 35:9–10 that it is only open to the *redeemed* and the *ransomed*, reminding us it cost the Lord a lot to build this highway for us. We will discover just how much in Isaiah 53.

understand it in 35:10 and they end the "Book of Judgment" with their happy singing.[13]

So how about you? Will you add your own voice to the sound of this bittersweet symphony? Will you celebrate the fact that God is far sterner than you thought? Will you rejoice, as Isaiah expects in 35:2, in *"the glory of the Lord, the splendour of our God"*?

---

[13] Jesus has paid the price for our salvation. We do not have to strive to receive anything. If we simply travel in faith along God's holy highway, 35:10 promises that all the blessings of the Gospel will *overtake* us.

Part Three

Half-time Substitution

(Isaiah 36–39)

Enemy at the Gates
(36:1–22)

Who of all the gods of these countries have been able to save their lands from me? How then can the Lord deliver Jerusalem from my hand?

(Isaiah 36:20)

When my oldest son performs one of his magic tricks to his friends, he has learned that it always helps to tell a story. If he needs to move an object from one hand to the other, a little anecdote distracts his audience while he makes a quick transfer. Now Isaiah isn't like my son. He isn't employing any sleight of hand. He expects us to guess why he now gives us four chapters of story. He does so in order to make a half-time substitution.

These four chapters are the only section of Isaiah which is written in prose. All the rest of the book is written as poetry. That in itself should be enough to make us sit up and pay attention, but what is even odder is that we already have an account of these events in 2 Kings 18:13–20:19 and in 2 Chronicles 32:1–31. Isaiah can't therefore be recording these events in order to inform us. He must have a deeper reason, which only becomes evident when we try to date the stories. Chapters 36–37 form "Story A", and we are told in 36:1 that it took place in 701 BC. Chapter 38 forms "Story B", and we are told in 39:1 that it took place before the events of "Story C". Chapter 39 forms that third story, and it must have taken place before 701 BC because Marduk-Baladan was deposed as king of Babylon in 702 BC. In other words, the correct order for these stories is not A–B–C, but

B–C–A. Isaiah has put them the wrong way round for a reason. Like my son, he uses these stories to make a quick substitution.

"Story A" in chapters 36–37 explains how the Lord drove the Assyrian Empire off the stage of world history. The superpower which dominated the pages of the "Book of Judgment" in Isaiah 1–35 will no longer dominate the "Book of Comfort" in Isaiah 40–66. "Story B" in chapter 38 marks the point at which Isaiah's prophecies stop being primarily national (about a single nation-state in the eighth century BC) and become primarily personal (about God's invitation for us all to become part of his New Jerusalem). "Story C" in chapter 39 introduces us to the new arch-villain who will oppose God in his plan. It also shows us that the kings of Judah are far too weak to save God's people. A better Saviour is needed. These stories prepare us for the message of Isaiah 40–66: God is calling you to become part of his New Mount Zion. The Devil will try to use the spirit of Babylon to stop you, but he will ultimately fail because he is no match for God's Messiah.

Let's therefore read the first of these four chapters together, seeing them as Isaiah's way of making an important half-time substitution. There are two main characters in chapter 36: the royal cupbearer of King Sennacherib of Assyria, and Eliakim, the messenger of King Hezekiah of Judah.[1] We have already seen in the "Book of Judgment" that Assyria often speaks for the Devil and that Eliakim is a prophetic picture of the Messiah. Their interaction is therefore the outworking of the threats and promises in Isaiah 1–35.

The king of Assyria is full of himself. When his spokesman opens his mouth in 36:4–10, it sounds just like the Devil talking. He ignores the rebuke of chapters 13–14 and postures about *"the great king, the king of Assyria"*. He dismisses the idea of the Lord helping Jerusalem in the same way that he sneers at the

---

[1] The Hebrew *Rab-Shākēh* could be a man's name, but it means literally *chief cupbearer*, a very important official for rulers paranoid about being poisoned (Genesis 41:9; Nehemiah 1:11).

treaty promises made by Pharaoh. He taunts the men of Judah, *"On whom are you depending, that you rebel against me?"* Then he tries to fool them that, anyway, God is on his side and not theirs. He treats Hezekiah's removal of the sinful high places of Judah as an act of rebellion, not of obedience to God's Law. He even claims that *"The Lord himself told me to march against this country and destroy it."*[2] No deception is too low-down and dirty for a man inspired by the Devil. He has made his choice about which side he is on. He is about to be destroyed.

In 36:11–12, Eliakim's response to this is every bit as godly as we were led to expect in 22:15–25. In order to emphasize that he is acting as a prophetic picture of the Messiah, the Lord ensures that the disgraced Shebna is standing right next to him, demoted to court secretary but not yet taken into exile. They stand together to emphasize how different Eliakim is from Shebna's sinful and superseded order. There is not a single word of blame on Eliakim's lips towards his master, even though the Assyrian invasion was provoked by King Hezekiah's folly. Eliakim does not point out that his master should never have disobeyed the Lord by trying to forge an alliance with Egypt, provoking Sennacherib to invade. Nor does he mention that his master disobeyed the Lord a second time by plundering the Temple treasures in a vain attempt to buy off Sennacherib before he reached the walls of Jerusalem.[3] Eliakim is the model of obedience. To use Isaiah's metaphor in 28:9–13, he obeys God both in the baby language of the kindergarten of Judah and in the sophisticated language of the university of Assyria.

This is Sennacherib's last opportunity for repentance. Instead of taking it, his messenger delivers another great tirade of defiance, claiming that he is *"the great king, the king of Assyria... Do not let Hezekiah persuade you to trust in the Lord."*

---

[2] 2 Kings 18:3–4; 2 Chronicles 30:12–14; 31:1. Isaiah 5:26, 7:18–20 and 10:5–7 tell us that the Lord did indeed summon Assyria against Judah, but not in the way that Sennacherib pretended.

[3] Isaiah 36:6; 37:9; 2 Kings 18:13–16.

He even has his own satanic parody of what the Lord told Israel about the Promised Land: if the people of Jerusalem repent and serve him, he promises to lead them into his own land flowing with milk and honey.[4] The messenger tries to tempt the people of Judah with clever reasoning to disobey the Lord, pointing out that Sennacherib has already won his fights against the gods of the Mesopotamians, Arameans and Israelites.[5] If those idols were powerless to stop him, *"how then can the Lord deliver Jerusalem from my hand?"*

Eliakim leads the people of Judah in a godly response to this in 36:21–22. He must have been very tempted to correct the Assyrian messenger's muddled thinking, yet he submits completely to the orders he received from Hezekiah.[6] The people of Judah who are listening from the walls of Jerusalem follow his lead. Eliakim shows them what to do next by tearing his clothes in repentance and as a fervent prayer to the Lord. Even wicked Shebna is impressed and follows Eliakim's lead. We need to see this as a clash between Nineveh and Jerusalem, Assyria and Mount Zion, the Devil and the Messiah.

We will have to wait until the following chapter to know the outcome of the battle but, for now, let's simply note what Isaiah has said so far. Assyria has chosen the path of defiance and it will exit the world stage. The Lord is about to call time on an evil nation.

---

[4] Compare 36:16–17 with Leviticus 20:24, Micah 4:4 and Zechariah 3:10. The messenger deceives God's people by failing to mention that he is actually describing a land of captivity and slavery.

[5] Since Israel's God, at least nominally, was the same as Judah's this logic was deadly. It tested whether they truly believed the message of 17:8, that the Lord had judged the Israelites for worshipping idols.

[6] Satan is an expert at redefining vice as virtue. Eve's folly in Genesis 3 was to start debating with him.

The Real King of Judah
(37:1–38)

Hezekiah prayed to the Lord: "Lord Almighty, the God of Israel, enthroned between the cherubim, you alone are God over all the kingdoms of the earth."

(Isaiah 37:15–16)

In the political drama *The West Wing*, the head of the US military reminds President Bartlet that *"Presidents don't make new friends. That's why they've got to hang onto their old ones."*[1] Leadership is always lonely, and never more so than for King Hezekiah in 701 BC. Although he had Eliakim, most of his courtiers were pragmatic men like Shebna. If he hadn't listened to their advice over Egypt, he would not be in this predicament now.

The imperial annals of King Sennacherib boast that, during his Judah campaign, he captured forty-six fortified cities, carried away 200,150 of their citizens as slaves and reduced Hezekiah to *"a prisoner in Jerusalem his royal residence, like a bird in a cage".*[2] We still have the stone reliefs which he commissioned for his palace in Nineveh to depict his brutal slaughter. Hezekiah must have felt terribly lonely in his hour of need.

Crises often bring out the very worst and very best in a leader. In 7:9, Isaiah observed that in such moments, *"If you do not stand firm in your faith, you will not stand at all."* Hezekiah had

---

[1] Admiral Fitzwallace says this in *The West Wing*, Season 1, Episode 3 – "A Proportional Response" (1999).

[2] See the Sennacherib Prism and the Lachish Reliefs, on display in the British Museum in London.

been listening, and the way that he responded to Sennacherib's letter marked a major turning point in history. Instead of panicking, he realized that it was time to do away with religious hypocrisy and Egyptian gullibility. It was time for him to pay a visit to the real King of Judah.

Hezekiah tore his clothes and dressed in sackcloth as an expression of his repentance and his desperate need for God to help him.[3] He sent Eliakim to ask Isaiah to pray, and then he went alone to the same Temple courtyard where Isaiah had seen *"the Lord, high and exalted, seated on a throne"*. He took out the letter from King Sennacherib and he spread it out in front of the Lord. He remembered the words which his predecessor King David had prayed in Psalm 5:2 – *"Hear my cry for help, my King and my God, for to you I pray"* – and he made it his own prayer. Sennacherib's letter was the Lord's problem and not his. After all, the Lord was the real King of Judah.[4]

We do not truly understand Hezekiah's prayer in 37:14–20 unless we grasp this. It is a speech of abdication. He is stepping off the throne and calling on the Lord to be the true ruler of his people. He worships the Lord as the one who is *"enthroned between the cherubim"*, reigning from the Temple in Jerusalem, as the earthly extension of his heavenly throne. He worships the Lord as the Almighty God and as the Creator of the heavens and the earth. He is the one against whom Sennacherib has really boasted. If Jerusalem falls as easily as any other city, the world will assume that the Lord is as weak as the Sepharvite sun-god Adrammelek or the Israelite fertility-goddess Asherah. That can never be. Hezekiah makes an impassioned plea to the real King of Judah: *"Lord our God, deliver us from his hand, so that all*

---

[3] Less than a century earlier, a sinful Assyrian king had been forgiven for responding this way in Jonah 3:6.

[4] Hezekiah uses a vivid Hebrew metaphor in 37:3 to say effectively, "All of my outward show of strength for the past few months has been exposed as a lie by this sudden moment of truth."

the kingdoms of the earth may know that you, Lord, are the only God."[5]

This was the moment that the Lord had been waiting for. The leader of the people of Judah had finally confessed him as the Holy One of Israel. In the very place where Isaiah had seen a vision of God's holiness in the year that King Uzziah died of his leprosy, the sinful king's great-grandson had uttered his own echo of that vision. His humble prayer sings the same song as the angels: *"Holy, holy, holy"*. It unleashes one of the most astonishing reversals of fortune in the whole of military history.

Having spoken words of comfort to Eliakim in 37:5-7, Isaiah now sends a letter to Hezekiah in 37:21-35. It sounds just like an excerpt from his "Book of Judgment", only this time it isn't predicting events in the distant future. It is promising deliverance for Jerusalem that very night.[6] The Lord addresses Jerusalem tenderly as his *"Daughter Jerusalem"* and, despite her many sinful acts of spiritual adultery, as his *"Virgin Daughter Jerusalem"*. He promises to treat the king of Assyria's boasting as a personal affront to the Holy One of Israel (37:23). Since King Sennacherib has become the boastful mouthpiece of the Devil (37:24-25) and has forgotten that he is merely an item in God's toolbox (37:26-27), the Lord will send him home in shame, like a beast of burden (37:28-29). Isaiah even says that he will give Hezekiah a sign to prove it, although it's interesting that the sign will not become visible until long after the siege has been lifted. The sign promises that this deliverance of Jerusalem is a down payment on the Lord's far bigger promise to recreate a New Jerusalem on a New Mount Zion (37:30-32).[7]

The chapter therefore ends with an astonishing miracle.

---

[5] Hezekiah prays, *"It is true, Lord"* (37:18). Faith does not deny facts. It simply believes that heavenly facts trump earthly facts every time.

[6] 2 Kings 19:35 adds this detail that Isaiah's prophecy was fulfilled that very night.

[7] For similar "signs" that are only visible after the fact, see Exodus 3:12 and John 7:17.

For perspective, bear in mind that 80,000 people were killed when the atomic bomb was dropped on Hiroshima in 1945. Isaiah tells us that a single angel killed more people in one night than were killed by the two bombs which were dropped on Hiroshima and Nagasaki combined, fulfilling the Lord's promise in 31:8 that *"Assyria will fall by no human sword; a sword, not of mortals, will devour them."* This is actually the largest number of people that have ever been killed in battle on a single day in history, and it was accomplished as a one-sided rout by a single angel! No wonder the Lord recounts this story for us three times in three different places in the Bible. He really wants us to understand what happens when we confess that he is far bigger than we think. It attracts the help of the real King of Judah.

Isaiah condenses his history of what happened next. Remember, he is far more interested in performing a half-time substitution between his "Book of Judgment" and his "Book of Comfort" than he is in laying out the strict order in which events happened. Sennacherib woke up in the morning and discovered that most of his soldiers were dead. He panicked and quickly fled back to his palace in Nineveh, ordering craftsmen to create enormous reliefs that majored on his victory at Lachish in order to downplay his defeat at Jerusalem.[8] It didn't work. The power of the Assyrian Empire had been fatally broken. In 681 BC, after the Lord had given him twenty gracious years to repent, his sons assassinated him as he was worshipping the Assyrian fertility-god Nisrok. A few decades later, the Assyrian Empire was destroyed by the king of Babylon.

Act One of this three-part interlude is therefore over. The empire of the arrogant king of Assyria has exited the stage. The final chapters of Isaiah are going to be very different from the ones which have gone before.

---

[8] The Hebrew text of 37:7 says literally that the Lord sent a *rūach* or *spirit* into him, handing him over to a demon of fear so that he fled. See 2 Timothy 1:7.

The Big and the Small
(38:1–22)

Go and tell Hezekiah, "This is what the Lord, the God of your father David, says: I have heard your prayer and seen your tears."

(Isaiah 38:5)

One day in 703 BC, Hezekiah began to feel unwell. Up until now he had not been too concerned about the mysterious boil which had appeared on his skin, but now it was definitely spreading. Some of the oldest people in his kingdom still remembered the death of his great-grandfather from leprosy, and he could hear them whispering. Finally, he received an unwanted message from the prophet Isaiah: *"This is what the Lord says: put your house in order, because you are going to die; you will not recover."*

Up until now almost all of Isaiah's prophesying had been to nations. This time, it was personal. Hezekiah was reeling from the news. He went into an inner room of his palace, turned his face to the wall so that none of his courtiers could see it and wept bitterly.[1] He prayed and pleaded with the Lord not to let him die before he had even had the chance to celebrate his fortieth birthday.[2]

Hezekiah knew how to lay hold of God's Word when it came to the grand sweep of his purposes for Israel. He was

---

[1] 2 Kings 20:4 adds some extra detail, telling us that Hezekiah rushed so quickly to prayer that Isaiah was still on his way home when God told him to turn around and go back to correct what he had said.

[2] 2 Kings 18:1–2 tells us that Hezekiah was aged 25 when he became king in 715 BC.

comfortable fulfilling Judah's national mission by sending missionaries to the ruined towns of the northern kingdom and calling the people there to come and worship the Lord at his Temple.[3] He knew that God was interested in massive, nation-sized prayers. What he was unsure about was whether God also cared about smaller, individual-sized prayers. Isaiah wants us to walk this path of discovery with him, because the "Book of Comfort" is far more personal in its prophesying than the "Book of Judgment". He wants to show us that God cares deeply about individuals.

First, Hezekiah discovers that the Lord is the God of individuals as well as of nations. Isaiah prophesies, not to Judah in general, but to Hezekiah in particular. He tells him in 38:5, *"This is what the Lord, the God of **your father** David, says: I have heard **your** prayer and seen **your** tears."* Suddenly the emphasis of the book of Isaiah changes. The New Jerusalem is a gathered community, but it is made up of many individuals who are personally known and loved by God.

God is glorified by his concern over the big things. Think about the sun. It emits more energy every second than all the human beings who have ever lived have managed to produce since the dawn of time. The amount of solar energy which reaches the earth in a year is twice as great as we could obtain if we took all the coal, oil, gas and uranium that have ever existed on the earth and blew it all in a single year. The sun, which goes on producing all of that energy year after year, owes its continued existence to the sustaining power of God. God's concern over the big things proclaims his immense glory whenever we look up, but here's the point: so does his concern over the small things whenever we look down. There are over 300,000 different species of beetle in the world, when most of us would have thought that only one would do. Every single

---

[3] 2 Chronicles 30:1–11. This is one of the good works which he brings to God's attention in 38:3, although he eventually confesses in 38:17 that none of them has made him any less a sinner in need of mercy.

microscopic string of DNA in your body contains many times more information than the whole of Wikipedia. These tiny things glorify God too. He isn't just interested in saving the nations. He is also interested in helping people like you and me.

Second, Isaiah builds on this by telling us that God wants to build a deeply fulfilling friendship with us as individuals. He is not building the New Jerusalem because he wants a city of faceless people who will worship him. He is building the New Jerusalem because he wants to create an urban paradise in which he can know each one of us as neighbours and friends. He emphasizes his desire to work with us shoulder-to-shoulder by saying something astonishing to Hezekiah. One of Isaiah's prophecies will fail to come to pass. He has afforded such power to our prayers that, at least in one sense, they are able to change his mind.[4] Because Hezekiah turned to prayer so quickly and so fervently, God has decided to bless him with a further fifteen healthy years.[5] To prove his commitment to deepening his friendship with Hezekiah, the Lord performs a miracle using the sunshine on the staircase of his home. God wants us to do life together.[6]

Hezekiah is so excited about this fresh revelation that he writes the personal testimony that Isaiah records for us in 38:9–20. Note how the words *"I"* and *"my"* and *"me"* occur thirty-seven times in these twelve short verses.[7] He wants the subjects of his kingdom and the pagans in the surrounding nations to know that God wants to get personal.[8]

---

[4] Knowing that God has ordained everything in our lives is not to become a recipe for fatalism (Psalm 139:16; Ephesians 1:11). It is meant to stir us towards active co-operation with God.

[5] The Lord also treated David as a much-loved and loyal friend in 37:35.

[6] The Hebrew of 38:8 could refer to the notches on Hezekiah's sundial rather than the steps on his staircase.

[7] Isaiah particularly emphasizes this. These words of testimony are absent from the other two accounts.

[8] We discover in 39:1 that the news about his testimony even travelled all the way to Babylon.

Third, Isaiah shows us that our little chats with God have massive ramifications. Some people argue that Hezekiah was wrong to pray for fifteen more years of life, because he used them to make some very foolish choices in chapter 39, but this isn't Isaiah's take on the story. If Hezekiah had died in 702 BC, he would have been succeeded by his son Manasseh, who was the most evil king who ever sat on the throne of Judah. Just imagine what would have happened if Manasseh had been at the helm of Judah the following year when the Assyrians invaded! Isaiah wants to show us that an individual's personal walk with God can change world history. In fact, it is the only thing that ever has.

Hezekiah's personal victory of faith over his illness would prove the training ground which opened the door towards a national victory of faith the following year.[9] His prayers about his personal disappointments resulted in the amazing national promise of 38:6 – *"I will deliver you and this city from the hand of the king of Assyria."*

When we reach the "Book of Comfort", Isaiah will encourage you to respond personally to God's Messiah. Don't wait for chapter 40 to start doing so. Learn from Hezekiah now and start a daily routine of bringing your personal needs to the Lord, both the big and the small. I have made this my own daily habit. Following Hezekiah's lead in 37:14, I have learned to spread out each day's to-do list before God. As I tell him that he is the real King of my life, I have lost count of how many prayers he has answered: about parenting and parcels, about marriage and money, about massive holidays and little habits, about absolute traumas and absolute trivia.

We studied Isaiah 1–35 through a panoramic lens, seeing God's power over the nations. We are about to study Isaiah 40–66 through a zoom lens, seeing God's power over every little aspect of our individual lives.

---

[9] Hezekiah senses this, praying in 38:17, *"Surely it was for my benefit that I suffered such anguish."*

Enter the Dragon (39:1–8)

Hear the word of the Lord Almighty: the time will surely come when everything in your palace... will be carried off to Babylon.

(Isaiah 39:5–6)

Isaiah has only one story left in the four chapters which form a bridge between the "Book of Judgment" and the "Book of Comfort". He really has to make it count, so he teaches us three big lessons through this story instead of just one. These three things enable him to complete his half-time substitution. If we understand them, we will be fully prepared to experience the amazing promises which follow.

First, Isaiah wants to introduce us to a new arch-villain. The Assyrian Empire has exited the stage. Now the city of Babylon is on the rise under a new king named Marduk-Baladan. An ambitious upstart who seized the throne, he derives his name from Babylon's patron deity, a god who was normally depicted walking with a dragon. He managed to secure independence from Assyria in 721 BC and to hold it for eleven years before the city was reconquered in 710 BC, so his return to the throne at the head of a fresh rebellion in 703 BC should be taken as an ominous sign. Hezekiah ought to know better than to receive his envoys on their tour of the Middle East in search of allies against Assyria.[1] Perhaps it is simply part of his flirtation with Egypt, or perhaps he is flattered to discover that even Babylonians are

---

[1] Sennacherib managed to topple him from the throne a second time in either late 703 BC or early 702 BC. We should therefore see this visit as part of his attempt to build an alliance ahead of a decisive battle.

interested in hearing his story about how the Lord healed him and gave him a miraculous sign on the staircase of his home.[2]

Looking back, it is easy to see how foolish Hezekiah was to befriend Marduk-Baladan. The true identity of his dragon-hugging demon-idol could hardly have been more thinly disguised. Nevertheless, Hezekiah gladly received the envoys and took them on a tour of his palace treasure rooms. Isaiah was furious. It didn't matter that they came *"from a distant land"*. Babylon is the bitter enemy of Zion. Showing off his treasures had simply whetted its greed to launch an attack ahead of time. Isaiah prophesied that a day was coming when the Babylonians would come and plunder Jerusalem, stealing all of the treasures that Hezekiah had just shown them.[3] Members of the royal dynasty of Judah would be castrated and taken into slavery in Babylon. The Lord wants to make Zion the home of the brave and the free. The Devil wants to emasculate and enslave them through the spirit of Babylon. As we shall see, this forms a significant theme in the "Book of Comfort", as the Lord sets about building his New Jerusalem on his New Mount Zion.

Second, Isaiah wants to remind us through this story of our need for God to send us his Messiah. Some of the greatest Old Testament prophecies about Jesus are found in the "Book of Comfort", so Isaiah wants to prepare us to receive our Saviour. Hezekiah was a good king. In fact, 2 Chronicles 30:26 suggests that he was better than any other king of Judah except for David and Solomon. He represented the monarchy of Judah at its very best, and yet even he committed several foolish blunders.

We have already examined Hezekiah's hypocrisy, his sinful alliance with Egypt and the way he plundered the Temple in a

---

[2] Isaiah emphasizes that Marduk-Baladan had heard about his healing, perhaps through the personal tract he wrote in 38:9–20. 2 Chronicles 32:31 emphasizes that he had heard about the sign on his staircase.

[3] As an initial act of judgment, Hezekiah would empty these treasure rooms in 701 BC in a futile attempt to buy off Sennacherib in 2 Kings 18:13–16. A larger fulfilment would only come later, in 2 Kings 24:10–15.

panicked and vain attempt to buy off Sennacherib and his army. Now in chapter 39 we see him at his worst. He fails to detect the demonic spirit at work behind Babylon. He boasts about his treasures to the enemy. Worst of all, instead of crying out to God for mercy when Isaiah prophesied the future destruction of Jerusalem at the hands of Babylon, he responded with short-sighted and self-centred complacency: *"The word of the Lord you have spoken is good. There will be peace and security in my lifetime."* The man who wept over the thought of his own premature death did not shed a single tear over the future destruction of God's holy city. Perhaps Isaiah is also hinting here at his failure as a parent, since his son Manasseh would be the worst king of Judah. The man who talked in 38:19 about the importance of parents bringing up their children in the Lord did not seem to bother about the next generation.

All of this is simply meant to show us that the best of human kings are only human kings at best.[4] People may not always do what their leaders say, but they never fail to copy what their leaders do, so Hezekiah's tragic example is meant to show us that God's New Jerusalem could never be established until a better type of King came to the throne of Judah. It is meant to make us look back to 9:6–7 and long for our Mighty God to come and rule personally on David's throne. It is meant to make us look back to 11:1 and long for God to raise up a new and better Branch from the fallen dynasty of David. It is meant to make us look back to 32:1 and long for the day when the Lord will cry out, *"See, a king will reign in righteousness!"* The "Book of Comfort" is an amazing proclamation that all of these verses are about to be fulfilled. They tell us what the Messiah will do for his people.

Third, Isaiah wants to use this story to remind us that a better Eliakim is waiting in the wings. As the king of Babylon

---

[4] 2 Chronicles 32:31 expresses this as *"God left him to test him and to know everything that was in his heart."*

rises up to perform Satan's work in the world, so does the Messiah who holds the true house key of David. As Hezekiah shows the foreign envoys around his treasure rooms, we are meant to recall God's promises about his Messiah in 22:15–25: *"I will place on his shoulder the key to the house of David; what he opens no one can shut, and what he shuts no one can open."* The "Book of Comfort" is about to describe the many treasures that are ours through the Gospel, but for now Isaiah merely reminds us in miniature. We have the riches of salvation, the spices of answered prayer, the fine olive oil of our anointing with the Holy Spirit, the armour of God and the weapons of righteousness – everything we need to assert the victory of Zion over Babylon.

These four transitional chapters are over. Isaiah has built his bridge between the "Book of Judgment" and the "Book of Comfort". He has performed his half-time substitution. Exit Assyria and enter Babylon. Sideline nation-states and bring the New Jerusalem centre stage. End Hezekiah's reign in failure and let the Messiah's reign begin to shine brightly, like the rays of dawn puncturing the night sky.

Part Four

God is Stronger Than You Think

(Isaiah 40–55)

Isaiah Sawn in Two (40:1–5)

Comfort, comfort my people, says your God.

(Isaiah 40:1)

An ancient Jewish oral tradition tells us that King Manasseh executed Isaiah by commanding that he be sawn in two. There is evidence in 2 Kings 21:16 and Hebrews 11:37 which suggests that this tradition may be true. What we know for sure is that many modern scholars are still trying to saw Isaiah in two today.

Here is how their argument goes: Isaiah 1–39 and 40–66 are so different in their content that they simply cannot have been written by the same person. The first section is full of judgment and the second full of comfort. The first section is all about sin and retribution, whereas the second is all about salvation and redemption. The first section is all about Judah and Assyria, whereas the second is all about Zion and Babylon. What is more, Isaiah uses by far the largest Hebrew vocabulary in the Old Testament (almost 2,200 different words) and there are subtle differences in his choice of words in the two sections. To top it all, these scholars argue that several of the prophecies in the "Book of Comfort" are so insightful about the future that they must have been written in retrospect rather than ahead of time. They find it particularly hard to believe that Isaiah could have named Cyrus as the Persian king who would capture Babylon and send the Jewish exiles home, if he were prophesying 100 years before Cyrus was born.

As a result, many Old Testament scholars state categorically that there must have been more than one Isaiah. They try to saw Isaiah in two by describing the author of the "Book of Judgment" as "Proto-Isaiah" ("the first Isaiah") and the author of the "Book of Comfort" as "Deutero-Isaiah" ("the second Isaiah"). A few scholars even go one step further and saw Isaiah in three by citing further textual differences between chapters 40–55 and chapters 56–66, thereby creating an additional "Trito-Isaiah" ("the third Isaiah"). I hope that our brief study of the way in which Isaiah bridges the two main sections of his book has already convinced you that he wrote it all, but this point matters so much to our understanding of the message of Isaiah that I want to give you four additional reasons to be confident about the unity of this book of prophecies as a whole.

First, the differences have been dramatically overplayed. One of the big themes of Isaiah is to call the Lord *"the Holy One of Israel"*. Isaiah uses this name twelve times in Isaiah 1–39 and fourteen times in Isaiah 40–66. Another big theme is *Zion*, which is named more often in Isaiah than in any other book of the Bible: thirty-one times in Isaiah 1–39 and eighteen times in Isaiah 40–66. The differences in vocabulary have also been exaggerated, and what differences there are can be explained by the fact that Isaiah completed the "Book of Comfort" by the end of 701 BC and then continued to prophesy for at least a further fifteen years.[1] We can even see the unity of this book of prophecies in the way in which both sections start and end. They both begin with the old city of Jerusalem (1:1 and 40:2) and they both close with God's new city on Mount Zion (35:10 and 66:20).

Second, it's worth noting that those who seek to saw Isaiah in two have the heavy weight of history stacked against them. There is not a single ancient manuscript of Isaiah, either in Hebrew or in Greek, which is divided in the manner they expect. To put it mildly, this is a very major weakness in their theory. When a shepherd-boy discovered the Dead Sea Scrolls in 1947,

---

[1] There are at least 25 words which are used nowhere in the Old Testament except in Isaiah, but which are used in both halves of his book of prophecies. Isaiah's vocabulary points to unity, not disunity.

one of those 2,000-year-old scrolls was the book of Isaiah set out as one seamless book of prophecies. Add to this the testimony of the famous Jewish rabbi Ben Sira in around 200 BC and that of the Jewish historian Josephus in around 95 AD, and the weight of evidence stacked against their theory is devastating.[2]

Third, we should really not be surprised that Isaiah foretold the future so accurately. Predicting the future is, after all, precisely what the prophets claimed that God had given them the supernatural ability to do! John 12:37–41 particularly draws our attention to Isaiah's amazing insights into the future, not to deny them but to warn us not to be like his stubborn contemporaries who refused to take his words seriously. His predictions about Cyrus should not make us try to saw him in two. They should make us marvel that his other prophecies will just as surely all come true.

Fourth, Jesus and the writers of the New Testament bear united testimony that Isaiah wrote the entire book. For me this is the absolute clincher. John 12:37–41 quotes from both sections of Isaiah and attributes both quotes to a single author. So do Matthew 3:3 and 4:14, Mark 1:2 and 7:6, Acts 8:30 and 28:25, and Romans 9:27 and 10:16. In fact, the New Testament is so clear about this and so often that the failure of so many scholars to recognize it seems to illustrate the truth of Isaiah 29:14: *"The wisdom of the wise will perish, the intelligence of the intelligent will vanish."*

All of this matters. When we recognize that Isaiah's "Book of Comfort" is the sequel to his "Book of Judgment", it actually makes an enormous difference. It helps us understand what he means when he begins his second section with the words, *"Comfort, comfort my people, says your God. Speak tenderly to Jerusalem, and proclaim to her that her hard service has been completed, that her sin has been paid for."*[3] It means that Isaiah

[2] Sirach 48:20–25 and Josephus's *Antiquities of the Jews* (11.1).

[3] 40:2 is not saying that Israel has earned its salvation through its suffering. It is saying that their Messiah has fulfilled for them the promise of 35:9–10 by

is announcing that he is moving on from words of judgment to words of comfort. He is about to prophesy what the Messiah has done to earn our forgiveness and to turn us into the New Jerusalem.

Recognizing the integrity of the book of Isaiah also helps us understand what the prophet means when he continues, *"A voice of one calling: 'In the wilderness prepare the way for the Lord; make straight in the desert a highway for our God… The glory of the Lord will be revealed, and all people will see it together.'"*[4] All four gospels quote from these verses and apply them to the ministry of John the Baptist, the one who preached in the desert that people needed to be baptized in preparation for the imminent revelation of God's Messiah.[5] In addition to prophesying about him, these verses also describe the whole of Isaiah 1–35 as a kind of John the Baptist for us too. The first half of this book has prepared us for a detailed revelation of the Messiah in the second half of the book. These verses link back to imagery of the "Book of Judgment" and they promise that the Messiah will turn the wasteland into God's pastureland paradise. He will clear the rough ground so that God can build his holy highway for all people.

So let's not separate what God has joined together. The sixty-six chapters of Isaiah flow together as one whole. Everything that God whetted our appetite for in Isaiah 1–35 is about to be revealed as ours through faith in his glorious Messiah in Isaiah 40–66.

"Comfort, comfort my people, says your God." We are about to receive real comfort indeed.[6]

---

paying the full price for their forgiveness with his own blood.

[4] In 40:5, Isaiah says literally in Hebrew that *"all flesh"* will see the Lord's glory. God will come in human flesh and all people will be able to gaze upon his holiness without being destroyed (Exodus 33:20).

[5] Matthew 3:3; Mark 1:2–3; Luke 3:4–6; John 1:23.

[6] The command to *"comfort my people"* is not a singular command for Isaiah alone, but a plural command for us to become preachers of the glorious message of Isaiah 1–66 too.

Pure Muscle (40:6–26)

See, the Sovereign Lord comes with power, and he rules with a mighty arm.

(Isaiah 40:10)

Isaiah never told us in his "Book of Judgment" what God looked like when he saw him in his vision in the Temple courtyard. Instead of describing the beauty of the Lord's face, the "Book of Judgment" is all about what the Lord is doing with his hand.

Isaiah warned the people of Judah that the Lord had resolved, *"I will turn my hand against you"* (1:25). He told them that *"the Lord's anger burns against his people; his hand is raised and he strikes them down"* (5:25). He prophesied long swathes of judgment and then warned that *"for all this, his anger is not turned away, his hand is still upraised"* (9:12, 9:17, 9:21, 10:4). In many ways, the entire "Book of Judgment" was a warning about God's hand: *"This is the plan determined for the whole world; this is the hand stretched out over all nations. For the Lord Almighty has purposed, and who can thwart him? His hand is stretched out, and who can turn it back?"* (14:26–27).

That's why the "Book of Comfort" opens with such amazing news. It shifts the focus away from God's hand of judgment and onto God's arm of salvation. In 40:2, the Lord commands Isaiah to *"speak tenderly to Jerusalem, and proclaim to her that her hard service has been completed, that her sin has been paid for, that she has received from the Lord's hand double for all her sins."* By double payment, he does not mean that he has judged Judah excessively. In the same way that we might say an angry wife gave her husband "both barrels" when she shouted at him, or that a boxer gave his opponent "both right and left" when he laid him out on the canvas, the Lord is saying that the people of Judah have heard more than enough about his hand. He is about to tell them about his arm, which is one of the names he gives his Messiah throughout Isaiah 40–66.[1] The "Book of Comfort" prophesies that the Messiah will succeed wherever Israel failed and that the blood which he will shed for them on the cross will bring full atonement for their sin. Don't miss the move away from God's hand of judgment when Isaiah exclaims, *"See, the Sovereign Lord comes with power, and he rules with a mighty arm."*

Isaiah 40:1–5 has been likened to the overture of a great musical symphony, since it introduces the major themes to be played in full in the chapters which follow. Those first five verses prophesy that the Messiah will bring forgiveness and comfort to anyone humble enough to confess that they are weak and sinful and that the Lord is strong and holy. He will reveal the glory of the Lord, which Isaiah alone saw in the Temple courtyard, not just to the people of Judah but also to the nations of the world. Isaiah emphasizes the continuity between the first and second sections of his book by saying that this prophecy is certain to come true because *"the mouth of the Lord has spoken."*[2]

In 40:6–11, Isaiah contrasts the Lord's power with our own. The Hebrew word *zerōa'*, which is used for God's *arm* throughout the "Book of Comfort", is a word which specifically describes the muscles of the arm – the forearm, the biceps and the shoulder.[3] Human strength is weak. It is as fragile as grass and flowers under the scorching skies of Israel. The Messiah, on the other hand, is pure muscle.[4] He speaks strong words

---

[1] For example, in 51:5, 9; 52:10; 53:1; 59:1, 16; 63:5.

[2] Compare 40:5 with 1:2, 20; 21:17; 22:25; 24:3; 25:8; 34:16.

[3] Two examples of Isaiah using the word *zerōa'* to mean "human muscle" can be found in 17:5 and 44:12.

[4] 1 Peter 1:24–25 quotes 40:6–8 from the Greek Septuagint translation and therefore speaks about human *glory*, but Isaiah actually speaks in Hebrew

which cannot be broken (40:8) and rules with strong commands which cannot be defied (40:10).[5] Since his heart is as pure as his muscle, his strong and loving arms will bring deep comfort and protection to God's people (40:11).[6]

In 40:12–17, Isaiah contrasts the Lord's power with that of the nations. For all the boasting of the rulers of Babylon, their own campfire stories confessed that their god Marduk was unable to create the world without the help of the wise sea-god Ea. The Lord appears to have this Babylonian creation myth in mind when he points out that he needed no help from anyone when he created the universe. The oceans which cover two-thirds of the earth's surface fitted into his hand. The vast stretches of space which defy human telescopes fitted into his handbreadth. The atoms which make up all matter fitted into his basket, and the mountains which tower over the earth fitted onto his scales. The Spirit of the Lord had no need of advisers.[7] God is far stronger than we think. To him, the combined might of the nations is like a drop of water that goes unnoticed in the corner of an empty bucket, or like the dust which goes unnoticed on a set of scales.[8]

In 40:18–26, Isaiah contrasts the Lord's power with that of foreign idols. He points out that they are the handiwork of human craftsmen. They are made of wood which will rot unless

about human *loving faithfulness*. Because the Messiah will be fully God as well as fully man (40:9), he will be everything that humankind has failed to be.

[5] In talking about the Messiah, the "Book of Comfort" will also talk much about the work of the Holy Spirit. The Hebrew word translated as *breath* in 40:7 is *rûach*. The Spirit of God holds the power of death and life.

[6] The mighty Messiah is also the meek shepherd, becoming a lamb to save his flock in 53:6–7. See John 10:11.

[7] The Hebrew word *tākan* in 40:13 is the same word that describes God *measuring* the heavens in 40:12. Paul quotes from 40:13 in Romans 11:34 and 1 Corinthians 2:16 in order to remind us that human minds can never *get the measure* of the Spirit of the Lord.

[8] This is also how God views any man-made attempt to get right with him. 40:16 warns us that there are not enough animals or wood in the fields and forests for us to sacrifice our own way to salvation.

it is given man-made treatment. They are made of metal which will fall over unless it is given a man-made base. They are takers and not givers. They cannot even save themselves, let alone anybody who is foolish enough to put their trust in them.

They are nothing like the Lord, who created the vast reaches of space with less effort than it takes you or I to erect a tent, and who created more stars than all the world's astronomers have yet to name. His throne towers over the earth, making even mighty rulers look like insects.[9] He isn't just the Creator of the universe. He is also its Sustainer. Were it not for his strength, even the sun and stars would cease to exist in a moment.[10]

This is what it means for the Lord to be the Holy One. It means that he is in an entirely different league from every person, every national ruler and every national idol. That's why God commands Isaiah and why Isaiah commands his readers in 40:9 to proclaim to the world *"Here is your God!"*[11] It's why the "Book of Comfort" begins with the question: *"'To whom will you compare me? Or who is my equal?' says the Holy One."*

The "Book of Judgment" is over. Isaiah has finished talking about God's hand. He has begun to reveal God's arm, and he says that all salvation starts by realizing that God is stronger than we think.

---

[9] Although 40:22 says that God sits enthroned above the *circle* of the earth, it isn't right to see this as early divine revelation that the earth is spherical. The Hebrew word *hūg* can refer to a flat disc as easily as to a globe. Isaiah uses decidedly unscientific language when he tells us in 40:26 that God "brings out" the stars.

[10] Isaiah has no time for deism, the idea that God created the world and then left it to run by itself like a wound up clock. Stars are the largest of all created things, yet 40:26 tells us that even they depend on God's active daily intervention for their ongoing existence. See also Colossians 1:17 and Hebrews 1:3.

[11] The Hebrew text is deliberately ambiguous in 40:9. It can be read either as God commanding Isaiah to proclaim this to Zion and Jerusalem, or as God commanding Zion and Jerusalem to proclaim it to Judah.

Lowly Worm and Popeye
(40:27–41:16)

"Do not be afraid, you worm Jacob, little Israel, do not fear, for I myself will help you," declares the Lord, your Redeemer, the Holy One of Israel.

(Isaiah 41:14)

When I was a child, one of my favourite cartoon characters was Lowly Worm. He was so ridiculously weak in Richard Scarry's books about Busytown that I felt sorry for such a tiny worm in such a great big city. I found him cute and endearing, but the people of Judah can't have been flattered when Isaiah likened their nation to Lowly Worm. They liked to think of themselves as a major player in global politics – after all, the might of Assyria had been shattered at the walls of Jerusalem – but the Lord was insistent. Until they learned to confess their own weakness, he could never make them strong.

That's why he is prepared to offend them in 41:14 by saying, *"Do not be afraid, you worm Jacob, little Israel, do not fear."*[1] He calls them Jacob to remind them that they are descended from Isaac's younger son and not from his natural heir Esau. While Esau hunted animals like a warrior, Jacob preferred to stay at home with mum. When Esau got angry, Jacob ran away from home and was too scared to return for twenty years. When he finally came home, Jacob was so scared of his Canaanite neighbours that he didn't even complain when one of them

---

[1] Don't be surprised that the Lord refers to the southern kingdom of Judah as "Israel" throughout the "Book of Comfort". He includes all 12 tribes in the promises he makes to Judah.

raped his daughter. He told his sons feebly that *"We are few in number, and if they join forces against me and attack me, I and my household will be destroyed."*[2] The Lord reminds the people of Judah that they are descended from a weakling and that they are just as weak as their father.

To reinforce this, the Lord also reminds them in 41:8 that they are descended from Abraham. Jacob's grandfather was so weak that he lied to the locals that his beautiful wife was his sister, for fear that they would kill him in order to marry her. He was too afraid to protest on two separate occasions when a local ruler took her into his harem. His successes never came from his muscles, from his mates or from his money, but from his relationship with the Lord. As soon as Abraham confessed to God that he was as weak as Lowly Worm, he received such divine strength that kings bowed down and begged him to make peace treaties with them.[3]

All of this forms the background to Isaiah 41. The Lord declares that he is about to raise up a new and powerful ruler, somewhere to the east of Judah, who will conquer the entire region (41:2–4).[4] The ruler's military campaigns will terrify the nations (41:5–7), but the people of Judah can rest assured that his successes are part of God's master plan to bless his people (41:2 and 4).[5] The swift collapse of the nations that worship pagan idols will enable the Lord to shout a great *"But you!"* in contrast over the descendants of Abraham and Jacob (41:8). As his hand of judgment falls on their proud neighbours,

---

[2] Genesis 25:24–28; 27:41–45; 31:41; 32:7–12; 34:30. *Israel* was the new name that the Lord gave to Jacob.

[3] Genesis 12:10–20; 20:1–13; 21:22–34.

[4] King Cyrus the Great of Persia would not be born for about a century, but Isaiah will prophesy much more about him in 41:25, 44:28–45:6, 45:13 and 46:11. The Hebrew is deliberately ambiguous in 41:2, since it can mean either *"whom victory meets at every step"* or *"who is called to serve [the Lord] in righteousness"*.

[5] Jesus is referring back to Isaiah 41:4, 44:6 and 48:12 when he calls himself *"the First and the Last"* in Revelation 1:8, 1:17, 2:8, 21:6 and 22:13.

the Lord will extend his hand of help to his people. *"But you, Israel, my servant, Jacob, whom I have chosen, you descendants of Abraham my friend... Do not fear, for I am with you; do not be dismayed, for I am your God. I will strengthen you and help you; I will uphold you with my righteous right hand"* (41:8–10).

The Lord assures the people of Judah that they will be the real winners in that day of foreign empire-building. Though in their own strength they are mere maggots,[6] they will become mountain movers when God takes hold of their hand like a father and his little child (41:11–16).[7] God is not looking to strike up a manly partnership with his people, in which we take his left hand in our right hand. He is calling us to express the same humility as a toddler learning to walk, supported in its first faltering steps by its father who holds its right hand firmly in his own as he walks lovingly behind (41:10 and 13).

Now that we have understood what God is saying in these verses in chapter 41, we are able to go back and read the end of chapter 40. If we are willing to admit we are like Lowly Worm, God promises to make us like another cartoon character: like Popeye. The comic-strip sailor is a weakling too. He is powerless to resist the evil bully Bluto. But then he eats a little of his trademark spinach. As soon as Popeye gives up on his own strength and reaches out for the green vegetable, he is endued with supernatural strength and always overcomes his oversized enemy.

God gives us a far better offer than spinach to Popeye. He offers us his own strength: the same power through which he lives forever, through which he created the universe and through which he never grows tired or weary or confused about what to do (40:27–28).[8] All we have to do to receive this power is

---

[6] The Hebrew word *tōla'ath* in 41:14 can mean either a *worm* or a *maggot*.

[7] Operated by a human farmer, a threshing-sledge crushed grain to remove chaff from the wheat. Operated by the arm of God, a threshing-sledge would crush mountains to remove nations from the earth.

[8] See Psalm 121:3–4; Isaiah 27:3; John 5:17.

repent of our fatal reliance on our own weak and weary muscles (40:29–30),[9] trading in false hope in our own strength for true hope in the Lord's strength working through us (40:31–41:1).[10] The Hebrew word Isaiah uses for *renewing* our strength in 40:31 and 41:1 is *hālaph*, which means literally *to exchange*. It therefore isn't a promise that God will restore our tired human strength, but a command for us to do away with it altogether! God invites us to exchange it for his own divine strength instead. This is the same promise which he gave to the apostle Paul in 2 Corinthians 12:9: *"When you admit your complete weakness, my complete power is given you."*[11]

Martin Luther's Commentary on Isaiah is never more insightful than it is on these verses. He had been like Lowly Worm himself when he nailed his Ninety-Five Theses to the church door in Wittenberg in October 1517, yet the scribbled thoughts of an obscure German monk had brought spiritual revival to Europe. He reveals the secret of his extraordinary fruitfulness in his commentary on these verses. He says he owes it all to confessing that he is like Lowly Worm and allowing the Lord to turn him into Popeye:

> *It is as if God were saying: "You must be weary and emptied, so that there is no way out for you. Then I will give you strength. First you must become nothing, then consolation and strength will come." This happened to me, Martin Luther, who against my will came up against the whole world, and then God helped me.*

---

[9] God does **not** say in the Hebrew text that he will multiply the power *of* the weak, but that he will multiply power *to* the weak. This distinction is crucial. We don't need increased human strength, but divine strength.

[10] The Hebrew word *qāwāh* in 40:31 means *to wait*, *to hope* or *to expect*. Our problem is that we are often unwilling to wait for God, strengthening ourselves because we expect to receive so little strength from him.

[11] The word *hālaph* is used to describe people changing clothes in Genesis 35:2. Jesus uses this same metaphor in Luke 24:49 when he promises that God will *clothe* our naked weakness with his divine power.

Dumb and Dumber
(41:17–29)

Tell us what the future holds, so that we may know you are gods.

(Isaiah 41:23)

If you want to understand the astonishing growth of the church in China during the twentieth century, you need to read the writings of some of its leaders. Watchman Nee tells us that it came about because they learned the same lesson as Martin Luther. Astonishing spiritual breakthrough always accompanies anybody who confesses that they are like Lowly Worm and who asks the Lord to make them strong like Popeye.

As a young church leader, Watchman Nee and six friends spent two weeks preaching the Gospel on a Chinese island which was home to an idol named Ta-Wang. They expected God to give them enough converts in two weeks to plant a church on the island, so when the Gospel fell on deaf ears they began to wonder why.

They found the answer to their question in Isaiah 41:17–20, where the Lord warns that he lets his people go through periods of spiritual drought in order to teach them to rely on his power instead of on their own. It was not because the Lord was weak that the Assyrians had destroyed the northern kingdom of Israel in 722 BC.[1] It was not because the Lord was weak that the Babylonians humiliated the southern kingdom of Judah in 651, 605 and 597 BC, eventually destroying it in 586 BC. The problem

---

[1] He remains *"the God of Israel"* and *"the Holy One of Israel"* in 41:17 and 20.

is never that the Lord is weak, but that his people think that they are strong. He takes drastic action to convince us of our poverty and neediness. If the church in your nation is struggling, take a moment to consider whether the Lord might have led you into a spiritual desert in order to increase your thirst for his power. Whenever churches respond to defeat and decline by repenting of their reliance upon their own strength, God quickly turns their barren deserts into fertile fields.[2] As soon as we take off the ragged clothes of self-reliance, God quickly clothes our naked weakness with power from on high.

Watchman Nee explains:

*On January 9th we were outside preaching. Brother Wu with some others was in one part of the village and suddenly asked publicly: "Why will none of you believe?" Someone in the crowd replied at once: "We have a god – **one** god – Ta-Wang, and he has never failed us. He is an effective god." "How do you know that you can trust him?" asked Wu. "We have held his festival procession every January for 286 years. The chosen day is revealed by divination beforehand, and every year without fail his Day is a perfect one without rain or cloud," was the reply. "When is the procession this year?" "It is fixed for January 11th at eight in the morning." "Then," said brother Wu impetuously, "I promise you that it will certainly rain on the 11th." At once there was an outburst of cries from the crowd: "That is enough! We don't want to hear any more preaching. If there is rain on the 11th, then your God is God!"... We stopped our preaching at once, and gave ourselves to prayer.[3]*

---

[2] Do not assume that what happened to Watchman Nee could never happen in your community. Isaiah assures us that no barren height, no dry valley and no parched desert is beyond the reach of God's power.

[3] Watchman Nee recalls this showdown at the end of his book *Sit, Walk, Stand* (1957).

Watchman Nee and his friends were about to learn the lesson of Isaiah 41:21–29, where the Lord tells the idols of the ancient world that he is *"Jacob's King"* – he is such a mighty ruler that he can strengthen any weak believer.[4] He defies the idols to prove their influence over events by making a few predictions about the future. When they remain speechless, he makes a few predictions of his own. He promises to raise up a new ruler to the north-east of Judah, who will conquer every nation and even capture the mighty walls of Babylon.[5] Israel's God can freely utter such predictions because he is the Lord of History. The pagan idols cannot do so because they are dumb, and anyone who chooses to worship them is even dumber.[6]

Watchman Nee and his friends knew that the people of the island were fishermen and experts at reading the weather. If they predicted clear skies at eight o'clock on the 11th, only a miracle would bring them rain. For two days they prayed.

I was awakened by the direct rays of the sun through the single window of our attic. "This isn't rain!" I said. It was already past seven o'clock. I got up, knelt down and prayed. "Lord," I said, "please send the rain…"

Even before our Amen we heard a few drops on the tiles… Soon we heard what had happened in the village. Already, at the first drop of rain, a few of the younger generation had begun to say openly: "There is God; there is no more Ta-Wang! He is kept in by the rain." But he wasn't. They carried him out on a sedan chair. Surely

---

[4] In Chinese, the idol's name Ta-Wang means *the Great King*. The Lord would expose him as an imposter.

[5] The Lord predicted in 41:2 that Cyrus would come from the *east*. Now he predicts with greater detail in 41:25 that he will come from the *north-east*. Although God does not name Cyrus until 44:28, he describes his reign as *"good news"* for Jerusalem in 41:27 because he would destroy its arch-nemesis Babylon.

[6] The Lord doesn't just call idols *worthless* in 41:24. He also calls those who choose to worship them *detestable*.

he would stop the shower! Then came the downpour. After only some ten or twelve yards, three of the coolies stumbled and fell. Down went the chair and Ta-Wang with it, fracturing his jaw and his left arm. Still determined, they carried out emergency repairs and put him back in the chair. Somehow, slipping and stumbling, they dragged or carried him halfway round the village. Then the floods defeated them... The procession was stopped and the idol taken into a house. Divination was made. "Today was the wrong day," came the answer. "The festival is to be on the 14th with the procession at six in the evening." Immediately we heard this there came the assurance in our hearts: "God will send rain on the 14th."

Watchman Nee and his friends used the next four days of glorious sunshine to preach the Gospel and saw over thirty people solidly converted. These could form the core of a new church on the island, but only if the idol Ta-Wang was humiliated a second time.

The 14th broke, another perfect day, and we had good meetings. As the evening approached we met, and again, at the appointed hour, we quietly brought the matter to the Lord's remembrance. Not a minute late, His answer came with torrential rain and floods as before. The next day our time was up and we had to leave. We have not been back... Satan's power in that idol had been broken, and that is an eternal thing. Ta-Wang was no more "an effective god". The salvation of souls would follow.

Do you want your church to advance like the church in China? Then learn the same lesson which its leaders learned from these verses in Isaiah. Don't be afraid to confront the idols in your nation – whether they are blatant images of wood and stone, or whether they are the subtler idols of money, sex, success and power. Don't be afraid to proclaim that they are dumb and that those who choose to worship them are even dumber.[7] Proclaim the Kingdom of God and expect God to back up your words with power. Take a risk in weakness and you will see God move in strength. Dare to speak God's Word like the leaders of old:

> *Do not turn away after useless idols. They can do you no good, nor can they rescue you, because they are useless... We too are only human, like you. We are bringing you good news, telling you to turn from these worthless things to the living God.*[8]

---

[7] There is a Hebrew play on words in 41:29, since the word for wind is *rūach*, which can also mean spirit. Idols fill their followers with wind, but the Lord promises to fill his followers with the Holy Spirit.

[8] 1 Samuel 12:21 and Acts 14:15. See also Jonah 2:8 and 1 Thessalonians 1:9. Note the way that Jesus follows the principle of Isaiah 41 in John 11:41–42, 13:19 and 14:29.

The Singing Servant
(42:1–9)

*Here is my servant, whom I uphold, my chosen one in
whom I delight.*

(Isaiah 42:1)

Richard Hannay finds himself in trouble in John Buchan's novel
The Thirty-Nine Steps. He has discovered vital information
that will ensure that Britain wins World War One, but German
spies are watching him. He is forced to disguise himself and to
reveal his identity to his allies secretly by singing an obscure
Scottish ditty. The plan succeeds. The watching Germans do not
recognize the song, so under their noses he is able to warn the
British how to save their fleet from swift destruction.

The people of Judah were about to be in far worse trouble
than Richard Hannay. They were about to be conquered by the
Babylonians, then by the Persians, then by the Macedonians,
then by the Seleucids and then finally by the Romans. The Lord
therefore gives them four songs in the "Book of Comfort" which
the Messiah will sing under the noses of their enemies so that
only those in the know will recognize him for who he is. They
are known as the four Servant Songs. The first is in 42:1–4, the
second is in 49:1–6, the third is in 50:4–9 and the fourth is in
52:13–53:12.[1] They prophesy about the Messiah, but their lyrics
are deliberately obscure to hide the truth from unfriendly ears.

For a start, it isn't clear in this first Servant Song who
the servant actually is. Is Isaiah talking about himself, since

---

[1] The first three Servant Songs also have encores in 42:5–9, 49:7–13 and
50:10–11.

the Lord called him *"my servant"* in 20:3? Is he talking about the ruler from the north-east who will destroy Babylon, since he told us in 41:2 that he would call that ruler to serve him in righteousness? The answer to both questions is yes. This song echoes chapters 40–41 because the Lord will make both Isaiah and Cyrus proof that he is able to take weak people by the hand and make them supernaturally strong.

At the same time, Isaiah also appears to be talking about the people of Judah. God has just told them in 41:8–9 that he regards them as *"Israel, my servant"* and that he promises them, *"You are my servant; I have chosen you and have not rejected you."*[2] Since the Hebrew word for *teaching* in 42:4 is *tōrāh*, most modern Jewish rabbis believe that this song is a promise that the Gentiles will one day embrace the Jewish Law. This isn't wrong, but it cannot be the complete picture, since the other Servant Songs tell us that the servant will bring Israel back to God (49:5–6) by being hated and killed by the Jewish nation (49:7) so that he can bring forgiveness to all of God's people (53:3–12).

Thankfully, we are not left guessing about the servant's identity. Like Richard Hannay's contact in the British government, we are in the know about the Song. Matthew 12:17–21 sings it from start to finish over Jesus and tells us that he came *"to fulfil what was spoken through the prophet Isaiah"*. Jesus is the true and better Isaiah, since he speaks deeper comfort to the weak by the power of the Holy Spirit. Jesus is the true and better Cyrus, since he conquers the nations, not with a sword, but with the Gospel he proclaims. Jesus is the true and better Israel since, unlike the weak descendants of Jacob, he has never failed to pursue justice and faithfulness. Those who are in the know about the Song can hear its echo in the words that God the Father speaks over Jesus: *"You are my Son, whom I love; with*

---

[2] The Lord will also address the people of Judah as *"my servant"* in 44:1–2, 44:21, 45:4, 48:20 and 49:3.

you I am well pleased," and *"This is my Son, whom I have chosen; listen to him."*[3]

Imagine how tragic it would have been for the outcome of World War One had the government official failed to recognize Richard Hannay when he sang his Scottish ditty. That's nothing compared to the tragedy which has befallen the Jewish nation for failing to recognize its Messiah when he came singing this first Servant Song. When the Holy Spirit descended on Jesus like a dove at his baptism (42:1), the Jewish priests and rabbis looked the other way. When he extended God's love to the poor and needy (42:3), warning them not to turn God's power into a sideshow by bragging loudly about how much his miracles had helped them (42:2), the Jewish priests and rabbis missed it again.[4] When he included the Samaritans and the pagans in God's offer of salvation (42:1 and 4), the Jewish priests and rabbis were so furious that they put him on trial for his life.[5] When he didn't fear or falter in their courtroom (42:4), again they missed their cue. This Servant Song was meant to reveal the identity of the Messiah to the Jews under the noses of the Greeks and Romans. Because the Jewish leaders refused to listen to him when he came, he was recognized by the Greeks and Romans under their noses instead.

The Lord therefore continues singing in 42:5–9. He is determined to persuade a remnant of Jews to defy their rabbis by laying hold of their Messiah. He sings first to the Messiah in 42:5–7, promising to take him by the hand and demonstrate what divine strength can do through human flesh and blood.[6]

---

[3] Luke 3:22; 9:35.

[4] If you feel weak, you should find 42:3 very encouraging. God never crushes the weak – only the strong.

[5] Isaiah uses the Hebrew word *tōrāh* to refer to the Gospel because the Gospel is the fulfilment of the Jewish Law. See Matthew 5:17, and Romans 3:31, 8:1–4 and 10:4.

[6] Though he was the Son of God, John 5:19–20 and Acts 10:38 both emphasize that Jesus did not minister out of his inherent divinity, but as a man who held his Father's hand and was empowered by the Holy Spirit.

Having empowered King Cyrus to conquer the walls of Babylon, he promises to empower the Messiah to conquer the evil spirits at work behind Babylon. He will strengthen him to give sight to the blind, freedom to the captives and light to those who sit in darkness.[7] Even though the priests and rabbis will reject him, the Lord promises that many Jews and many Gentiles will lay hold of his New Covenant and be saved.[8]

The Lord therefore sings to the people of Judah in 42:8–9. He repeats the message of the previous chapter when he points out that *"the former things have taken place"* (that many of the prophecies in the "Book of Judgment" have already been fulfilled) and that *"new things I declare; before they spring into being I announce them to you."* They must not miss this proof that the Holy One of Israel is far superior to the false gods of the nations. *"I am the Lord; that is my name! I will not yield my glory to another or my praise to idols."*

But this is more than repetition. It also explains why the Lord refuses to empower us until we admit our weakness. It echoes what he said to Gideon in Judges 7:2. He will only do extraordinary things through people who admit that they are ordinary. He will not display his glory through people who believe some of the glory ought to go to them.[9]

The Messiah will be perfectly humble, so he will be the perfect candidate for God to display his divine power through human weakness. The Lord has staked his glory on the accuracy of his predictions, so the people of Judah can rest assured that the Messiah will fulfil all the prophetic lyrics of this song. All they have to do is make sure that they are listening when he comes and that they are humble enough to start singing along.

---

[7] Don't miss the echo of 9:2 in 42:7. This servant is the same person as the Galilean Messiah.

[8] Luke 22:20 says this prophecy about God's New Covenant was fulfilled when Jesus died on the cross.

[9] This is why God actively resists the proud. See Proverbs 3:34, quoted in James 4:6 and 1 Peter 5:5.

Tone Deaf (42:10–25)

Who is blind but my servant, and deaf like the
messenger I send?

(Isaiah 42:19)

Some songs are so breathtaking that they demand an encore.
In the early days of Broadway, a new duet named "Little Peach"
broke all the records by eliciting eleven encores from the
captivated crowd.[1] We have already seen that the Lord was so
excited by his first Servant Song that he sang an encore in 42:5–
9. Now we discover that Isaiah is excited too. Together they sing
four more encores to the nations of the world.

Isaiah's first encore is in 42:10–13. He sings it to the pagan
nations who were on the receiving end of his fierce words in the
"Book of Judgment", inviting them to sing a new song of faith in
Israel's Messiah. He is so excited by the promise in 42:4 that *the*
islands will put their hope" in the Messiah that he calls out a song
of mercy to the far-off islands which felt God's judgment upon
the seafarers of Tyre and Sidon in chapter 23. Next he turns to
the Arabs, whom he called Kedar when he prophesied against
them in 21:13–17.[2] Although they have been persistently
hostile towards the people of Judah, he includes them in his
Gospel invitation. He even turns to Sela, the mountain fortress
of Edom, which most modern tourists know as Petra. Edom was

---

[1] The duet was sung by Mr Wilson and Miss Lyford at The Broadway Theatre.
Their record number of encores was reported by the New York *Evening*
Telegram on 5th August 1889.

[2] Kedar was a son of Ishmael (Genesis 25:13), whose name became
synonymous with the nomads of the Arabian Peninsula (Psalm 120:5; Song of
Songs 1:5; Isaiah 60:7; Jeremiah 49:28; Ezekiel 27:21).

so implacably hostile towards Israel that the Lord could use its name as shorthand for every sinful nation of the earth in 34:5–6. Nevertheless, Isaiah includes them in his Gospel invitation too. The Messiah has triumphed over their hostility and now invites them to become friends of God.[3] The Ishmaelites who were counted out of Abraham's blessing for the sake of Isaac are now counted back in for the sake of Jesus. The Edomites who were counted out of Isaac's blessing for the sake of Jacob are now counted back in for the sake of Jesus too.

Isaiah's song provokes the Lord to sing a fresh encore of his own in 42:14–17. He uses the same Hebrew word that is used to describe Joseph's attempts to hold back his emotions in front of his brothers in Genesis 43:31 and 45:1 when he confesses that it has been hard for him to wait to reveal his Messiah to the world.[4] He expresses his deep relief that, now that he has finally sung the first of his Servant Songs, he can finally vent his emotions at the top of his lungs, like a woman at long last entering the throes of labour.[5] He will still judge the pagans if they cling to their worthless idols, but his big announcement is that the gestation period for their salvation is almost over. Millions of pagans will be born again and will put their faith in a God their fathers never knew: *"I will lead the blind by ways they have not known, along unfamiliar paths I will guide them."*[6]

Suddenly the Lord turns to the people of Judah and sings

---

[3] In 42:13, Isaiah describes the Messiah as a *mighty hero* and as a *man of war*. As we will discover later, in 63:1–6, we dare not mistake the Messiah's meekness for weakness.

[4] Although the Hebrew word *mē'ōam* at the start of 42:14 can simply mean *"for a long time"*, its literal meaning is *"from eternity"*. The Lord has longed to reveal his Messiah since before the dawn of time.

[5] God's character is truly beyond fathoming. Only he could describe himself in one verse as a mighty warrior shouting a battle-cry and in the very next verse as a woman screaming out in labour!

[6] Note the way in which these references to levelled mountains, dried-up rivers and smoothed rough places all link back to the Lord's promise of a holy highway in 11:15–16, 19:23–25, 35:8–9 and 40:3–5.

another encore in 42:18–22. This time there is no doubt whom he means by *"my servant"*. It is the Jewish nation which has failed to recognize his prophet Isaiah and which will also fail to recognize his Messiah when he finally comes. *"Who is blind but my servant, and deaf like the messenger I send?"* the Lord demands. They were called to be his witnesses to the nations of the world, but they have been tone deaf to his songs and blind to his signs. Theirs is the covenant which he made with Israel at Mount Sinai. Theirs are the Scriptures and the prophets and the Temple and its sacrifices. *"It pleased the Lord for the sake of his righteousness to make his law great and glorious,"* yet they proved to be deafer and blinder than the surrounding nations which did not receive the Law. That's why the Lord warns them that the next few centuries of Jewish history will be a catalogue of slaughter, exile and occupation. He predicts they will ignore the words of Isaiah and will not even return wholeheartedly to their God when his prophecies about King Cyrus come true. They will prove to be tone deaf to the Messiah's first Servant Song. *"You have seen many things, but you pay no attention; your ears are open, but you do not listen."*

Isaiah is so upset by this that he sings a final encore of his own in 42:23–25. He makes a final appeal for the people of Judah to open up their ears and pay attention. He urges them to listen to the marching sound of many foreign soldiers invading their land in order to plunder and enslave them. Since they are about to experience the curses which Moses spoke in Deuteronomy 29 and 32 over anyone who broke God's Law, Isaiah pleads with them to have the common sense to look up quickly and to see who it is that is giving them such a severe beating. These are not natural disasters or simple shifts in geopolitics. These are acts of loving discipline from God the Father, determined to bring his wayward children to their senses and to call them to come back home.

Isaiah knows that the people of Judah will not listen to

him. He predicts that they will be tone deaf to his song and blind to the Lord's anger: *"It enveloped them in flames, yet they did not understand; it consumed them, but they did not take it to heart."*[7] Nevertheless, Isaiah ends this chapter with real hope for his tone-deaf nation.

First, he identifies himself with sinful Judah. He asks them, *"Was it not the Lord, against whom **we** have sinned?"* If God has forgiven Isaiah, there is hope for the rest of his countrymen too. Second, Isaiah responds to the first Servant Song himself. He fulfils the words of 42:4 by refusing to grow discouraged or to falter in the face of their stubborn refusal to listen to his words. Third, through this act of obedience, Isaiah proclaims that the Messiah is on his way. Judah may be a tone-deaf servant, but the Lord has a servant waiting in the wings who will be pitch-perfect in everything. The true and better Israel is coming and he will succeed wherever the people of Judah have failed.[8]

---

[7] The Lord's discipline does not automatically lead to repentance. Repentance only springs from humility, which in turn springs from Gospel preaching. Isaiah shows us that we must therefore persist in our appeals.

[8] The double reference to Judah as God's *servant* in 42:19 forms a deliberate contrast with the Messiah in 42:1, who opens the eyes of the blind (42:7) and has a perfect ear to hear whatever the Lord sings (50:4–5).

Irrevocable (43:1–44:23)

Remember these things, Jacob, for you, Israel, are my servant. I have made you, you are my servant; Israel, I will not forget you.

(Isaiah 44:21)

Many readers of Isaiah fall into one of two unhelpful extremes.

The first group of readers fail to notice that "Zion" must mean more than a mere mountain. They focus on how often Isaiah mentions it instead of grasping what he says about it: *"In the last days the mountain of the Lord's temple will be established as the highest of the mountains"* (2:2). Back in Isaiah's day, Mount Zion was less than a third of the size of Mount Sinai or Mount Hermon. During the past 2,500 years that ratio hasn't changed. Readers who rush to apply Isaiah's prophecies to modern-day Jerusalem and to the modern state of Israel fail to recognize that Zion must mean something more than a physical mountain. Hebrews 12:22 tells churchgoers that *"You have come to Mount Zion, to the city of the living God, the heavenly Jerusalem."*

The second group of readers make the opposite mistake. They focus on what Jesus said in John 4:20–23 to a Samaritan woman who wanted to know whether she should worship on Mount Zion or Mount Gerizim: *"Believe me, a time is coming when you will worship the Father neither on this mountain nor in Jerusalem."* In doing so, they fail to spot that he also told her that *"salvation is from the Jews"*. God hasn't finished with the Jewish nation. He hasn't replaced it in his affections with the Church. God's call to Israel is irrevocable.

That's why we need to read these chapters carefully. We

must avoid both misguided extremes. Isaiah isn't just known as "the Romans of the Old Testament" because it describes the Gospel in the same clear manner as Romans 1–8, but also because it outlines God's plan for the Jewish nation in the same manner as Romans 9–11. Having corrected the first of these two mistakes in chapter 42 by telling us that any Jew who rejects the Messiah will be destroyed as a pagan and that any pagan who receives the Messiah will be saved as a Jew, Isaiah now corrects the second mistake in chapters 43–44.

Isaiah encourages the people of Judah by emphasizing that the Lord still wants to be their national God. He is still *"the Holy One of Israel"* (43:3, 14 and 15). He is still *"your Saviour"* and *"your Redeemer"* (43:3, 43:14 and 44:6). He is still *"Israel's Creator"* and *"Israel's King"* (43:15 and 44:6). As for the people of Judah, the Lord still assures them that *"I have summoned you by name; you are mine... You are precious and honoured in my sight... I love you... for I am with you"* (43:1, 4 and 5).[1] He still calls them *"my people"*, *"my chosen ones"*, *"my servants"* and *"my witnesses"* (43:10, 43:12, 43:20, 43:21, 44:1, 44:2, 44:7, 44:8 and 44:21). Don't miss the myriad of ways in which the Lord insists his plan to save the Gentiles does not mean that he has finished with his plan to save the Jews.

The Lord encourages the people of Judah to trust that, even in judgment, he is faithful. He will punish them for their sinfulness, but his punishment will be measured (43:2). If they need proof of this, they need merely note the way that Assyria has given up on conquering Jerusalem and has turned its attention towards invading Egypt and Cush instead.[2] The Lord is about to divert punishment away from Judah so that a faithful

---

[1] These verses deliberately restate God's promise to Israel in Exodus 19:5–6 and Deuteronomy 14:2. This promise is expanded in 1 Peter 2:9–10 to include any Gentile who joins this faithful remnant of the Jews.

[2] The Lower Nile kingdom of Egypt and the Upper Nile kingdom of Cush were united under a single pharaoh. Seba was their neighbour and ally (Genesis 10:7). The Assyrians ravaged all three from 674 to 664 BC.

remnant of believing Jews can still be saved. They can trust him to bring them back from the four corners of the earth and to resettle them in the Promised Land (43:4–7).[3]

It gets even better for Israel. The Lord promises that he will shape the course of history for their sake, destroying Babylon in order to release them from captivity and bring them back to Zion (43:14–21). Despite their non-stop unfaithfulness towards him, he will direct world events in complete faithfulness towards them (43:22–28).[4] He will forgive them and so transform their weakness into strength through his Holy Spirit that they are finally able to live up to the name which Moses gave them when he warned that they could never obey the Law all on their own (44:1–5). *Jeshurun* means *Upright One*, and the Lord resurrects this name from Deuteronomy as a promise that he will so strengthen their weak hearts that people from every nation will be attracted to join them (44:5).[5]

This is where we need to turn to Paul's letter to the Romans in order to understand what God is saying. Although he does not quote from these two chapters, Paul quotes from at least fifteen verses in Isaiah during the course of Romans 9–11. He echoes Isaiah 42 when he tells us in 9:6 that *"Not all who are descended from Israel are Israel"* – in other words, any Jew who rejects God's Messiah will be numbered with the Gentiles, while any Gentile who receives God's Messiah will be numbered with the Jews. He echoes Isaiah 43–44 when he tells us in 9:4–5 that, nevertheless, God has not finished with the Jews: *"Theirs is the adoption to sonship; theirs the divine glory, the covenants, the*

---

[3] The Lord refers to Israel literally in 44:7 as *"my eternal people"*. Note, however, that Romans 4:13 says this promise has been upgraded from a tiny patch of land in the Middle East to encompass the entire world.

[4] Their forefather Abraham sinned, their judges sinned, their kings sinned, their prophets sinned and their priests sinned (43:27–28). Nevertheless, the Lord repays evil with good. He will forgive and restore Israel.

[5] Other than in 44:2, the only place in the Bible where the name Jeshurun is used is in Deuteronomy 32:15, 33:5 and 33:26. God is deliberately restating his promises to Israel.

receiving of the law, the temple worship and the promises. Theirs are the patriarchs, and from them is traced the human ancestry of the Messiah." He echoes Isaiah when he warns us in 11:29 not to think that the Church has supplanted the Jewish nation, "for God's gifts and his call are irrevocable".[6]

Paul picks up on Isaiah's reference to Jeshurun and goes back to the closing chapters of Deuteronomy for an explanation of what God is doing. Since only a remnant of Jews will receive their Messiah (Deuteronomy 32:15-18 and Romans 11:1-5), God has decided to make the rest of the Jews jealous by saving millions of Gentiles (Deuteronomy 32:19-21 and Romans 11:11-32). This strategy will work. Not only will it enable the Lord to save vast numbers of Gentiles, but it will also vindicate his utter faithfulness to Israel in the eyes of the watching world (Deuteronomy 32:26-27 and Romans 11:33-36). The Church hasn't replaced Israel in God's purposes, because the Church is Israel. It is the continuation of the Jewish story which began with Abraham and which will end with a countless crowd of worshippers from Israel and from every other nation of the world.

No wonder Isaiah is excited as he announces this good news to the people of Judah in 44:21-23. "Remember these things, Jacob, for you, Israel, are my servant. I have made you, you are my servant; Israel, I will not forget you. I have swept away your offences like a cloud, your sins like the morning mist. Return to me, for I have redeemed you." Isaiah is so excited that he cries out for the heavens and the earth to sing an encore of their own, "for the Lord has redeemed Jacob, he displays his glory in Israel."

So don't fall for either of these two errors about Zion. Sing a little encore of your own.

---

[6] In 48:12, even after the Babylonian captivity, the Lord still refers to the Jews as his "called ones".

Forget It (43:1–44:23)

This is what the Lord says – he who made a way through the sea... "Forget the former things; do not dwell on the past. See, I am doing a new thing!"

(Isaiah 43:16–19)

The people of Judah were exceedingly forgetful. If you don't believe me, just take a look at the account of their history in Psalm 106. It repeatedly tells us that all their troubles as a nation flowed from their forgetfulness: *"They did not remember your many kindnesses... They soon forgot what he had done.... They forgot the God who saved them, who had done great things in Egypt."* The Lord had a solution for this. He commanded them to celebrate the Passover as an annual feast during which they reminded one another all about how the Lord had freed their ancestors from slavery in Egypt through the Exodus.

We don't need good memories ourselves to spot the many references back to the Exodus in Isaiah 43:1–7. The prophet refers to the God of Israel as *Yahweh*, the name by which he revealed himself to Moses at the burning bush and which means "the I AM", "the Eternal One" or simply "the Lord". When Isaiah reminds us that the Lord *redeemed* his people, he uses the same Hebrew word *gā'al* which the book of Exodus uses to describe what was accomplished through the death of the Passover lambs. Isaiah doesn't have to name the Red Sea when he reminds us that the Lord has a track record of helping his people to pass through large bodies of water at the expense of the Egyptians.[1] Isaiah uses this Exodus imagery to assure us

---

[1] Exodus 3:13–15; 6:6; 14:21–31; 15:13.

that the God of Israel is still Israel's Saviour. No matter what disasters may befall his people, they can rest assured that they are still his children and have still been created for his glory. They can expect a second Exodus from him after their sin takes them into captivity in Babylon.[2]

The references back to the Exodus continue in 43:8–13. The Lord reminds the people of Judah that, unlike the pagan idols, he is strong enough to predict and shape the future course of human history.[3] However deaf and blind the people of Judah may be, they are still God's witnesses of how he did this when he promised to defy the odds by forcing the superpower of Egypt to free its slaves.[4] Quite apart from the stunning accuracy of his predictions in the "Book of Judgment", this Exodus prediction had already proved that *"I, even I, am the Lord, and apart from me there is no saviour."*[5] Nothing can ever stop the Lord from saving or can ever reverse his finished work of salvation. God not only saves his people, but he also keeps them saved. *"I have revealed and saved and proclaimed – I, and not some foreign god among you. You are my witnesses that I am God."*

The Lord therefore warns the people of Judah not to forget the Exodus. Have you got that? If so, then you are ready for the message of 43:14–44:23. The Lord tells the people of Judah to forget the Exodus! He is about to do something far greater for their nation.

---

[2] Isaiah is talking primarily about the Jewish return from the Babylonian exile, but the remarkable resurrection of the state of Israel in 1948 is a reminder that God still hasn't finished with the Jewish nation.

[3] We can hear an echo of 43:10 in Philemon 6, since both verses tell us that the more we witness the more we will know and believe the Gospel for ourselves. Active evangelism carries its own reward.

[4] The unfaithfulness of the people of Judah has not disqualified them as God's witnesses (43:10, 12; 44:8). Proclaiming God's greatness isn't optional. He tells us in 43:21 that it lies at the very heart of his calling on our lives. See also John 15:27, Acts 1:8 and 1 Peter 2:9.

[5] We can hear an echo of 43:11 in John 14:6, Acts 4:12 and 1 Timothy 2:5–6. There are many man-made religions but there is only one God-given path to salvation.

In 43:14, he mentions Babylon by name for the first time in the "Book of Comfort". He promises that he will redeem the people of Judah from their Babylonian captivity, just as he redeemed their ancestors from their Egyptian slavery. He promises to break the power of Babylon in the same way that he broke the power of Egypt, through the redemption price of a Passover Lamb. In 43:16–17, the Lord commands the people of Judah to look back a final time at the miracle which he performed at the Red Sea, then in 43:18–19 he commands them to shift their eyes forwards: *"Forget the former things; do not dwell on the past. See, I am doing a new thing! Now it springs up; do you not perceive it?"*

The "new thing" which needs to capture their full attention is the second Exodus, which the Lord is about to perform for the people of Judah. He will bring them home from their Babylonian captivity, leading them across the deserts to rebuild their homes in the Promised Land. However, this "new thing" must also be something far greater than this. The return from Babylon was good but it wasn't *that* good. It was nowhere near as breathtaking as the first Exodus from Egypt. No, Isaiah is predicting something even greater than the Jewish return from Egypt and Babylon.

In 43:22–28, Isaiah says that the new Exodus will bring a better experience of God's forgiveness. The Babylonian army would destroy the Jewish Temple because even its priests were sinful, but a new and better priest will proclaim to God's people: *"I, even I, am he who blots out your transgressions, for my own sake, and remembers your sins no more."*[6] In 44:1–5, Isaiah promises that this new priest will also pour out God's Holy Spirit on all his people. Moses built a tent so that the Lord would come and dwell inside it at the heart of the camp of Israel, but the Messiah will cause the Lord to come and dwell inside each

---

[6] Although the New Testament never quotes from 43:25, it quotes from a similar Old Testament promise in Hebrews 8:1–13. Our new priest saves us, not because of anything we have done, but for his own sake alone.

one of us, turning us into walking, talking tabernacles. Suddenly we begin to see why this new Exodus makes even the mighty miracle of the Red Sea entirely forgettable.

In 44:6–20, Isaiah tells us that this new Exodus will expose human idols for the weak and feeble phoneys that they are. The accurate fulfilment of all God's promises to Moses exposed the weakness of the idols of Egypt, but the accuracy of all God's promises about the Messiah will expose the weakness of every man-made religion.[7] Metal gods are forged with the weak and faltering arms of a human blacksmith, so they will fail when the arm of the Lord is finally revealed (44:12). Wooden gods are chiselled out of fuel for the fire, so they will be reduced to ashes when the Messiah comes to baptize people with God's Holy Spirit and with fire (44:14–20).[8] Moses proved to Egypt that the Lord is the only true God, but the Messiah will prove it to every nation of the world.[9]

In 44:21–23, Isaiah therefore commands the people of Judah to sing a better song than the one which their ancestors sang on the far side of the Red Sea in Exodus 15. They are to forget the Exodus but they are to *"remember these things, Jacob, for you, Israel, are my servant. I have made you, you are my servant... Return to me, for I have redeemed you."*

These verses close with Isaiah exclaiming that even the earth and skies ought to sing along with the people of Judah. We need to sing too. Forget the Exodus. God is about to perform something far better. Moses was just Moses, but the Messiah is the Messiah.

---

[7] Exodus 12:12; Numbers 33:4. Since wooden idols were plastered over and painted, the Lord points out in 44:18 that the eyes of idolaters have been plastered over and blinded too. See 2 Corinthians 4:4.

[8] Matthew 3:11. Note the way in which 44:14 reminds us that even the wood men use to make their idols only grows through God-given rain. God alone is the Creator.

[9] When Luke 9:30–31 tells us that Moses appeared to Jesus in order to discuss his new "departure", the Greek word is actually "Exodus". 1 Corinthians 5:7 describes Jesus as the true and better Passover Lamb.

Suddenly Cyrus
(44:24–45:8)

… who says of Cyrus, "He is my shepherd and will accomplish all that I please."

(Isaiah 44:28)

The people of the ancient world didn't have Wikipedia, but it didn't matter. They had their own companion to help them while away their evenings: they had *Cyropaedia*. If you have never heard of it, it's the name the Greek historian Xenophon gave to his bestselling biography of King Cyrus the Great of Persia. It meant *"The Education of Cyrus"* and it promised to tell its readers everything they needed to know about the most successful ruler and general that the world had ever seen.

Isaiah's account of the life of Cyrus differs in two major ways from that of Xenophon.

The most obvious difference is that Xenophon wrote over a century after Cyrus died, whereas Isaiah wrote over a century before Cyrus was born! This fact alone convinces many scholars that the author of the "Book of Judgment" cannot possibly have written the "Book of Comfort", but let's slow down before we start redating Isaiah. The Lord has just spent the past four chapters telling us that he is about to prove his mastery over history by predicting future events with astonishing accuracy. Saying that the prophet Isaiah cannot have prophesied these words because they are too prophetic is therefore as obtuse as denying someone the Oscar for Best Actor because their performance is too convincing to be acting![1] If Isaiah could make such accurate predictions about Israel, Judah, Assyria, Babylon and Jesus, it should not surprise us that he did the same about Cyrus. The Lord shows he is far stronger than we think by inspiring Isaiah to prophesy about the conqueror of Babylon over a century before the man was even born.

The other big difference is less obvious but it matters hugely. Xenophon seeks to emphasize the strength and wisdom of King Cyrus, but Isaiah seeks to emphasize his weakness and his folly. Xenophon of Athens had been a soldier in the Persian army and wanted to use the reign of Cyrus to extol the virtues of Persian dictatorship over Athenian democracy. In total contrast, Isaiah prophesies that Cyrus will be nothing to write home about. The Lord will use him in spite of his own natural weakness.

In 44:28, when Isaiah prophesies that Cyrus will be *"my shepherd"*, he means more than that Cyrus will be God's chosen ruler. The Greek historian Herodotus tells us that Cyrus grew up as the child of a humble cattle herder from Anshan, a kingdom so small that it had long since been gobbled up into the empire of the Medes.[2] Expecting a man from Anshan to create a mighty empire was like expecting Luxembourg to win the football World Cup final.

When he suddenly names Cyrus in 44:28 and 45:1, Isaiah also tells us that he will be a pagan idolater. His name labels him as a devotee of the Persian sun-god Khor, one of the idols that the past few chapters have taught us are unable even to help themselves. The flattering picture that Xenophon paints of Cyrus is therefore fiction. In reality, he was weak and foolish, the kind of idolater who provoked the Lord to exclaim in 44:18: *"They know nothing, they understand nothing; their eyes are*

[1] As if anticipating the reluctance of many scholars to believe him, the Lord reminds us in 44:25 that he *"overthrows the learning of the wise and turns it into nonsense"*.

[2] Herodotus in his *Histories* (1.110–117). Like Xenophon, Herodotus romanticizes the life of Cyrus, whereas Isaiah revels in the man's weakness.

plastered over so that they cannot see, and their minds closed so that they cannot understand." Cyrus will therefore be perfect as a case study in how the Lord can make even the weakest humans supernaturally strong.

In 44:26–28, the Lord predicts that he will use this weak man's ignorance for good. God is stronger than we think, so no amount of human weakness can ever scupper his plans. He can declare that Cyrus *"is my shepherd and will accomplish all that I please"*, because he will turn around for good the fact that Cyrus has all the spiritual discernment of a cattle herder. Unlike the Babylonians, whose religious sophistication made them pursue a harsh policy of forcing their subject peoples to renounce their own gods in favour of the gods of Babylon, Cyrus tried to hedge his bets by pacifying each local god in his vast empire. We have a copy of one of his royal edicts, found among the ruins of Babylon, which reveals the extent of his spiritual confusion: *"May all the gods that I have returned to their sanctuaries ask Marduk and Nebo daily that I may have a long life."*[3] When we read in Ezra 1:1–4 the proclamation by which he sent the Jews back to Jerusalem in 538 BC, it carries the same tone of multi-faith tolerance:

> *The Lord, the God of heaven, has given me all the kingdoms of the earth and he has appointed me to build a temple for him at Jerusalem in Judah. Any of his people among you may go up to Jerusalem in Judah and build the temple of the Lord, the God of Israel, the God who is in Jerusalem, and may their God be with them.*

The Lord is strong enough to shape world history through the ignorance of a pagan idolater.

In 45:1–7, the Lord explains how he will pass such global power into the hands of such a weak leader. He refers us back

---

[3] The "Cyrus Cylinder" is now in the British Museum in London. Marduk (also known as Bel) and Nebo were the two main gods of Babylon.

to what he taught us about Lowly Worm and Popeye in chapters 40–41 when he tells us that he will help Cyrus succeed by taking his right hand in his own, like a father teaching a toddler to take faltering steps while he walks carefully behind.[4] Cyrus will only become strong through the Lord anointing him with his Holy Spirit (45:1a). How else could he ever secure independence for puny Anshan from the Medes when he came to the throne in 559 BC? How else could he shock the world by conquering the Median Empire in 549 BC (45:1b)? How else could he ever breach the impregnable gates of Babylon in 539 BC (45:2)? How else could he defeat the fabulously wealthy King Croesus of Lydia in 547 BC (45:3)? How else could he create the largest empire so far in history, stretching all the way from the Black Sea to India (45:4)? It could only happen through the fact that the strong arm of the Lord is able to make the weak and feeble strong.[5]

Cyrus would only succeed because he was an item in God's toolbox (44:28). Although he drew his name from the Persian sun-god, he drew his power from the true God of Israel (45:3–4). He would only succeed because the Lord had determined to make his life proof that he is able to shape the course of history through anyone, even through one too blind to recognize his Maker's hand upon him (45:5). He would succeed in order to fulfil the Lord's predictions, and thereby prove the Lord is the true Master of History. The sudden success of Cyrus would make the nations recognize that God's words in 45:6–7 are true:

> *I am the Lord, and there is no other. I form the light and create darkness, I bring prosperity and create disaster; I, the Lord, do all these things.*

---

[4] The Lord promised earlier that he strengthens people by taking their *right hand* with his own *right hand* (41:10, 13). This is not the hand-holding of equals, but the hand-holding of a parent and a toddler.

[5] God is so excited about this plan that he calls the heavens to celebrate with him in 45:8. He celebrates the goodness of his sovereign plan even as he unfolds it to the world.

Giveaway (45:1–25)

*This is what the Lord says to his anointed, to Cyrus,
whose right hand I take hold of…*

(Isaiah 45:1)

When we read the beginning of Isaiah 45 in English, we generally
fail to notice how offensive the prophet's words must have been
to the people of Judah. Our Bibles simply describe Cyrus as the
Lord's *"anointed"*, but this is a translation of the word *"messiah"*
in the original Hebrew text and of the word *"christ"* in the Greek
Septuagint.

Think about that for a moment. Even for us, it appears odd
that God should promise to anoint a sinful unbeliever with his
Holy Spirit.[1] For the people of Judah it was outrageous. They
reserved the term "messiah" for their kings: first for Saul and
then for David and his sons. When they therefore heard Isaiah
describe Cyrus as the Lord's messiah, it must have prompted at
least two worried questions.

First, it must have made them wonder if the Lord had
somehow given up on them. If he had found himself a new
messiah in the foreign lands of the north-east, did it mean he
had no further need of David's dynasty? By the time Isaiah
prophesied these words, King Hezekiah was ageing and
Manasseh had become co-ruler in 697 BC – the wickedest
king of Judah, who filled the Temple courtyards with idols and
sacrificed his own children to the false god Molech.[2] Had the

---

[1] It should encourage us that God fills sinful people with his Holy Spirit. See
Acts 3:12; Galatians 3:5.
[2] 2 Kings 21:1–16; 2 Chronicles 33:1–9; Jeremiah 15:4.

Lord finally given up on the house of David and found a foreigner more righteous than Manasseh through whom to fulfil Isaiah's prophecies instead?[3]

Their second question must have been equally angry and confused. How could this Cyrus ever save God's people if he himself was a Gentile sinner? They had been promised a righteous deliverer in 41:2 and 42:6. What good was a saviour to whom the Lord had to say in 45:4, *"I summon you by name and bestow on you a title of honour, though you do not acknowledge me"*? What good was a deliverer who needed to be told by the Lord in 45:5 that *"I will strengthen you, though you have not acknowledged me"*? Like an excited child on Christmas morning who discovers that her parents haven't bought her the present that they promised, the people of Judah must have felt bitterly disappointed.

Isaiah replies to their second question in 45:9–14. He reminds them that a clay pot ought not to lecture its potter and that a child ought not to lecture its parents. In the same way, the people of Judah ought not to offer advice to their Maker. Paul quotes the words of 45:9 in Romans 9:20, because this particular temptation is common to us all. It is very human to want to tell God what he should do, despite the fact that he created billions of stars and billions of humans without us. He is quite capable of orchestrating his master plan for history without our wisdom now. He tells the people of Judah to trust him to raise up for them a righteous deliverer[4] and to bring them back from their captivity in Babylon without any need of their assistance.[5]

Isaiah replies to their first question in 45:15–17. He tells

---

[3] Perhaps this is why the Lord reassures them in 45:4 that Israel is still his servant and his chosen one.

[4] The Lord does not actually name Cyrus in the Hebrew text of 45:13. He simply says *"him"*. This deliberate ambiguity continues with the promise of free salvation. See 1 Peter 1:18–19.

[5] The *Sabeans* in 45:14 are the people of Seba, echoing the promise God made in 43:3. Some readers believe that Paul is quoting from 45:14 in 1 Corinthians 14:25. God wants to be seen through his people.

them that he deliberately used the word *"messiah"* as a giveaway. It was a deliberate clue as to who is singing the Servant Songs. The people of Judah are absolutely right to say that they require a better deliverer than Cyrus, but they need to allow this giveaway to take them one step further. They need to recognize that they have a bigger enemy than Babylon and that God has a better home for them than the physical Mount Zion. Isaiah is so excited that they have noticed his deliberate giveaway that he exclaims in praise: *"Truly you are a God who has been hiding himself, the God and Saviour of Israel."*

We have the advantage of the New Testament, so we know where this giveaway ought to lead the people of Judah. A far better deliverer is hiding in the shadow of the weak and sinful Cyrus. When the Lord calls Cyrus his shepherd in 44:28, he is making him a picture of Jesus the Good Shepherd (John 10:11). When he prophesies in 44:28 that Cyrus will command the rebuilding of the Temple in Jerusalem, he is making him a picture of Jesus, the builder of a better Temple than Solomon (Luke 11:31 and John 2:19). When he calls Cyrus righteous in 45:13, he is making him a picture of Jesus the Righteous One (Acts 22:14). When he predicts the stunning victories of Cyrus in 45:1, he is making him a picture of Jesus the Victor (Colossians 2:15 and Revelation 3:7). The reason why King Cyrus does not seem good enough to the people of Judah is that – well – he isn't good enough! Hiding in his shadow is their real deliverer, the *"God and Saviour of Israel"*. The word messiah was a deliberate giveaway, predicting that *"Israel will be saved by the Lord."*

Cyrus would continue to be blind to the God who had raised him up suddenly. In the royal edict from which I quoted in the previous chapter, found by archaeologists in the ruins of Babylon in 1879, he actually uses very similar language to these verses when he attributes all of his successes to the demon-god of Babylon: *"The most high Marduk... inspected and searched every country, looking for the upright king of his choice. He took* the hand of Cyrus, king of the city of Anshan, and called him by his name, proclaiming him aloud to be king over everything." Perhaps that's why the Lord repeats his warning against idols in 45:18–25. He urges the Gentile nations to spot his deliberate giveaway and to recognize that he has not proclaimed this good news in secret. He has distinguished himself from their dumb idols by predicting the sudden rise of Cyrus. Time is running out for them and they are every bit as much in need of a deliverer as the people of Judah.[6]

So hear the voice of Jesus as he proclaims to the pagan nations, *"There is no God apart from me, a righteous God and a Saviour; there is none but me. Turn to me and be saved, all you ends of the earth; for I am God, and there is no other."* Respond to him as your only true Deliverer from Babylon, as the only one who can bring you to Mount Zion and as the only one who can overcome your human weakness by strengthening you with divine power. Jesus ends these verses with a warning that he is stronger than you think:

> *By myself I have sworn, my mouth has uttered in all integrity a word that will not be revoked: before me every knee will bow; by me every tongue will swear. They will say of me, "In the Lord alone are deliverance and strength."*[7]

---

[6] The Lord encourages the Gentiles in 45:20 to see themselves as fugitives, just like the Jews, longing for Zion.

[7] Paul quotes from 45:23 in Romans 14:11. It probably also inspired him as he wrote Philippians 2:10–11.

The Fall of Babylon
(46:1–47:15)

Go down, sit in the dust, Virgin Daughter Babylon;
sit on the ground without a throne, queen city of the
Babylonians.

(Isaiah 47:1)

Most people can remember where they were when they heard
the news that two hijacked passenger planes had been flown
into the Twin Towers of the World Trade Center in New York
City. When the Twin Towers suddenly came crashing to the
ground on Tuesday 11th September 2001, their echo was heard
all around the world.

That's how it was with the sudden fall of Babylon, only
more so. America would survive the destruction of its Twin
Towers, but the Babylonian Empire could not survive the
capture of its mother city. Nobody expected Cyrus to breach its
walls. He confessed to his advisers that *"I am unable to see how
any enemy can take walls of such strength and height by assault."*[1]
Belshazzar was so unconcerned by the Persian upstart at his
gates that he threw a party in his palace on the very night his
city fell. Nevertheless, the Lord had spoken. Sure enough, on the
evening of 6th October 539 BC Babylon was defeated.

The Lord had prophesied that this would happen 150 years
earlier in Isaiah 46:1–13. *Bel* was another name for Marduk,
the city's dragon-hugging patron deity. *Nebo* was his son, and
together they were worshipped throughout Babylon. Many of

---

[1] Xenophon records these words in his *Cyropaedia* (7.5.7). Daniel 5 describes
Belshazzar's drinking party.

its rulers were named in honour of them: Marduk-Baladan, Nebuchadnezzar and Belshazzar. The Lord therefore begins his attack on Babylon by squaring up to its two main idols. He accuses them in 46:1–4 of inflicting a heavy burden on their worshippers, promising them strength but merely making them weary.[2] The Lord contrasts this with his own arm, which has carried Israel from its infancy in Egypt to its old age in captivity in Babylon.[3] No Babylonian idol has the muscle to resist God's plan to break open its city and to bring the Jewish remnant home.[4] Cyrus can ponder and Belshazzar can party, but the battle belongs to the Lord.

Not only do idols weaken instead of strengthening their worshippers, but the Lord also accuses them in 46:5–8 of impoverishing them. The Babylonians have squandered their gold and silver on making images of Marduk and Nebo, gods which cannot even move or talk or lift a finger to deliver them from the Lord's hand.

Nebo was the Babylonian god of wisdom and of writing. He was often pictured holding the "Tablets of Destiny", which were supposed to contain written plans for the future fate of humankind. The Lord therefore revels in the irony when he insists in 46:9–13 that he is the true writer of history. He has already made enough accurate predictions in the past to be taken seriously when he boasts that *"My purpose will stand, and I will do all that I please."* He likens Cyrus to a great bird of prey, flying in swiftly from the east to liberate the Jewish exiles with a sudden pounce and to bring them safely back home to Zion.

[2] This is equally true of our own secular idols. Much of our stress and tiredness is caused by serving the insatiable demands of the false gods money, possessions and loved ones. See Proverbs 13:8; 15:16.

[3] Exodus 19:4; Deuteronomy 1:31. Although the Lord is specifically describing his dealings with Israel, we can take 46:3–4 as a wonderful promise that the Lord will also carry us through every season of our lives.

[4] The Lord uses three different Hebrew verbs to state five times in 46:3–4 that, while Marduk and Nebo make their worshippers carry them, he has perpetually carried Israel.

The Lord therefore turns to the city of Babylon itself in 47:1–15. He declares an end to the days of its military hegemony (47:5), of its merciless slaughter (47:6),[5] of its complacent pride (47:7),[6] of its pleasure-seeking (47:8) and of its twisted state religion (47:9).[7] Because the city has boasted blasphemously that *"I am, and there is none besides me,"* it is about to feel the strong arm of the one who declares that *"I am God, and there is none like me"* (46:9 and 47:10). They have fooled themselves that he will never judge them, so they are about to feel the full force of his anger. On that day, none of the magic charms of their idols will be strong enough to protect them (47:10–15).[8]

When Revelation 17–19 echoes the words of Isaiah by using the fall of Babylon as a picture of the Final Judgment Day, it calls the spirit of Babylon *"the great prostitute"*. Many readers are therefore surprised when Isaiah addresses the city as *"Virgin Daughter Babylon"*. Don't be fooled. He merely calls her this in order to form a contrast with his prophecies to *"Virgin Daughter Zion"*.[9] Babylon is never as innocent as she pretends, which is why the Lord vows to tear off her veil and force her to hitch up her skirts so that the world will see her for the common prostitute she really is. The Holy One of Israel will display his strength to the world by exposing Babylon's sin and weakness.

Herodotus tells us that the walls of Babylon were 25 metres thick and 100 metres high (that's roughly as wide as a basketball

---

[5] The Babylonians were always merciless, but the Lord particularly promises that he will judge them for their excessive cruelty towards Judah when he used them as his tool of judgment in 586 BC.

[6] It is easy to tell if your own culture is contaminated by the spirit of Babylon. It will be marked by an irrational confidence that the current spiritual state of affairs will never change.

[7] Another sign that your own culture is contaminated by the spirit of Babylon is that it only tolerates religion which turns God into our servant, never faith which recognizes him as our Master.

[8] The word which is translated as *power* in 47:14 means literally *hand*. Isaiah knows that flames do not have hands, but he wants us to see the fall of Babylon as the work of God's strong hand and of his mighty arm.

[9] Isaiah 1:8; 10:32; 16:1; 37:22; 62:11.

court and 15 times higher than the tallest sections of the Great Wall of China).[10] Even if he is exaggerating wildly, there can be no doubt that the walls were far too strong for a cattle herder from Anshan. Nevertheless, the Lord had promised to make the career of Cyrus a case study in what happens when he anoints weak and foolish people with his Spirit of wisdom. Suddenly Cyrus noticed that the River Euphrates passed under the walls of Babylon. After dark, he instructed his men to raise up dams which diverted its flow away from the city. While Belshazzar partied in the palace, the Persians watched in wonder as the river bed emptied to expose a broad and undefended passageway under the wall. By the time the drunken Babylonians knew that their walls had been breached, the battle was all over. Xenophon tells us that the Persian soldiers *"fell upon them as they were drinking by a blazing fire, and without waiting they dealt with them as with foes"*.[11]

All fifteen verses of chapter 47 are addressed to Babylon except for one. In verse 4, Isaiah suddenly breaks into a spontaneous shout of praise. It's as if he cannot contain his excitement at the thought that God will turn the tables on Babylon in order to end the Jewish captivity. Let's join with him as he celebrates the fact that *"Our Redeemer – the Lord Almighty is his name – is the Holy One of Israel."*

Let's do so because of the better Exodus that Isaiah says is coming. In the same way that Cyrus breached the walls of Babylon in 539 BC, Jesus will destroy the spirit of Babylon and free us in a moment on the Final Day. He will transform us into the New Mount Zion and we will sing eternal songs of wonder that our God is stronger than we thought.

---

[10] Herodotus in his *Histories* (1.178). He goes on to describe the fall of Babylon in 1.191.
[11] Xenophon in his *Cyropaedia* (7.5.27).

Leave It All Behind
(48:1–22)

Leave Babylon, flee from the Babylonians!

(Isaiah 48:20)

Not everyone among the exiles of Judah was happy in 538 BC when Cyrus granted the Jews permission to return home to Mount Zion. Some of them had become rather attached to their lifestyle in Babylon and they didn't want to leave it all behind. Ezra tells us that fewer than 50,000 Jews responded to their new ruler's proclamation. Those who chose Babylon over Jerusalem would later pay a heavy price for their sin.

We observed earlier that the Bible is a tale of two cities. The struggle began early on in Genesis 11. We make two mistakes when we refer to this story as the "Tower of Babel". First, we forget that this was as much about a city as a tower: *"Come, let us build ourselves a **city**, with a tower that reaches to the heavens, so that we may make a name for ourselves."* Second, we fail to grasp that the Hebrew name for that city is translated everywhere else in the Bible as Babylon.[1] Add to this the first mention of Jerusalem three chapters later in Genesis 14:18–20, and we can tell that Babylon and Zion have been locked in mortal combat since the earliest of times.

We saw in Isaiah 14:12–14 that the spirit of Babylon always entices people to make a bid to ascend to God's throne in order to act like little gods alongside him. We saw in Isaiah 47 that the

---

[1] Genesis 11:1 confirms that this is the account of the initial building of Babylon by telling us that the city was built on the plain of Shinar. Daniel 1:2 tells us that this was the site of Babylon.

spirit of Babylon always tempts us to place our trust in human power, in earthly pleasures and in self-centred religion. That's why the book of Revelation depicts the spirit of Babylon as a ravishing woman dressed in sumptuous clothes and sparkling jewels.[2] The Devil wants to seduce us into thinking that we can be citizens of both Zion *and* Babylon, living both for heaven *and* for this world. An Israelite named Achan discovered the hard way that this is impossible when he rescued some of the baubles of Babylon from the ruins of Jericho. Before his execution he confessed in Joshua 7:20–21 that *"I have sinned against the Lord, the God of Israel. This is what I have done: when I saw in the plunder a beautiful robe from Babylonia, two hundred shekels of silver and a bar of gold weighing fifty shekels, I coveted them and took them."* Nobody can mix a little Babylon with Zion. We can only ever make a choice between them.

In 48:1–2, the Lord therefore appeals to anyone who claims to truly follow him. It isn't enough for us to invoke the name of Zion by calling ourselves *"citizens of the holy city"* or to invoke the name of the Lord by declaring that we have put our faith in Israel's God. We need to make an active choice between living by the values of heaven or the values of the spirit of Babylon. That's what the writers of Psalm 137 were trying to express when they sang during their captivity, *"By the rivers of Babylon we sat and wept when we remembered Zion."* It is why their harpists cursed themselves, *"If I forget you, Jerusalem, may my right hand forget its skill."* It is why their singers cursed themselves, *"May my tongue cling to the roof of my mouth if I do not remember you, if I do not consider Jerusalem my highest joy."* They wrote their psalm as a plea for the exiles to leave Babylon behind when Cyrus called. Tragically, many of them chose to walk the path of Achan instead.

In 48:3–11, the Lord therefore calls us to see his strong arm at work in the fall of Babylon. Knowing how stubborn we are to believe that turning to him also means turning away from

---

[2] Revelation 17:1–5; 18:16.

idols,[3] he foretells the destruction of Babylon over 150 years before it happens in order to convince us that if we feel at home in Babylon, we will share its fate. Of course we will. How could God not judge us if we betray him for the sake of fleeting earthly pleasures?[4] If we look to anything other than the Lord to satisfy and fulfil us, we are idolaters. Our lifestyle is therefore a battle for God's glory.[5] He postpones his judgment long enough for us to come to genuine faith: *"For my own name's sake I delay my wrath; for the sake of my praise I hold it back from you, so as not to destroy you completely."* But if we despise his patience, we must share in Babylon's fate: *"For my own sake, for my own sake, I do this. How can I let myself be defamed? I will not yield my glory to another."*[6]

In 48:12–22, both Isaiah and the Lord plead with us together to leave it all behind.[7] God has presided over this tale of two cities from the beginning and he will preside over its end.[8] He wants to use his strong arm to save us, but since that arm is firmly committed to destroying Babylon, we can only be saved if we throw in our lot with the right side.[9] The Lord is not trying

---

[3] Paul also makes this point in 1 Thessalonians 1:9, and in Acts 14:15 and 26:18. Don't be confused by the way God uses past tense verbs to describe the fall of Babylon. Whatever he prophesies is as good as done.

[4] The Hebrew verb *bāgad* in 48:8 was used to describe a husband or wife *being unfaithful* to their marriage vows. God considers it spiritual adultery when we flirt with the great prostitute Babylon.

[5] Verse 8 tells us literally that we are *"transgressors from the womb"*. We do not become sinners by sinning. We sin because we are born sinners. Our only hope of change is to be born again through the Gospel.

[6] This may explain much of the church decline in our own day. When congregations claim to be Zion but blow kisses at Babylon, the Lord refuses to let them prosper while they misrepresent him to the world. Our church-growth strategies simply wear us out (47:13). Only repentance can reverse the decline (30:15).

[7] The Lord speaks in 48:12–16a, 17–19 and 22. Isaiah speaks in 48:16b and 20–21.

[8] Jesus is referring back to 48:12, as well as to 41:4 and 44:6, when he calls himself *"the First and the Last"* in Revelation 1:8, 1:17, 2:8, 21:6 and 22:13.

[9] The Lord calls Cyrus his *arm* in 48:14 in order to emphasize that the ancient struggle between Cyrus, Babylon and Zion represents something far bigger.

to spoil our fun by forbidding us from sampling what Babylon is selling. He is simply trying to wean us off this world's bread and water so that we can feast on the delights of heaven. *"I am the Lord your God, who teaches you what is best for you, who directs you in the way you should go. If only you had paid attention to my commands, your peace would have been like a river, your well-being like the waves of the sea. Your descendants would have been like the sand, your children like its numberless grains."* Those who reject Babylon and choose Zion always reap a wonderful reward for their faith.

The fall of Babylon to Cyrus in 539 BC was not the city's only fall. Within a few years it reaped its own reward for rebelling against its Persian masters. In around 520 BC, King Darius the Great of Persia recaptured the city and showed none of the previous mercy of King Cyrus. Those Jews who were not in Jerusalem rebuilding the Lord's Temple and who had managed to survive a siege so terrible that the hungry Babylonians strangled their own wives to eat them were caught up in the city's slaughter.[10] That's why the Lord ends this chapter by reminding us that *"There is no peace for the wicked"* and by urging us to *"Leave Babylon, flee from the Babylonians!"*

The writers of the New Testament take this graphic picture and apply it to our own lives. They urge us to embrace the new Exodus which God has brought about through Jesus, his new and better Passover Lamb.[11] They plead with us to wake up to the dangers of flirting with Babylon. They tell us that there is no dual citizenship in God's salvation. We must leave Babylon behind. True believers in the Christian Gospel always do.[12]

See 51:5, 9; 52:10; 53:1; 59:1, 16; 63:5.

[10] Herodotus tells us this in his *Histories* (3.151–159).

[11] Note the clear reference back to the Exodus in 48:21. See Exodus 17:6 and Numbers 20:11.

[12] The words of 48:20 and 52:11–12 are both echoed in 2 Corinthians 6:17 and Revelation 18:4.

You're Gonna Need a Bigger Boat (49:1–6)

It is too small a thing for you to be my servant to restore the tribes of Jacob... I will also make you a light for the Gentiles, that my salvation may reach to the ends of the earth.

(Isaiah 49:6)

After Isaiah 48, the name of Babylon is whispered no more. Cyrus has won and it is therefore time for Zion to taste the fruits of his victory. We need to listen very carefully when the Messiah sings his second Servant Song to tell us what this means. These six verses celebrate a victory which is far bigger than the people of Judah can imagine.

169

Initially the tune sounds very familiar. It reaches out to the same distant nations and far-off islands as the first Servant Song in 42:1–4. It is just as cryptic about who the servant is, since in verse 1 he sounds like Cyrus, in verse 3 he sounds like Israel and in verse 4 he sounds like Isaiah! But as soon as we listen carefully to the lyrics of the Song it becomes clear that something big has changed. There is a progression taking place. Whereas the first Song described the servant, this second Song is sung by the servant himself. Whereas the first Song proclaimed him a victorious king and general, this second Song describes him as a prophet, whose rejection leads to total vindication.

Thanks to the New Testament, we are in the know about who the singing servant is. Paul quotes from 49:6 in Acts 13:47 and explains that these words were first sung in all their fullness by Jesus the Messiah. He was called by God the

Father long before his birth (1 Peter 1:20) and given the name Jesus from the moment he was conceived in Mary's womb (Luke 1:26–35 and Matthew 1:18–23). The Father kept him in obscurity for many years in Nazareth while he turned him into a perfect weapon against the Devil (Luke 3:23). Only fools rush into battle. Jesus was happy to be hidden in the shadow of his Father's hand while his mouth became sharp enough to minister with the precision of a surgeon's scalpel.[1] He was happy to be concealed in his Father's quiver while he grew in his knowledge of the Scriptures and of how to fly unswervingly in ministry.[2] We tend to assume that Jesus had nothing to learn, but Hebrews 5:8 tells us that this isn't true at all. If Jesus needed thirty years of preparation before he was ready to be revealed to Israel, we mustn't grow impatient that the Lord seems slow in using our own lives.[3]

Modern-day Jewish rabbis take verse 3 to mean that the singing servant is the nation of Israel. They are not wrong; they are simply not completely right. Because they refuse to listen to Paul, they miss the meaning of the Song. They do not understand that Jesus is claiming to be the true and perfect Israel. Matthew emphasizes this in his gospel, since he writes primarily for Jews, presenting the early life of Jesus as an echo of the great Jewish story. He is the true son of David and the true seed of Abraham (1:1). He becomes a fugitive in Egypt and experiences his own mini-Exodus (2:15). After his own equivalent of crossing the Red Sea (3:13–15), he spends forty sinless days in the desert, which parallel Israel's forty sinful years (4:1–11). Having succeeded wherever Israel failed, he then climbs up a hill to

---

[1] Matthew 8:16; Mark 1:27; John 6:68; Hebrews 4:12; Revelation 1:16; 2:12; 19:15.

[2] A fletcher spends a long time making the shaft of an arrow perfectly straight and its feathers perfectly balanced, all for a single moment of flight. Its success rests on the quality of this patient preparation.

[3] John 7:6–8, Romans 5:6 and Galatians 4:4 all remind us that the Lord is the God of perfect timing.

deliver the Sermon on the Mount as his own re-enactment of Israel receiving the Law at Mount Sinai (5:1). Isaiah prophesies to the people of Judah that their Messiah will be the true and perfect Israel.

They needed him to be. In the very next verse, Isaiah prophesies that their nation will largely reject him. Those Jews who receive him will only be saved through faith in his work, not in their status as a nation. As a Gospel preacher, I find the words of verse 4 extremely encouraging. They tell us that even Jesus had moments when he was tempted to be discouraged by his apparent lack of fruitfulness in ministry and cried out to his Father, *"I have laboured in vain; I have spent my strength for nothing at all."* Knowing that Jesus felt as I do gives me strength to overcome my own discouragement and to finish the prayer: *"Yet what is due to me is in the Lord's hand, and my reward is with my God."* Suddenly the Messiah's prayer of faith blows this Servant Song wide open and Isaiah prophesies that his eventual fruitfulness will be out of this world.

One of the most famous moments in the Steven Spielberg movie Jaws sees Roy Scheider on a fishing boat, throwing bait into the ocean to locate a great white shark that is terrorizing the local beaches. Suddenly the shark leaps out of the water. It is enormous – over twenty-five feet long and weighing at least three tons. He staggers back into the cabin and tells the owner of the fishing boat the news: *"You're gonna need a bigger boat."*[4]

The first Servant Song only gave us part of the picture. This second Servant Song tells us much more because, if God can empower a cattle herder from Anshan to defeat Babylon and conquer the world, he is able to do much more through the sinless carpenter from Nazareth. He will do more than simply fish for souls within the Jewish nation. Isaiah gives us a God-sized vision. We are going to need a bigger boat.

In verse 5, the Messiah prophesies that *"God has been my*

---

[4] *Jaws* (Universal Pictures, 1975).

strength."[5] He will be strong enough to rescue many Jews.[6] But verse 6 tells us that the Father has made an even bigger promise to his Messiah. Jesus will have the full reward of his suffering by rescuing many Gentiles too: *"It is too small a thing for you to be my servant to restore the tribes of Jacob and bring back those of Israel I have kept. I will also make you a light for the Gentiles, that my salvation may reach to the ends of the earth."*

This is the verse that Paul quotes as he leaves the synagogue in Acts 13:47, but note that he does not simply put these words in the mouth of the Messiah. He proclaims that *"this is what the Lord has commanded **us**."* In other words, the victory of Jesus over Satan is so colossal that, when Christians make puny plans for ministry, they are not being humble. They are insulting the Lord. If Jesus is truly greater than Cyrus, if the gates of Babylon are truly powerless to resist him and if he has the nations of the world in his sights, then only God-sized plans are worthy of him.

Take a moment to consider what that means for your own life every day. What does God want to do through your life, your family, your church? Whatever the specifics, at least one thing is certain. One glimpse of the Messiah means that you are going to need a bigger boat.

---

[5] As we will see in Isaiah 52–53, Jesus deliberately came in human weakness. He is the ultimate fulfilment of the Father's promise throughout this section of Isaiah to grant weak humans his divine power.

[6] Verse 5 can be translated, *"Even though Israel is not yet gathered, I shall be honoured in the eyes of the Lord."*

Three-Year-Old Theology (49:7–50:3)

*Can a mother forget the baby at her breast and have
no compassion on the child she has borne? Though
she may forget, I will not forget you!*

(Isaiah 49:15)

The first Servant Song provoked several encores. The second
Servant Song is just the same. The Lord sings five separate
encores, interrupted only briefly by a short interjection from
Isaiah and another from the people of Judah.

The Lord sings his first encore in 49:7. He reiterates his
promise that the Messiah's ministry will be very fruitful. Yes,
the nation of Israel will despise and detest him, but that is only
because many ethnic Jews are spiritually pagans.[1] The Holy
One of Israel has chosen Jesus to be his Messiah, so we can
trust that a faithful remnant of Jews will choose him too. In the
meantime and in order to make the Jews jealous, God declares
that he will make the Messiah his servant to the rulers of the
pagan world. Kings and princes from every nation will rise from
their thrones and bow down before him as the mighty King of
kings. God's arm is big and strong enough to embrace the entire
world.

The Gospel has already spread remarkably from little
Israel all across the globe. If you feel that it is not advancing
quickly enough where you are, note the conditions laid down

---

[1] The normal Hebrew word for the *nation* of Israel is *'am*. The normal word
for a pagan nation is *gōy*. The Lord deliberately uses the word *gōy* in 49:7 to
emphasize that many within Israel are not true Jews at all.

in the Song. Are we truly proclaiming the Word of God like a sharpened sword or have we blunted its edges in the face of people's outrage and derision? If the Messiah was despised and detested for his words, we dare not back off from speaking his words because we find that people despise and detest us too. Only if we are happy to be treated in like manner to our Master can we ever expect to see like manner of reward.[2]

This leads into the Lord's second encore in 49:8–12. He promises to answer the Messiah's prayers by making him a fruitful Saviour to both Jews and Gentiles. Note the way in which he uses the Jewish return from captivity in Babylon as a metaphor for his general work of salvation.[3] Note also the way he uses his earlier promise of a holy highway as a general metaphor for the salvation of the Gentiles throughout the centuries too.[4] This should give us personal encouragement as we seek to proclaim the New Covenant about which the Lord sings in these verses. Paul quotes from 49:8 in 2 Corinthians 6:2 and applies the words of this encore to *us*. God promises to make us joint heirs with Jesus to all of these messianic blessings too.

This gets Isaiah so excited that he interjects in 49:13, calling the heavens and earth to sing their own encore of praise to God for such magnificent salvation. The people of Judah refuse to sing, however. Isaiah reports in 49:14 that Zion is complaining that all this talk of saving Gentiles sounds as if *"The Lord has forsaken me, the Lord has forgotten me."*

The Lord replies to this complaint with a third encore in 49:15–21, using pictures that even a toddler can understand. A few days ago I was carrying my three-year-old son on my

---

[2] See Matthew 10:24–25; 2 Timothy 3:12; Hebrews 13:13.

[3] In describing the nation of Israel more positively in 49:8, the Lord reverts to the Hebrew word 'am.

[4] Some Hebrew texts of 49:12 refer to Aswan in southern Egypt; others to Sinim, the ancient name for China. Revelation 7:16 quotes from 49:10 and uses it to describe our enjoyment of our salvation in the age to come.

shoulders and I was trying to explain the faithfulness of God to him by pointing out the blossom on the trees. It was a bit too much for him to understand, but he put it better in his own words: *"Sometimes my mum calls me by my brother's name, but God is the one who never forgets your name."* It wasn't sophisticated, but it was beautiful. The Lord says something similar to the people of Judah in this third encore.

Everybody knows how indestructible a mother's love is for her children. Nevertheless, as my three-year-old son points out, even a mother's love has its limits. The Lord tells the people of Judah that his love towards them has none. They may feel forgotten and barren. They may feel their share in Zion is too small. But they are wrong. The Jewish high priests engraved the names of the twelve tribes of Israel on their uniform, but the Lord has engraved the names of every single Jew upon his mighty hands.[5] He has not forgotten that the walls of Zion are first and foremost *"your walls"*. He is still their loving Father and Husband, who will make the faithful remnant of Jews like a fertile bride and mother. He will make them so fruitful in witnessing to their fellow countrymen that they will start to complain that Zion is overpopulated with Jews!

The Lord's fourth encore in 49:23–26 also offers reassurance that even a three-year-old can understand. When I am out with my son in the park, it only takes one glimpse of the bread in our hands to bring the ducks and squirrels rushing towards us. In the same way, by raising up his Messiah as the Bread of Life before the pagan nations, the Lord promises to fulfil his purposes for the Jews. Many pagans will come and lick at the dust around their feet in search of their bread.[6] Having turned to the Jewish Messiah, those converted Gentiles will

---

[5] The Lord is probably also referring back to Exodus 28:9–21 in Isaiah 54:11–12.

[6] The Lord described the Messiah as his *banner* in 11:10–12, and he will do so again in 62:10. Jesus refers back to this picture in Isaiah when he promises to save the pagans in John 12:32.

reach out to the unconverted Jews and will save them out of God's judgment on the pagans. The people of Judah will not be disappointed if they wait in faith for the Holy One of Israel.[7] Far from forgetting the Jews, the Lord insists that he is still *"your Saviour, your Redeemer, the Mighty One of Jacob"*.

The Lord's fifth and final encore also uses a picture which any toddler can understand. When a mother and father fight, their children always feel the pain. The Lord therefore assures any Jew who has come to know him as Father through his Messiah that he never wanted a rift to come between him and their mother Israel. They cannot accuse him of divorcing her (or else they would have a certificate) and they cannot accuse him of selling her down the river (or else they would be able to name her buyer). They know full well that Mother Israel has sold herself to sin. It is not the Lord who has forsaken the Jewish nation, but the Jewish nation that has forsaken the Lord!

God has finished singing all five of his encores. He is about to make room for the Messiah to sing again. He therefore ends by assuring the little children of Judah that he is still strong enough to save their Jewish family. He echoes his question to Moses in Numbers 11:23, pointing out that his hand has not grown too short to save their nation. They can trust him to make many Jews part of his New Mount Zion. Their nation may be stubborn and foolish, but he is stronger than they think.

---

[7] The Hebrew word *qāwāh* in 49:23 means *to wait, to hope* or *to expect*. It is the same word that was used in 40:31. Our faith is often expressed by waiting, which in turn is often key to our receiving God's strength.

Righteous (50:4–51:8)

*He who vindicates me is near. Who then will bring
charges against me? Let us face each other! Who is
my accuser? Let him confront me!*

(Isaiah 50:8)

If you want to understand what is happening in the third Servant
Song, it helps to know the little Hebrew word *tsedeq*. The word
means *righteous* or *righteousness* and it comes from the verb
tsādaq, which means *to vindicate* (proving something righteous)
or *to justify* (making something righteous). Knowing this little
Hebrew word helps to unlock the Song which the servant now
lifts his voice and starts singing.

One of the most confusing aspects of Isaiah's prophecies
about King Cyrus is the fact that he describes the man as
tsedeq in 41:2. Translated literally, it sees Cyrus as the Lord's
"righteous one", but what could a pagan idolater know about
God's righteousness? What could a man who had picked up his
morals in the marketplace of Anshan know about the righteous
requirements of God's laws? Confused by this, most English
Bibles find more neutral ways of translating the text, usually
stating that the Lord merely called him *"in righteousness"*. It is
all a bit unsatisfactory, but when the Messiah starts singing his
third Song the mystery is solved. Isaiah could describe Cyrus
as *tsedeq* because his military victories pointed to the true and
better Victor over spiritual Babylon.

The Messiah sings the third Servant Song in 50:4–9. It
is the only one of the four which is never quoted in the New
Testament, but it predicts that the New Testament will call the

Messiah *"the Righteous One"*.[1] It tells us that God woke Jesus up early each morning and whispered words in his ear so that he would know what to say to the weak and weary people to whom he ministered during the day.[2] Against the background of God's stern accusation in the past few chapters that the people of Judah are deaf to his commands, the Song predicts that God will open the Messiah's ears to enable him to walk in total obedience as the true and perfect Israel.

Obedience to God never makes a person very popular with sinners. The Song therefore predicts that the Messiah will be physically abused by those he comes to save. Jesus fulfilled these words before his crucifixion, when he allowed the Jewish leaders and the Roman soldiers to spit in his face, to pull out his beard, to mock him and to flog him.[3] As his weak body was tortured, he was strengthened by God's power to persevere in his obedience.[4] Therefore at the end of his Song he is able to turn to the nation that condemned him to death and to defy them to name a single sin he has committed.[5] He knows in 50:8 that the Lord will vindicate him (*tsādaq*) because he is the only truly righteous person who has ever lived. He is beyond the reach of any accusation.

All of the encores to this third Servant Song celebrate the fact that the Messiah is the Righteous One. The Lord sings the first to the people of Judah in 50:10–11, calling them to recognize that their own imperfect attempts at obedience are

---

[1] See Acts 3:14; 7:52; 22:14, as well as 1 John 2:1. The closest that the New Testament ever comes to quoting from this third Servant Song is in Romans 8:33–34.

[2] For example in Mark 1:35–38 and John 7:15–16. Jesus tells us to minister the same way in Matthew 10:27.

[3] Matthew 26:67–68; 27:26–31.

[4] Luke 9:51 tells us that Jesus fulfilled 50:7 when *"he set his face to go to Jerusalem."*

[5] While judging him, Pontius Pilate confessed three times that he knew that Jesus was innocent (Luke 23:4, 14–15, 22). He only condemned him to crucifixion because his righteousness was inconvenient.

like flickering torches. In contrast and as promised in 42:6 and 49:6, the Messiah is the Light of the World. Jesus referred back to these Servant Songs when he claimed this as his name in John 8:12, but he didn't stop there. He told his followers that he was also passing this title on to them: *"While I am in the world, I am the light of the world"* (John 9:5), and after I ascend to heaven, *"You are the light of the world"* (Matthew 5:14).

That's where we start to find these verses a little difficult. We are happy to be told that all the promises in the first two Servant Songs apply also to us, because the Songs are full of victory and fruitfulness. We find it harder to accept that this third Servant Song applies to us too, since its marching tune sounds over-demanding to our disobedient ears. Nevertheless, Isaiah is insistent. He tells us that the reason why we currently have so little strength to help the weary is that we are being little strengthened by early morning fellowship with our Father. He tells us that the reason why we currently experience little righteousness under pressure is that we have so little resolve to obey. He tells us that we have so little experience of Christ's resurrection power because we have too little experience of sharing in Christ's sufferings.

Isaiah therefore sings a second encore in 51:1–3. He addresses the few Jews who are pursuing God's righteousness (*tsedeq*) and reminds them that their nation was quarried from a single rock named Abraham, a weak and sinful man who chose to obey the Lord. The Lord can therefore certainly rebuild their nation from the rubble which the Babylonians left on Mount Zion, if they choose to obey him like Abraham.[6]

This prompts the Lord to sing a third encore in 51:4–6, assuring the remnant of Jews that they are still his people and his nation. They are about to see his righteousness (*tsedeq*) because he is about to reveal his arm to the world. The

---

[6] Reviewing our personal history with God increases personal faith for the future. Studying Church history increases our corporate faith for the future. Paul models 51:1–3 for us in 1 Corinthians 1:26–31 and 6:9–11.

Messiah will reveal God's mighty strength, becoming *"a light to the nations"* and saving people right across the globe with an imputed righteousness (*tsedāqāh*) which never flags in its power to save.[7]

In the fourth and final encore in 51:7–8, the Lord expands this invitation to believers from every nation. He addresses anyone who understands this message of righteousness (*tsedeq*) and who embraces the Gospel as good news.[8] He encourages them to imitate their Messiah by standing firm against those who pursue, persecute and punish them for their faith in God's Word. Those enemies may seem strong now, but they will very quickly demonstrate that their human strength wears out as fast as a moth-eaten sweater. On the other hand, the Messiah will demonstrate that God's saving righteousness (*tsedāqāh*) remains strong throughout every generation.

The arm of the Lord is gradually being revealed in all its glory. Each successive Servant Song predicts slightly more about how glorious the Messiah's reign is going to be. Let's therefore sing an encore of our own in response to this emerging vision of Jesus.

Let's worship him as the righteous arm of the Lord. Let's celebrate him as our great Saviour.

---

[7] *Tsedāqāh* is simply a slightly different form of the word *tsedeq*. It is the word used in 48:1 when the Lord accuses the people of Judah of playacting at being Israelites, lacking any genuine righteousness.

[8] The Hebrew word that is used for *instruction* in 51:4 and 7 is *tōrāh*, the Jewish name for the Law of Moses. We noted earlier that Isaiah often uses this word as shorthand for the Christian Gospel.

Wake-Up Call (51:9–52:12)

Awake, awake, Zion, clothe yourself with strength!
(Isaiah 52:1)

You have probably heard the joke: *"I'm not lazy. I do fifty sit-ups every morning. I sit up and press my snooze button once, I sit up and press my snooze button twice..."* Whether you have heard the joke or not, you must know the feeling. We have all experienced the strong temptation to ignore an urgent wake-up call and to sleep a little more. Isaiah refuses to let us. He is so excited about what he is prophesying and so aware of what hangs in the balance that he suddenly sounds a wake-up call that is deafening. The Lord presses the snooze button, but only so that he can sound two more deafening wake-up calls of his own. I hope you aren't feeling too sleepy because these verses are very noisy.

The most surprising thing about 51:9–11 is who Isaiah thinks is asleep. He doesn't sound his wake-up call for the Jews or for the Gentiles or even for us. He sounds his wake-up call for the Messiah! *"Awake, awake, arm of the Lord, clothe yourself with strength! Awake, as in days gone by, as in generations of old."* Isaiah recognizes that, if the Messiah is the strong arm of the Lord, then it must have been him who sent the ten plagues on Egypt (51:9) and who parted the Red Sea (51:10).[1] Why wait, then, to perform a new and better Exodus from Babylon (51:11)? The people of Judah need his intervention now! They

---

[1] *Rahab* means *Proud and Insolent One* in Hebrew. It was the name of a famous sea monster mentioned in Job and Psalms, so the Lord uses the name in 30:7 to refer to the superpower Egypt.

need him to personify the lesson of 40:29–31 by clothing himself with divine strength and saving his people. Why wait for King Manasseh's outrageous behaviour to provoke the destruction of Jerusalem? Even if the city has to fall, why wait such a painfully long time before delivering the Jewish survivors from Babylon? Promises about the Messiah in the distant future are all well and good, but surely it is wake-up time for him now![2]

The Lord is polite but firm as he presses the snooze button in 51:12–16. If Isaiah had listened to the words of his own prophecy in 49:1–2, he would know it is not yet time for the Messiah to arise. Now is the time for his people to trust in their God's wisdom and sovereignty and perfect timing. Now is the time for Zion to be hidden in the shadow of his hand, meditating on his words while it awaits the perfect moment for the Messiah to come. They need not fear during the long delay.[3] He is still *"the Lord your Maker"* and *"the Lord your God"*, and he still says to them *"You are my people."*[4]

No sooner has the Lord pressed the snooze button for his Messiah than he sounds a fresh wake-up call of his own in 51:17–23.[5] It is the Jewish exiles in Babylon who need to look lively, because their reaction to the destruction of Jerusalem will dictate how long they have to spend in far-off Babylon. *"Awake, awake! Rise up, Jerusalem, you who have drunk from the hand of the Lord the cup of his wrath."* They are not to be like the sleeping drunkard, who opens his eyes only to look for a fresh

---

[2] 51:11 is a repeat of 35:10, the final verse of the "Book of Judgment". Isaiah wants the "Book of Comfort" to be over too. He wants to stop prophesying God's salvation and to see it happen!

[3] Fear of God ends fear of man (51:12), but those who stop fearing God always start fearing people (51:13).

[4] We need to exhibit this same patient faith ourselves. Psalm 121:3–4 tells us that the Church is never in disarray because the Lord is asleep. It is only ever in disarray because we are.

[5] Isaiah's wake-up call in 51:9 was the simple *'ûrî 'ûrî*, meaning *"Awake, awake!"* The Lord intensifies his wake-up call in 51:17 by making the verb reflexive: *hith'ôrî hith'ôrî*, meaning *"Wake yourself, wake yourself!"*

bottle of wine for breakfast. Their days of heavy drinking from the cup of the Lord's judgment are over.[6] Now it is Babylon's turn. The Jewish exiles need to be clear-thinking, as they commit themselves to swift repentance and to a speedy return to Mount Zion.

The Lord sounds a final wake-up call in 52:1–12. This time he cries out to Zion itself, declaring to this great symbol of his people throughout history that its problems never stem from his sleepiness, but only ever from their own. *"Awake, awake, Zion, clothe yourself with strength! Put on your garments of splendour, Jerusalem, the holy city."*[7] He tells them that the promise which he made in 40:29–31 about clothing weak human flesh with divine strength was not a promise for the Messiah alone. Divine strength is to be their everyday attire! Knowing that his people always struggle to believe this, God spells it out for us by saying literally, *"clothe yourself with **your** strength"* and *"put on **your** garments of splendour."* God is stronger than we think and he offers to clothe us with his strength whenever we admit our naked weakness. We don't have to work hard to obtain God's strength. God has already given it to us while we were sleeping!

I feel excited writing this, so hopefully you feel excited reading it too. Let's therefore look at the three things which the Lord says we need to do to live in the good of this.

First, we need to recognize that God has called us to be very different from the world (52:1–6). The Holy One of Israel has called us to be his *"holy city"*, so we must not allow any room in our lives for things that are *"uncircumcised and defiled"*. If we have learned anything from the history of Israel in Egypt and

---

[6] Matthew 20:17–23 and 26:39 tell us that Jesus has now drunk God's cup of judgment for us. As Isaiah 52:3 reminds us, our soberness was bought by the redemption price of the Messiah's blood.

[7] Now the Lord returns to the same simple command as 51:9 – *'ū̄n 'ū̄n*, meaning *"Awake, awake!"* Interestingly, Ezra 1:5 uses this same verb to tell us God *woke up* Jewish hearts to leave Babylon in 538 BC.

Assyria and Babylon, it is that sin never pays. It merely drags those who ought to be reigning on thrones with the Lord down into the dust with Satan.[8] It merely causes the Lord's name to be despised by unbelievers, who assume his people's actions must be a reflection on his character.[9]

Second, we need to recognize the Messiah for who he is (52:7–10). The Lord exclaims in both the Hebrew text and the Greek Septuagint, *"How beautiful on the mountains are the feet of **the one** who brings good news!"* He is therefore talking primarily about his Messiah. It is Paul who expands on his meaning by changing the words slightly in Romans 10:15 to *"How beautiful are the feet of **those** who bring good news!"* Our strength depends on our seeing the Messiah for who he really is, and other people's strength depends on our proclaiming this good news to them. Most people around the world are longing, like Isaiah, for God to flex his muscles and help them. We get to tell them that he has. We get to fulfil the prophecy that *"The Lord will lay bare his holy arm in the sight of all the nations."*

Third, we therefore need to recognize that we have a powerful opponent in this mission (52:11–12). Although Isaiah no longer utters the name of defeated Babylon, these verses are an obvious reprise of his warning in 48:20.[10] The earthly city of Babylon fell in 539 and 520 BC, but Paul quotes from these verses in 2 Corinthians 6:17 to warn us that the struggle between spiritual Zion and Babylon still carries on. Zion must not only come out of Babylon, but it must also drive what belongs to Babylon out of Zion!

---

[8] Satan loves to drag Christians down into the dust through his voice of condemnation. We need to remind him of 49:23 and 52:2. We are seated on heaven's throne in Jesus. Satan needs to grovel in the dust before us!

[9] Paul quotes 52:5 in Romans 2:24. It is a sobering thought that our sin and weakness makes other people despise God, but it is also encouraging. It means he longs to raise us up to vindicate his own power.

[10] The Israelites left Egypt in a hurry (Deuteronomy 16:3), so the Lord points out that this new Exodus is better by telling us that we have all the time we need to leave it all behind.

Make no mistake about it. There is a war on. You are weak, but God has given you his strength to wear as your everyday clothes. You don't need him to wake up and help you further. You simply need to respond to his wake-up call. It's time to take off the pyjamas of your old way of living and to put on your new God-given clothes.

Naked (52:13–53:3)

Like one from whom people hide their faces he was despised, and we held him in low esteem.

(Isaiah 53:3)

Jesus of Nazareth was weak. Very weak. If you don't believe me, just read Mark's gospel. He goes out of his way to convince us that Jesus was a man of fragile flesh and blood.[1]

Jesus never put up a front with people. It's easy for us to imagine that he had a six-pack like Superman, the self-confidence of Captain America and the debonair looks of James Bond, but he didn't. He felt so thoroughly exhausted that he slept through a storm which made the seasoned fisherman Peter think his boat was going under. At times he felt so peopled out that *"He entered a house and did not want anyone to know it."* He once grew so lonely that he reached out urgently to his friends for support, confessing that *"My soul is overwhelmed with sorrow to the point of death."*[2] Jesus was the Son of God, but he never put on a show of human strength. He only ever put on a show of his weakness.

That's why we need to read the first six verses of the fourth Servant Song very slowly. We will look at the Song itself in the next chapter, but first let's just take a look at what its opening verses tell us about the Messiah and about the God who makes weak people strong. Unlike the last two Servant Songs, where the Messiah sang, this time it is a duet between God and Isaiah. The

---

[1] If you are offended by this, be offended in the right way. The Messiah sang in 49:5 that *"my God has been my strength"* because he ministered, not out of his divinity, but out of receiving divine power (Acts 10:38).

[2] Mark 4:37–38; 7:24; 14:33–34.

Lord predicts in 52:13 that the Messiah will be highly exalted, endowed with the heavenly glory that his disciples glimpsed on the mount of the transfiguration.[3] At the same time, 53:2–3 predicts that he will be incredibly lowly. I love the way that the Greek Septuagint translates 53:3: *"His form was ignoble, and inferior to that of the children of men."* It is crucial that we grasp this. Jesus didn't just become as weak as we are. He became even weaker to show us how to put on our new clothes.

Jesus was born as the lowest of the low. The Judeans despised him because he came from Galilee, the Galileans despised him because he came from Nazareth and the Nazarenes despised him because he had been conceived before his mother married. He was therefore a despised man in a despised village in a despised region. Strangers looked down on him because an unmarried thirty-year-old was an oddity in their culture. His neighbours looked down on him because he was the village carpenter and because they had climbed trees with his brothers and played hide-and-seek with his sisters.[4] Jesus came from such an unflattering background that the prophet predicts, *"He grew up before him like a tender shoot, and like a root out of dry ground."*

As for his looks, he did not have the supermodel features of religious paintings. Isaiah does not say that he will have dashing blue eyes or long and beautifully conditioned hair. He simply tells us that *"He had no beauty or majesty to attract us to him, nothing in his appearance that we should desire him."* People who passed Jesus in the street did not remark on his halo or on his otherworldly beauty. He didn't come to show off that he was different. He came to point the way for weak people to follow.

If you are not yet a follower of Jesus, well done for reading

---

[3] Mark 9:2–9. The same combination of Hebrew verbs which is translated as *"raised and lifted up"* in 52:13 is only ever used elsewhere in Isaiah to describe God himself (6:1; 33:10; 57:15). The Messiah is God.

[4] Mark 6:3. Jesus came as the perfect demonstration of what God taught Paul in 2 Corinthians 12:8–10.

so far into this commentary. Now here is your reward. If you have ever asked the question "Why would God ever want a person like me?" then the way that Jesus came answers your question. God is looking for weak and sinful people that he can forgive and clothe with his divine power. It makes no sense to say, "I could never become a Christian because I wouldn't be strong enough to keep it up."[5] Admitting that you could never be strong enough to live the way that God commands is one of the most Christian things a person can ever do.

If you are a follower of Jesus then – well – follow him! Understand that your Messiah came to earth in weakness for a reason. God hates the boasting arrogance which makes Christians declare that "I'm going to do something significant with my life for God." He isn't looking for heroes. He is looking for people who admit that they are absolute zeros. He is looking for people who are willing to take off the ragged clothing of their own strength and to stand before him naked. He is looking for people who are willing to respond to his invitation in 40:29–31: *"Those who stop their striving and fix their eyes on God instead will be able to change out of clothes of human weakness and to put on divine strength."*[6]

Following Jesus means walking on the Calvary road. It means treading in the footsteps of Christ's humility. These verses tell us that *"he was despised and rejected by mankind... and we held him in low esteem."* People were so wedded to their own self-esteem that they found his frank display of naked weakness repulsive and treated him *"like one from whom people hide their faces".*[7] They disfigured him so much through their beatings

---

[5] Verse 3 also answers the question "Why does God allow suffering?" God doesn't answer with a theological treatise. He answers by becoming *"a man of suffering, and familiar with pain"*. He isn't a spectator of pain.

[6] This is my own paraphrase, emphasizing that the Hebrew word *qāwāh* means to stop striving and *to wait*, and that the Hebrew word *hālaph* means more than simply *to renew*. It means *to change* a set of clothes.

[7] Mighty seraphim angels covered their faces in 6:2 because of Christ's intense glory. People cover their faces in 53:3 because of his intense weakness. Jesus knew our weakness so that we might know his strength.

and crucifixion that he was barely recognizable as part of their proud human race at all. *"There were many who were appalled at him – his appearance was so disfigured beyond that of any human being and his form marred beyond human likeness."* Yet because of this, he became strong enough to amaze nations and to square up to kings. The more we admit our human weakness, like Jesus, the more we will be made strong by God's same power.

We will look at the rest of the Song in a moment, but first let's make sure we have fully understood the introduction. Have we grasped why Martin Luther, after bringing massive spiritual revival to Europe, pointed to Isaiah 40:29–31 as the secret? Have we understood that the man who proclaimed what Abraham discovered about being justified through faith did so through what Abraham discovered about being strengthened through that same faith too? Can we tell why he wrote in his commentary on those verses that *"Abraham hardly had the strength to chase away the flies, and yet he conquered four kings"*?

Jesus didn't simply come to grant us God's salvation. He also came to grant us God's strength. He didn't simply come so that we could be forgiven, but so that we could become fruitful too. He came in abject weakness in order to teach us that *"'You must be weary and emptied, so that there is no way out for you. Then I will give you strength. First you must become nothing, then consolation and strength will come.' This happened to me, Martin Luther, who against my will came up against the whole world, and then God helped me."*

Get naked. The same God who saves us also wants to clothe us in his divine strength today.

Stronger Than Strength
(52:13–53:12)

Therefore I will give him a portion among the great,
and he will divide the spoils with the strong, because
he poured out his life unto death.

(Isaiah 53:12)

The first-century Jews found the fourth Servant Song the most confusing. They didn't think it sounded very much like their Messiah at all.[1] They were expecting a great King, a perfect priest, a mighty warrior. The suffering servant didn't sound like any of those things, so they concluded that this song must be describing Israel, not Israel's Saviour.[2]

But they were wrong. The Song reveals the strong arm of the Lord, but it also reveals that God's strength looks quite different from our own. It tells us in 52:13–15 that the Messiah is the Most High God, a powerful priest and a mighty conqueror,[3] but it also warns us not to miss it just because he plays by heaven's rules rather than by our own: *"Who has believed our message and to whom has the arm of the Lord been revealed?"* This song

---

[1] The confusion is not helped by the fact that the person singing is no longer the Messiah (as in 49:1–6 and 50:4–9). It is now God the Father (as in 42:1–4). Nor is it helped by Isaiah's prophetic past tenses.

[2] Both John 12:38 and Romans 10:16 quote from 53:1 in order to tell us that these words were fulfilled by the Jewish crowds rejecting Jesus. John links this verse back to the Lord's earlier warning in 6:9–10.

[3] The Hebrew wording of 52:13 deliberately points us back to the wording of 6:1. The Hebrew word used for the Messiah *sprinkling* many nations was the word normally used to describe a priest sprinkling blood.

describes the Messiah, but it warns us that his strength is far stronger than ours.

This is the longest of the Servant Songs, and is divided into five three-verse stanzas. We have already looked at the first two in the previous chapter, so let's pick up where we left off.

In 53:4–6, the prophet describes *sin*. The third Servant Song was all about the righteousness of the Messiah. It therefore seems to make no sense when Isaiah says he will be *"punished by God"* for *"transgression"* and *"iniquity"*. But read a bit more carefully. Isaiah is saying that the Jewish nation will mistakenly assume he must be a sinner when he is crucified like one. They will fail to notice that his punishment is *"**our** pain"* and *"**our** suffering"* for *"**our** iniquity"*. Our sins caused his suffering. His punishment brought us peace. Long before the Persians ever invented death by crucifixion, Isaiah prophesied that Jesus would be *"pierced"*, not just for Jewish sins but for *"the iniquity of us all"*.

In 53:7–9, the prophet describes *substitution*. In order to explain why the Messiah should pay the penalty for our sin, the Lord uses a powerful picture from the Jewish Temple: the daily sacrifice of an innocent lamb for the forgiveness of sins. Having pointed out in 53:6 that *"we all, like **sheep**, have gone astray"*, he says that the Messiah will be *"led like a **lamb** to the slaughter, and as a **sheep** before its shearers"*. Sinful humans try to seize God's place, so God took our place: Jesus was the substitutionary Lamb of God.[4] John Stott observes:

> *The concept of substitution may be said, then, to lie at the heart of both sin and salvation. For the essence of sin is man's substituting himself for God, while the essence of salvation is God substituting himself for man. Man asserts himself against God and puts himself where only*

---

[4] Although some scholars hate the idea of substitutionary atonement, 53:4–6, 8 and 11–12 are extremely clear.

God deserves to be; God sacrifices himself for man and puts himself where only man deserves to be. Man claims prerogatives which belong to God alone; God accepts penalties which belong to man alone.[5]

In 53:10–12, the prophet describes *satisfaction*. In what surely qualifies as one of the most mindboggling verses in the entire Bible, the Lord tells us literally that it was his *pleasure* to crush the Messiah under the weight of our sin.[6] God was pleased to make his Son the focal point of a collision between his justice and his mercy, *"so as to be just and the one who justifies those who have faith in Jesus"*. That's how Paul describes the cross in Romans 3:26 and it demonstrates why Isaiah 53 has been called "the gospel of the Old Testament". This is the most important chapter that the prophet ever wrote. It is quoted more in the New Testament than any of his other chapters because if we fail to understand it, we fail to understand the book at all. This chapter is the clearest explanation of the cross of Jesus anywhere in the Old Testament. These verses should be read very slowly.

The Lord describes the death of the Messiah as an *'āshām*, or *guilt offering*, which was one of the five main sacrifices which he commissioned for the Jewish Temple. He therefore predicts that the cross of Jesus will be the perfect fulfilment of the ancient covenant which he made with the Jews.[7] When the Lord describes the resurrection of the Messiah, it becomes obvious why he is able to take pleasure even in the death of his Son. Through it, the despised and childless singleton of

---

[5] John Stott in *The Cross of Christ* (1986).

[6] The same Hebrew word *hāphēts*, which is used at the start of 53:10 to describe God's *pleasure* with the Messiah's crucifixion, is also used in 1 Kings 10:9 to describe his *pleasure* with Solomon's enthronement. The word is used again at the end of 53:10 to describe his *pleasure* with the Messiah's vindication. Translating it merely as God's *will* is not wrong, but it misses the full extent of God's mercy.

[7] Hebrews 9:1–10:25 explains this amazing truth in great detail. See also Matthew 26:28 and John 1:29.

Nazareth has become the most prolific parent ever, and the one whose days were cut off prematurely has become the longest ever living human! The risen Messiah will look around and be satisfied that his sufferings were worth it, and his Father will look around and be satisfied that both justice and mercy have won. The righteous servant (*tsaddīq*) who was rejected by the Jewish crowds and crucified with Gentile nails will justify (*tsādaq*) people the whole world over. The one who refused to open his mouth to save himself will open his mouth constantly to intercede with God for everyone.[8]

The Song hasn't quite finished. It began with colossal human weakness but now it ends with colossal divine strength: *"Therefore I will give him a portion among the great, and he will divide the spoils with the strong."* This fourth, last, longest and most elaborate Servant Song ends with rejoicing that the Messiah's willingness to put his naked human weakness on show means he can be fully clothed with divine power.[9] He has become the ultimate example of God's promise in 40:29–31. The apostle Paul puts it this way:

The message of the cross is foolishness to those who are perishing, but to us who are being saved it is the power of God... For the foolishness of God is wiser than human wisdom, and the weakness of God is stronger than human strength... God chose the foolish things of the world to shame the wise; God chose the weak things of the world to shame the strong. God chose the lowly things of this world and the despised things – and the things that are

---

[8] Most of the Hebrew verbs in this song are perfect tenses, expressing the fact that this will take place once and for all. The tense here, however, is imperfect, telling us that Jesus goes on making intercession for us in heaven right now. See Romans 8:34 and Hebrews 7:25.

[9] Although religious artists usually give Jesus a loincloth, the Romans crucified people naked.

not – to nullify the things that are, so that no one may boast before him.[10]

For to be sure, Christ was crucified in weakness, yet he lives by God's power. Likewise, we are weak in him, yet by God's power we will live.[11]

---

[10] 1 Corinthians 1:18, 25, 27–29.

[11] 2 Corinthians 13:4.

What They Saw
(52:13–53:12)

*Who has believed our message and to whom has the
arm of the Lord been revealed?*

(Isaiah 53:1)

Isaiah 53 comes right in the middle of the 27-chapter-long
"Book of Comfort", but it's also fair to say that it lies right at the
very heart of the Old Testament. Before we move on, let's take
a moment to examine what different people have seen in the
words of this chapter. Let's see what happens whenever people
reply positively to Isaiah's question: *"Who has believed our
message and to whom has the arm of the Lord been revealed?"*

The first person was an out-and-out sinner. We know
very little about him except that he was one of the two thieves
crucified on either side of Jesus. Matthew and Mark tell us that
they both heaped insults on Jesus as they died, but Luke adds
the sequel to the story. Even as the lights began to go out on
his own life, the light of revelation began to dawn in the thief's
heart. Perhaps he had heard this chapter read as a child in the
synagogue. Perhaps he had heard it sung by one of the devout
Jews from whom he stole. No matter how he knew the lyrics, he
saw in them what had eluded the rabbis. The Messiah would be
both strong and weak at the same time.[1]

The man hanging next to the thief had been pierced
through his hands and feet, just as the Song had predicted in

---

[1] Luke 22:37 and Mark 15:28 point out that the words of 53:12 were fulfilled
when Jesus was crucified between two thieves, therefore being *"numbered
with the transgressors"*.

53:5. Although most death-row criminals died protesting their innocence, this one had fulfilled the prophecy in 53:7: *"As a sheep before its shearers is silent, so he did not open his mouth."*[2] He had run rings around the rabbis when he debated with them in the Temple courtyards, so now he said nothing at his trials in case it resulted in his walking free. Since the thief knew that this man had been the toast of all Jerusalem only a few days before, he had also fulfilled the words of 53:8 when his countrymen closed ranks against him and unanimously called for his execution.[3] The thief had seen enough to believe that the beaten and bloodied figure dying next to him was Israel's Messiah. Turning to him, he expressed his confidence that the words of 52:15 would be fulfilled: *"Jesus, remember me when you come into your kingdom."* The Messiah smiled at his faith and looked back at him with eyes of love: *"Truly I tell you, today you will be with me in paradise."*[4]

The second person was equally unlikely to believe the Gospel. He lived in Ethiopia, a nation so far away from Jerusalem that Isaiah used its neighbours Cush and Seba as shorthand for "the ends of the earth". Even if he made the 4,000-mile round trip to Jerusalem, eunuchs were barred by the Jewish Law from entering the Temple courtyards.[5] Nevertheless, he made the trip anyway. We can read about his journey home in Acts 8:26–40, and about how a Christian named Philip overheard him reading Isaiah 53 in his chariot and getting confused. We are told that *"Philip began with that very passage of Scripture and told him the good news about Jesus."*[6] We can only guess at what he said.

---

[2] This fourth Servant Song is almost as long as the other three put together, yet to accentuate 53:7 the Messiah does not speak even a single word. Marvel at the silence of the lamb.

[3] Although 53:8 can also be translated *"who can speak of his descendants?"*, the Hebrew probably means *"who of his own generation spoke up for him?"*

[4] This perfect illustration of why Isaiah 53 is such powerful Scripture is recorded in Luke 23:32–43.

[5] Deuteronomy 23:1. Despite his evident interest in the Jewish religion, a eunuch could only get so far.

[6] Acts 8:32–33 quotes from 53:7–8 in order to tell us he was reading the entire Song. None of the four gospels had been written yet, but the Lord considered Isaiah 53 a good enough gospel for the time being.

Did Philip tell this governor of Ethiopia that 52:15 promised that the Messiah would save rulers from every nation?[7] Did he explain from 53:4–12 that we need to step into the Messiah's death and resurrection? We do not know for sure, but we do know that when the Ethiopian came to an oasis he immediately acted on what he had heard: *"Look, here is water. What can stand in the way of my being baptised?"*

The third person is the disciple Matthew. It can't have been easy for him to be one of the dozen men who led the Gospel charge across the world. Matthew knew that his only hope of success lay in following his Master's example and healing people in every town. But how could he know for sure that it was God's will to heal, and how could he feed his faith that he had authority to command pain and sickness to leave? We aren't left guessing, because he tells us in Matthew 8:16–17. Having told us that Jesus *"drove out the spirits **with a word** and healed **all** who were ill"*, Matthew explains how he did it: *"This was to fulfil what was spoken through the prophet Isaiah: 'He took up our infirmities and bore our diseases.'"* If we examine his words carefully, we will also see what Matthew saw.

Matthew had noticed that the Hebrew words *mak'ōb* and *holī* in 53:3–4 are words that almost always describe physical, rather than spiritual, pain and sickness. He normally quotes from the Greek Septuagint but not this time, because it spiritualizes these promises, like many English Bibles: *"he bears our sins and is pained for us."* Matthew goes back to the Hebrew text and re-translates the words more accurately as *"he took our **sicknesses** and carried our **diseases**."*

Matthew had also noticed that the Hebrew words that Isaiah uses in 53:3–4 and 11 to describe the way that Jesus carried our sins and our sicknesses are exactly the same. *"He was despised and rejected by mankind; a man of pains (mak'ōb),*

---

[7] Paul quotes 52:15 in Romans 15:21 as one of the key verses which inspired him on his missionary journeys.

and familiar with sickness (holī)... Surely he took up (nāsā') our sicknesses (holī) and bore (sābal) our pains (mak'ōb)... He will bear (sābal) their iniquities... He bore (nāsā') the sin of many." Matthew uses these verses to explain the healing ministry of Jesus because it flows from his death and resurrection. Matthew uses the Greek word for "saving" to describe miracles of healing as well as miracles of forgiveness, because Jesus has dealt with the entire curse that sin brought upon us.[8] Whatever Adam lost, Jesus has restored. Matthew rebuked sickness, dispensed healing and expelled demons across the Roman Empire, not because he believed God might heal, but because he was certain that God had won healing for humanity through a definitive legal transaction on the cross.[9]

The fourth person was the high priest Caiaphas. He of all people should have known that Jesus had fulfilled the words of the fourth Servant Song. Caiaphas had seen his disfigurement, rejection and suffering. He knew his innocence and his refusal to open his mouth and walk free.[10] Caiaphas knew that his own guards had come back from the rich man's tomb in which Jesus was buried, claiming that the corpse of Jesus was a corpse no more. He should have seen this as the fulfilment of 53:9–11, but he didn't. The high priest of Israel failed to spot the Messiah when he came.

"Who has believed our message and to whom has the arm of the Lord been revealed?" Make sure that the answer is you. Be like the first three men and not like Caiaphas. Put down this book and worship Jesus. Tell the suffering servant that he is your Saviour and your Lord.

---

[8] Matthew uses the Greek verb *sōzō*, meaning *to save*, to describe Jesus' healing ministry in 9:21–22. He did not see a distinction between *saving* and *healing*. They are both part of a single great salvation package.

[9] Although Matthew 9:35–36 tells us that God's compassion is a significant factor in healing, it is first and foremost an expression of Christ's kingly authority through his death and resurrection.

[10] In quoting from Isaiah 53 several times, 1 Peter 2:21–25 reiterates both of these things about Jesus.

Gospel Explosion (54:1–3)

Enlarge the place of your tent, stretch your tent curtains wide, do not hold back; lengthen your cords, strengthen your stakes.

(Isaiah 54:2)

We know by now to expect an encore at the end of one of the Servant Songs, but nothing has prepared us for this sudden explosion. The Lord has been holding on to this Gospel secret since before the dawn of time, and he is clearly very excited that his arm has finally been revealed. Like drawing a sword out of its scabbard, like taking an arrow out of its quiver and like taking a strong arm out of its sleeve, the Lord has sung about his weapon of mass salvation. We really shouldn't wonder that he wants us to sing along.

Childlessness was seen as something deeply shameful in the ancient world. The Old Testament is full of examples of women who wept over their lack of children: Sarah, Rachel and Hannah are some of the most famous.[1] Thankfully, our culture is far more generous towards infertility, but we still feel its heart-wrenching tragedy. The Lord wants us to feel this way about our spiritual fruitfulness and about the spiritual state of our churches and our nations. He wants us to cry out like John Knox over his own nation: *"O Lord, give me Scotland or I die!"*[2] He wants us to cry out in faith that the final Servant Song guarantees that we will be fruitful: *"Sing, barren woman, you who never bore a child; burst into song, shout for joy, you*

---

[1] Genesis 11:30; 16:1–6; 29:31–30:8. Also 1 Samuel 1:1–28.
[2] John Knox's prayer was inspired by Rachel's in Genesis 30:1.

who were never in labour; because more are the children of the
desolate woman than of her who has a husband."

Most of us have plenty of excuses why these verses cannot apply to us. Some people argue that God is talking to the Jewish nation rather than to us, but Paul quotes this verse in Galatians 4:27 and tells us that it is not addressed to the bricks-and-mortar city of Jerusalem. It is addressed to Zion, the spiritual city which represents everyone who receives Jesus as the Messiah.[3] Other people counter that they must be an exception to this rule because their track record of fruitfulness is feeble. Not only is this foolish thinking (the small print on any investment plan reminds us that past performance is never a reliable indicator of the future), but it also fails to read these verses properly. The Lord addresses Zion as a barren woman (someone with a track record of zero fruitfulness!) and promises that her barrenness will actually play out to her advantage. Those who are a little bit fruitful can often be blinded to the true extent of their weakness, but barren people know they need a miracle from God. That's why the Lord tells Zion that she will be even more fruitful than if she had not endured such disappointments in the past. Jesus isn't joking when he promises you in John 15:16 that *"You did not choose me, but I chose you and appointed you so that you might go and bear fruit – fruit that will last."*

With that in mind, the Lord commands Zion to enlarge the size of her tent so that she will have room for a vast crowd of believers to come inside.[4] Note that this is often the problem in our churches. We wait for growth to happen before we make plans to accommodate it, but this is not how it works. The Lord commands us to make plans in faith ahead of time. I remember

---

[3] Paul is Jewish but very insistent about this. He insists that ethnic Jews who reject the Messiah are not real Jews (Galatians 3:15–4:31) and that any Gentile who accepts the Messiah is now part of Israel (Galatians 6:16).

[4] Contrast this with the promise in 33:20. Before we grasp the size and scale of the Messiah's victory, defensive promises are enough. Once we grasp how much Jesus has won, nothing but advance can satisfy.

God teaching me this in my earliest days as a church leader. In the miracle in Luke 5:1–11, we are told that *"they caught such a large number of fish that their nets began to break"* and they *"filled both boats so full that they began to sink"*. As I read those words I felt God speak to me: With stronger nets or an extra boat, they would have been given even more. God loves people too much to save them into your church if it isn't ready to receive them. Whatever plans you are making for the future, Isaiah says that in the light of the fourth Servant Song you're going to need a bigger boat.

An English shoemaker named William Carey understood this in 1786. Even though he was aged only twenty-five and had only been a Baptist minister for a year, he stood up at a minister's fraternal and shared the burden of his soul for the English Church to get a bigger vision for the world. Why were their eyes fixed on the inhabitants of one small island, when there were over twenty-five times as many people in India alone: a quarter of a billion souls, and rising? When he had finished pleading with his fellow ministers, one of the older men spoke up: *"Young man, sit down, sit down! You're an enthusiast. When God pleases to convert the heathen, He'll do it without consulting you or me."*[5]

William Carey was appalled but not dissuaded. In 1789, he published a tract entitled "An Enquiry into the Obligations of Christians to Use Means for the Conversion of the Heathens". It was not a snappy title but it was snapped up by English Christians. He was invited to address a larger group of Baptist ministers in 1792. He preached from these verses in Isaiah and he begged his hearers: *"'Enlarge the place of thy tent, and let them stretch forth the curtains of thine habitations: spare not, lengthen thy cords, and strengthen thy stakes'... Expect great things from God. Attempt great things for God... God is calling you*

---

[5] S. Pearce Carey in his excellent biography simply entitled *William Carey* (1923).

to a brilliant future, to preach the gospel throughout the world. My friends, you need this wider vision." As a result of this sermon, the Baptist Missionary Society was founded and William Carey became known as "the father of modern missions".[6]

The promises which the Lord gives us in this encore do not guarantee us an easy ride. When William Carey landed in India in 1793, he encountered a catalogue of problems. He was refused help by the British traders. He lost several children to tropical disease and buried them in the foreign soil. His wife became mentally ill, and he failed to see a single convert for the first seven years. Nevertheless, he was determined to do what the Lord commanded him and to keep on singing. He was convinced that if he persevered, he would see a massive harvest across India. He reflected later that *"If anyone should think it worth his while to write my life, if he give me credit for being a plodder he will describe me justly. I can plod. I can persevere... Few people know what may be done till they try, and persevere in what they have undertaken."* Sure enough, he saw his first convert in 1800. Suddenly the floodgates opened. By the time he died there were half a million believers in the region, many of whom manned the sixty mission stations he founded.

That was then and this is now. William Carey fought his battle of faith and won. Yours is only just getting started. Will you complain that your part of the world is spiritually difficult? Will you persuade yourself that this is not yet the right season for growth? Or will you start to sing this encore with the Lord? You're going to need a bigger boat.

---

[6] He preached this sermon in Nottingham on 30th May 1792. Paul tells us in Romans 15:21 that the fourth Servant Song gave him this big vision. Fittingly, he funded it by working as a tentmaker (Acts 18:1–4).

Extreme Makeover
(54:4–17)

Afflicted city, lashed by storms and not comforted,
I will rebuild you with stones of turquoise, your
foundations with lapis lazuli.

(Isaiah 54:11)

It feels as though just about every third programme on TV these days is about having an extreme makeover. Whether it is a home that is renovated, a car that is pimped, a fat waist that is slimmed or a person's dress sense that is transformed, it seems the viewing public just can't get enough of them. Well, hold on to your hats. Put all of those TV shows together and you still can't compete with what happens to Zion in this chapter. The Lord continues his encore by singing about the greatest makeover in history.

Bear in mind that Isaiah was prophesying in the final years of the ageing King Hezekiah. Eleven years before Hezekiah died, he had his sinful son Manasseh declared co-ruler. All around Isaiah, therefore, the early shoots of King Manasseh's evil reign must have been starting to sprout. Jerusalem must have looked on the brink of reaping the judgment it so richly deserved. Very soon the Babylonians would reduce it to a pile of scorched rubble. This song is therefore not just the announcement of some town-planning improvements – the urban equivalent of pimping a clapped-out car or renovating a bit of a fixer-upper. Zion was about to be down-and-out and destroyed. That's why the Lord is so excited about his promise to give her an extreme makeover.

In 54:4–8, the Lord promises to make the New Jerusalem his Bride. Her predecessor's flirtation with the great prostitute Babylon caused him to turn his back on her, but now he promises no longer to treat her like a jilted newlywed or a lonely widow. He will act as her husband again and, in so doing, he will give her back the full benefit of bearing his name. He spells this name out for her in five different ways in 54:5. He is her *"Maker"*, *"the Lord Almighty"*, *"the Holy One of Israel"*, her *"Redeemer"* and *"the God of all the earth"*. Given that her husband has these five names on his business card, it is not hard to see why Zion needed to increase the size of her tent in 54:1–3 in anticipation of a massive family of children. God's judgment has been brief and his grace will spring eternal.[1]

In 54:9–10, the Lord restates that this renewal of his covenant with Zion will last forever. The people of Judah could not understand the scope and scale of his forgiveness before they heard him sing his final Servant Song, but now they realize that the ink with which he writes his New Covenant is the righteous blood of his Messiah. Suddenly it all makes sense. If a rainbow in the sky proclaimed the permanence of the covenant achieved by righteous Noah and a wooden ark, how much more permanent is the covenant which has been achieved by the righteous Messiah and a wooden cross![2]

In 54:11–12, the Lord sings about the new walls and gates of Zion. She will not be rebuilt with stones quarried from a hillside, but with living stones – people quarried from the world and declared righteous through the substitutionary sacrifice of the Messiah.[3] The ancient high priests of Israel engraved the

---

[1] God is not downplaying the horrors of the Babylonian exile by calling it *"a brief moment"* in 54:7. He is simply contrasting it with his *"everlasting kindness"* in 54:8. Paul does the same in 2 Corinthians 4:17.

[2] See Genesis 6:9; 8:21–22; 9:8–17. Zion therefore needs to go forth, increase and multiply (9:7).

[3] 1 Peter 2:4–10 describes believers as God's new Temple rather than as God's new city, but the New Testament deliberately mixes its metaphors. Peter is very clear that we have become the New Mount Zion.

names of the twelve tribes of Israel onto twelve small jewels on the front of their uniform, but the Lord will turn every Christian believer into a jewel as large as one of the massive building blocks which ancient city-dwellers quarried to construct their mighty walls.[4]

If you have been a Christian for a long time, you may find verses like these a little hard to believe. A lot of the Christians you know may not look very much like jewels. You may have experienced churches that look a lot more like the blackened rubble of the Old Jerusalem than this glorious picture of the New Jerusalem. But wait a moment before you dismiss these words as fantasy. It is possible that those self-proclaimed believers and churches are nothing of the kind. If Paul tells us in Galatians 4:27 that not every Jew is truly part of Zion, it shouldn't surprise us that not everyone who claims to be a Christian is one either. On the other hand, if they are true believers and true churches, your cynicism is actually part of the problem.[5] Jesus meant it when he told people in Matthew 9:29, *"According to your faith will it be done to you."*

We need to believe that this is what the Church can be, because the task of making it happen falls squarely on the Lord. He knows more about the weaknesses of Christians and of churches than you do, which is why this promise comes as part of his pledge to make weak people strong. *"**I will rebuild** you with stones of turquoise... **I will make** your battlements of rubies,"* the Lord promises, putting the burden for this makeover on his own shoulders. Because the beautiful Messiah became grotesquely disfigured, the Lord can make even the weakest believer a work of art which dazzles with heaven's beauty.

---

[4] Exodus 28:9–21. The historian Josephus tells us in his *Antiquities of the Jews* (15.11.3) that some of the stones that were used for rebuilding Jerusalem were 11 metres long, 5.5 metres wide and 3.5 metres high.

[5] Paul warns us in Romans 15:7 that a proper response to the Gospel means viewing other believers as God views them and not as the lens of our own self-centredness perceives them to be.

Our faith that this is what the Church can be will never be disappointed, because the Lord says its fulfilment is already guaranteed. We can read a longer description of this beautiful Bride of Christ, the New Jerusalem, in Revelation 21 and it is amazing. Sinful men like Joseph's brothers form its gates. Slow learners like the twelve disciples form its foundation stones. The building materials are weak, but the builder is very strong.

That's why in 54:13, the Lord promises that even the weakest believer will experience this extreme makeover. Jesus quotes from this verse in John 6:45 when people doubt his authority because he is a humble carpenter. He uses this verse to declare that he is no longer in the furniture business. He is in the business of transforming ordinary lives. Any believer who reads the Bible, who worships, who prays and who pursues the place God has for them in Zion will find that they know God as their closest friend. They will discover that he is able to transform them into a very beautiful brick in the wall.[6]

In 54:14–17, the Lord ends with a promise that this makeover can never be undone. Fixed-up houses, pimped-up cars and slimmed-down tummies rarely stay that way. They represent the start of an ongoing battle. Zion is different. The Lord points out that even Satan is one of his creatures, so he can ensure every one of his attacks on Zion's walls ends in failure. Like Sennacherib breaking the teeth of his army on the walls of Old Jerusalem, any time Satan tries to reverse this makeover his plans will always backfire.

So stand back and admire the New Jerusalem. Marvel at what the Lord has made out of the smouldering ruins of Zion. Then marvel that this encore is a song that the Lord sings right now over you.[7]

---

[6] Verse 13 has profound implications for how we disciple people. The Lord takes the primary responsibility for discipling believers. We merely need to work alongside what he is doing.

[7] In the fourth Servant Song, the Messiah was the Lord's servant. In 54:17, you are now his servant too.

Food for the Weak
(55:1–13)

*Come, all you who are thirsty, come to the waters; and
you who have no money, come, buy and eat! Come,
buy wine and milk without money and without cost.*

(Isaiah 55:1)

When I used to work in business I was warned that there is no
such thing as a free lunch. It has generally been pretty good
advice over the years. Nevertheless, we need to recognize that
the Gospel is the one exception. Unless we are bowled over by its
lavish generosity, Isaiah warns us we haven't understood it at all.

Isaiah finishes this section of his book with an amazing
invitation to come and live in the good of what the Messiah has
won for us. The Lord invites anyone who reads these chapters
to come and eat for free: *"Come, all you who are thirsty, come
to the waters; and you who have no money, come, buy and eat!
Come, buy wine and milk without money and without cost."* We
must not wear ourselves out on idols, now that God has finally
revealed the New Covenant which he promised long ago to King
David.[1] The resurrection has proven once and for all that Jesus
is the Messiah,[2] that he is the King of kings and Lord of lords,
and that the nations must come streaming to his rule.[3]

---

[1] Paul quotes from 55:3 in Acts 13:34 and says it describes the resurrection
of Jesus. The New Covenant is *eternal* because every past covenant pointed
towards it and because, now revealed, it will endure forever.

[2] That's why the apostles preach far more about the empty tomb than the
cross in the book of Acts (see Acts 2:32; 4:2; 17:31). Paul even says in 2
Timothy 2:8 that *"Jesus Christ, raised from the dead… is my gospel."*

[3] Acts 2:36; Philippians 2:9–11; Hebrews 1:3–4; 2:9.

There is an easy way to tell if you have understood the outrageous generosity of the Gospel. Just take a look at the new king in Jerusalem. Isaiah began his book by telling us that he prophesied until the end of the reign of Hezekiah, who died in 686 BC and who appointed his son Manasseh to rule as king with him from 697 BC onwards. Since Isaiah 37:38 records an event that took place in 681 BC, the prophet's final years of ministry must have taken place in the early years of King Manasseh. Let's road-test our understanding of the Gospel by applying it to the life of the man during whose reign these words were prophesied. What do you think would have happened if Manasseh, the wickedest king of Judah, had repented of his sin?

Manasseh pursued an aggressive policy of paganizing Judah. He ignored Isaiah's warnings and filled the Temple courtyards with his idols. He turned the valley outside Jerusalem into a shrine to Molech, sacrificing at least two of his own sons to the demon-god and encouraging the people of Judah to do the same. He promoted witchcraft and divination throughout his realm. When people protested, he launched a violent wave of persecution against the remaining believers in Jerusalem.[4] According to Jewish tradition, he ordered his men to execute Isaiah by sawing him in two. It's no wonder that the Lord named Manasseh as the person chiefly responsible for the destruction of Jerusalem.

So here's the question: Could the evil King Manasseh have been forgiven through the Gospel which Isaiah proclaimed? How far is it true to say that God will forgive anyone?

It's a trick question, because we know what actually happened. The Lord brought the king of Assyria back to the gates of Jerusalem and he captured Manasseh. He put him in chains, put a hook through his nose and led him off as a prisoner to Babylon. The Bible records that, when finally stripped naked of his own strength, Manasseh finally believed the promise

---

4 2 Kings 21:1–18; 24:1–4; 2 Chronicles 33:1–20; Jeremiah 15:4.

of 40:29–31. He cried out to the Lord to forgive him and to clothe him with divine power. His prayer was answered and he experienced his own personal return from Babylonian captivity. He became an example of God's outrageous grace to sinners.[5]

Turning back to the final chapter of this section of Isaiah, the Lord tells us that it is crucial we believe this. First, our own salvation depends on grasping that God has done everything to save us. The only thing we need to do is to admit that we are thirsty and penniless: then we get to dine on it for free.[6]

Second, the Lord tells us that this truth lies at the heart of what he means when he tells us throughout this section of Isaiah that he is glorified by making weak people strong, wicked people righteous and foolish plans prosper. He is so strong that he has no need to be glorified through our strength. He derives his glory by being *"abundantly lavish in forgiveness"*.[7] He is glorified by demonstrating that his wisdom and strength are far wiser and stronger than our own: *"For my thoughts are not your thoughts, neither are your ways my ways. As the heavens are higher than the earth, so are my ways higher than your ways and my thoughts than your thoughts."*[8]

Third, the Lord says that the world will only grasp this amazing grace if Zion grasps it and displays it to the world. In 55:5, he likens us to advertising brochures for Mount Zion. His plan is for the splendour of our own lives to cause unbelievers to come running towards the gates of Zion. In 55:12, he underlines the fact that one of the most important features of our Gospel advertising must be the joy it gives us every day. People who

---

[5] King Ashurbanipal of Assyria did this to him in c.650 BC. See 2 Chronicles 33:10–13.

[6] Note the echo of 55:1–2 in passages such as Matthew 11:28–30, and John 6:35, 7:37–39 and 19:30.

[7] This is a literal translation of the final words of 55:7. God doesn't make this offer to the reformed and respectable, but to the *wicked* and the *unrighteous*. 55:13 says this is why the Gospel brings him such glory.

[8] Paul quotes from 55:10 in 2 Corinthians 9:10 and says the people of Zion should therefore sow generously.

believe they have to earn their way to God are generally miserable. Sadly, there are many such miserable churches, which dishonour God by singing the songs of Zion very badly out of key. Whenever churches understand that they have been forgiven through the work of Jesus, in spite of all their sin and weakness, they become the happiest communities in town.[9] The Lord says that Christian joy is so infectious that it makes the hills come alive with the sound of music (yes, God invented that line long before Julie Andrews), and it makes the trees clap their branches together like hands. Convincing unbelieving men and women to respond to the Gospel therefore isn't too difficult. The people of Zion simply have to start responding to it themselves.[10]

Fourth and finally, the Lord tells us that we need to understand this quickly because time is running out. As we are about to discover in the last section of Isaiah, the Messiah is coming back to bring world history to an end. Then, it will be too late for those in Babylon to confess that they are weak and that God is stronger than they thought. Now is the day of salvation. Isaiah ends this section of his book with an urgent appeal:

> *Seek the Lord while he may be found; call on him while he is near. Let the wicked forsake their ways and the unrighteous their thoughts. Let them turn to the Lord, and he will have mercy on them, and to our God, for he will freely pardon.*

---

[9] Isaiah repeatedly tells us that those who are truly redeemed will be joyful (9:3; 12:3; 30:29; 35:1–10; 51:3, 11; 52:8–9; 54:1; 61:3). A miserable Christian ought to be as much an oxymoron as a poor billionaire.

[10] We may need to wait a while to see this Gospel harvest, but the Lord assures us in 55:10–11 that it will come as surely as the one brought by the falling rain. The Hebrew phrase he uses for his Word *not returning empty* is used in 2 Samuel 1:22 to describe a warrior refusing to sheathe his sword without shedding blood.

Part Five

God is Closer Than You Think

(Isaiah 56–66)

No-Entry Signs (56:1–8)

My house will be called a house of prayer for all nations.

(Isaiah 56:7)

At the grand opening ceremony for Disney World Florida, a junior employee expressed his sadness that Walt Disney's death from lung cancer meant he had not lived to see the brand new theme park. One of his managers overheard and shot back a famous reply: *"Didn't live to see it? Didn't live to see it? Believe me, Walt Disney saw this theme park. It's the only reason that you and I are standing here!"*

If you hold that picture in your mind, it will help you as we move into this fourth and final section of Isaiah. The "Book of Judgment" described our sin (chapters 1–12) and its consequences (chapters 13–35). In the same way, the "Book of Comfort" describes God's solution (chapters 40–55) and its consequences (chapters 56–66).[1] Disney World owed its construction to somebody's clear vision of what they wanted it to be, and we are about to find that the same is true of the New Mount Zion. The Lord uses these eleven chapters to describe the city that he wants to empower his people to build.

Life is short. We only get one chance to play our part in God's plan to construct and expand Zion. It is therefore crucial that we take the time to discover what kind of Church the Lord is after. What kind of Church will generate saving faith in people

---

[1] These section divisions are not arbitrary. Remember, we saw earlier that Isaiah 40–55 and 56–66 are so different from one another that some scholars even try to argue they were written by two separate authors!

from every nation, provoking the Jewish nation to such jealousy that it turns en masse to Jesus, hastening his final return and the dawn of the bright new age to come? God tells us all that and more in these eleven chapters. There is an inscription over the main gates of the theme park in Florida that proclaims Walt Disney's vision: *"Here you leave today and enter the world of yesterday, tomorrow and fantasy."* Isaiah describes a far better vision here. This isn't fantasy. It is Zion as the Lord promises he will empower us to build her. It culminates in 66:1–2, which promises us that he will build Zion through us: *"Heaven is my throne, and the earth is my footstool. Where is the house you will build for me? Where will my resting place be? Has not my hand made all these things, and so they came into being?"*

In 56:1–8, the Lord therefore lays down **instruction #1: Zion is to be open to all**. Throughout this final section of Isaiah, the Lord will tell us that he is closer than we think, so he starts to spell this out for us by talking about those who felt the furthest away. Deuteronomy 23:1–14 gave a long list of people who were to be excluded from the Old Jerusalem.[2] Eunuchs were out (too infertile), illegitimate children were out (too shameful), foreigners were out (too sinful) and messy people were out (too dirty). Ancient Judaism was a religion of no-entry signs.[3] It proclaimed that God's presence in the Temple was out-of-bounds for most of us. God's guest-list was very short in the old city of Jerusalem.

That's why this first description of Zion as God wants her to be is so exciting. It begins with a promise that *"my salvation is close at hand and my righteousness will soon be revealed."* That's not simply saying that Jesus will return soon to end

---

[2] They were not simply excluded from the Tabernacle and Temple, but from the Israelite assembly altogether. The Greek Septuagint word for this assembly is *ekklēsia*, the New Testament word for *Church*.

[3] More no-entry signs can be found in Exodus 12:43, Leviticus 22:10–13, and Numbers 1:51 and 18:22. The Lord began to tear down these no-entry signs by saving an Ethiopian eunuch in Acts 8.

world history, although Isaiah will talk a lot about that Final Day in a few chapters' time. No, it is a promise which is echoed in Revelation 21, where the New Jerusalem is described in even greater detail. John says,

> *I heard a loud voice from the throne saying, "Look! God's dwelling-place is now among the people, and he will dwell with them. They will be his people, and God himself will be with them and be their God"... He carried me away in the Spirit to a mountain great and high, and showed me the Holy City, Jerusalem... On no day will its gates ever be shut.*[4]

The Lord is therefore declaring that, because of what the Messiah has done in the fourth Servant Song, all of the no-entry signs are to be taken down in Zion. The Church is to be a place where anyone can enter to taste and see that God is closer than they think.[5]

These eight verses are glorious. Foreigners enter Zion and are granted a share in sacrifices that were once reserved only for Jews. Eunuchs enter Zion and are granted a share in a building project which yields far greater posterity than children.[6] Sinners exchange their evil deeds for God's covenant and discover that even they can have a share in God's *"holy mountain"*. Those who are weary of following the insatiable demands of man-made religion discover that the no-entry signs have been replaced by signs which say "Sabbath". Babylon is all about slavery and striving; Zion is all about resting in faith. It

---

[4] Revelation strongly echoes Isaiah throughout, but never more so than in the strong parallel between Revelation 20–22 and Isaiah 56–66.

[5] I have said enough in previous chapters for you to know that I am not saying the Church has "replaced" Zion in these prophecies. The Church is Zion. Many Jews have stepped out of Zion but they will step back in.

[6] The Holocaust Memorial in Jerusalem is named after two Hebrew words in 56:5. *Yad Vashem* means either *"a hand and a name"* or *"a memorial and a name"*. But God has a far better memorial for Jews in the New Zion.

embodies what Isaiah celebrated earlier: *"In repentance and rest is your salvation, in quietness and trust is your strength."* It embodies what the New Testament also celebrates. It is home *"to the one who does not work but trusts God who justifies the ungodly".*[7]

Sadly, the Church has not always been very good at taking down the no-entry signs. A worker from the streets of Chicago recalls the time

> *A prostitute came to see me in wretched straits, homeless, sick, unable to buy food for her two-year-old daughter. Through sobs and tears, she told me she had been renting out her daughter – two years old! – to men interested in kinky sex. She made more renting out her daughter for an hour than she could earn on her own in a night. She had to do it, she said, to support her own drug habit. I could hardly bear hearing her sordid story... At last I asked if she had ever thought of going to a church for help. I will never forget the look of pure, naïve shock that crossed her face. "Church!" she cried. "Why would I ever go there? I was already feeling terrible about myself. They'd just make me feel worse."*[8]

That's why we need to take this first piece of building instruction very seriously. The Lord is not simply saying in 56:7 that Zion must be a place of prayer. He is saying that it must be *"a house of prayer **for all nations"***. This is the verse that Jesus quoted to explain his righteous anger when he cleared the Temple courtyards of anything that stopped it being a welcome lobby

---

[7] Isaiah 30:15; Romans 4:5.

[8] Philip Yancey shares this story in his book *What's So Amazing About Grace?* (1997).

for the foreigner, the eunuch, the tax collector, the prostitute and the sinner. I wonder how he feels about our churches.[9]

So let's take down the no-entry signs. There is no place for them in Zion. Let's put up signs that proclaim a Sabbath rest to anyone who believes God is closer than we think.

---

[9] Matthew 21:13; Mark 11:17; Luke 19:46. Intending to be welcoming is not the same thing as being welcoming. The Jews intended to be welcoming (1 Kings 8:41–43), but their self-centredness won the day.

Second Home (56:9–57:21)

I live in a high and holy place, but also with the one
who is contrite and lowly in spirit.

(Isaiah 57:15)

Everybody knew where God lived. He had his home in heaven.
Even though they talked a lot about his dwelling in the inner
room of their Temple, the people of Judah knew full well that
King Solomon had said the opposite at the dedication of his
Temple: *"Will God really dwell on earth? The heavens, even the*
highest heaven, cannot contain you. How much less this temple
I have built!" He went on to underscore this statement eight
times more during his official prayer of dedication.[1] Even
as he opened the Temple in Jerusalem as God's second home,
Solomon confessed that it could never rival his first home.

But now the Lord proclaims a new and better story over
Zion. The key verse is 57:15: *"For this is what the high and*
exalted One says – he who lives for ever, whose name is holy: 'I live
in a high and holy place, but also with the one who is contrite and
lowly in spirit.'" Go back and read that verse again, only this time
more slowly. It is quite phenomenal. It tells us that God is now
committed to living in two homes, not just one. The first half of
the verse uses similar language to Isaiah's vision of the Lord in
6:1, where he was enthroned in heaven and even the hem of his
robe was too much for Solomon's Temple. It emphasizes that
God is "transcendent" – far too lofty to dwell with the lowly. He is

---

[1] 1 Kings 8:27, 30, 32, 34, 36, 39, 43, 45, 49.

qādōsh: far holier than we think.[2] The second half of the verse, however, emphasizes his "immanence", that he is so attracted to humility that he wants to do a house-share with anybody who is willing to confess their human sinfulness and weakness. These verses tell us that God wants to turn Christian believers into his second home.

In 56:9–57:21, the Lord therefore lays down **instruction #2: Zion is to experience his tangible presence**. Again we need to turn to Revelation 21 for a fuller explanation. It tells us, *"Look! God's dwelling-place is now among the people, and he will dwell with them. They will be his people, and God himself will be with them and be their God."* Just in case we think that this is merely the promise of a slightly better Temple, John continues: *"I did not see a temple in the city, because the Lord God Almighty and the Lamb are its temple."* In the New Mount Zion, there are no inner rooms or outer rooms or walled courtyards. The Lord turns believers into his living Temple instead! The reference to Jesus as "the Lamb" is a reminder of how much it cost the Lord to be able to fill us with his Holy Spirit.

Having God up close and personal is wonderful but it also spells danger. The blood of Jesus makes us sinless; it does not make God more tolerant of sin. The tone therefore suddenly changes and begins to sound more like the "Book of Judgment" than the "Book of Comfort". Do not be surprised. The Lord's stern tone of voice reflects the depth of his desire to teach churches how to turn this promise into their daily experience.

In 56:9–57:2, the Lord tells us that it starts with church leaders. He warns them not to be like the Jewish leaders in the days of Manasseh: blind watchmen, mute dogs, idle dreamers, greedy guzzlers, stupid shepherds, money-grabbers, complacent

---

[2] It is not mistranslating the Hebrew words *shōkēn 'ad* in 57:15 when they are rendered *"who lives forever"*. However, a better translation is *"who lives in eternity"*. God's primary home isn't even in our time zone.

drunkards.[3] He even explains why he allowed so many godly men and women to be slaughtered by Manasseh in the bloodbath of 2 Kings 21:16. If you have ever lost a Christian loved-one too young and have cried out to God in anger and confusion, this answer may be for you: *"The righteous are taken away to be spared from evil."* God let them die early because it was better for them than being caught up in his judgment on this world. They were fast-tracked to heaven.[4] I hope that's helpful, but the main point of these verses is God's warning that, if those of us who are left want to experience his presence daily, we need to be led by people who love experiencing his presence every day themselves.[5]

In 57:3–13, the Lord tells us that it also depends on entire church congregations. The people of Judah still claimed to follow God during the evil days of Manasseh, but he saw past their Sabbath smiles and their religious self-delusion. They claimed to be the children of Israel, but the Lord calls them children of witches, the offspring of prostitutes, a brood of rebels and the offspring of liars. He is not fooled by their pretended desire for his presence. If they really wanted to walk with him, they would not be following their king's lead into witchcraft, sexual permissiveness, idolatry and child sacrifice.[6] This same principle has always been true throughout Church history. Not every generation that asks God for a daily experience of his Holy Spirit really means it.

---

[3] Don't mistake the nonchalance of 56:12 for faith. It is the sin of Luke 12:19–20 and it prevents people from crying out to be filled with the Holy Spirit. Ephesians 5:18 tells us that general drunkenness does this too.

[4] 2 Kings 22:18–20 echoes this. From an eternal perspective, many who die young are blessed, not cursed.

[5] Leaders always influence, either positively or negatively. The Lord says in 57:11 that the people of Judah rebelled because, by and large, the preachers of Judah failed to love and speak God's Word to them.

[6] The Hebrew word *melek* in 57:9 means *king*, but it is also a play on words. King Manasseh had led the people astray into sacrificing their own children to Molech.

The Lord is reminding us of the message of the first two sections of Isaiah, that he is far holier and sterner than we think. In 57:10, he also reminds us of the message of the third section, that he is far stronger than we think. The Lord allowed the people of Old Jerusalem to wear themselves out with their religion, just as he allows churches to wear themselves out today chasing church growth through the latest paperbacks and conferences. He brought them to the end of their own strength so that they might lay hold of his, yet tragically they refused. Rather than acknowledging their own spiritual nakedness so that the Lord could clothe them, the people of Judah simply gritted their teeth and attempted to patch their ragged clothes.[7] We can't be full of ourselves and of God's Spirit at the same time. We need to make an active choice. It's simple, really: *"Whoever takes refuge in me will inherit the land and possess my holy mountain."*

In 57:14–21, the Lord promises that if we repent he will fill us with his Holy Spirit and turn us into his second home. He reminds us that he wants to build a holy highway for all nations to come to Zion, so he is far more eager to forgive and restore than he is to judge and destroy. If we mourn over our sinfulness (57:18)[8] and give God the worship that only comes from a converted heart (57:19), he promises to grant us peace on the day when he destroys the wicked.[9] The consequences of our decision here are massive, so let's make the right choice.[10]

GOD IS CLOSER THAN YOU THINK

220

---

[7] 57:10 gives us a stern warning that God's discipline does not automatically lead us to repentance. We need to make an active choice to learn the lesson of 40:29–31.

[8] Jesus may have been thinking of 57:18 in Matthew 5:4: *"Blessed are those who mourn, for they will be comforted."* Only those who mourn over their own sinfulness and weakness can experience the Gospel.

[9] The Lord describes our worship literally in 57:19 as *"the fruit of our lips"*. God is only interested in words that come from a sincere heart (Luke 6:45; John 4:23–24). Repentance is the root; worship is the fruit.

[10] 57:21 is a direct repeat of 48:22. This final section of Isaiah forces us to choose between heaven and hell.

Let's ask God to fill us with his Holy Spirit, both as individuals and as churches.

Let's discover what Paul discovered in these verses and described in 1 Corinthians 3:16–17: *"Don't you know that you yourselves are God's temple and that God's Spirit lives among you? If anyone destroys God's temple, God will destroy that person; for God's temple is sacred, and you together are that temple."*

Street Repairs (58:1–14)

Your people will rebuild the ancient ruins and will raise up the age-old foundations; you will be called Repairer of Broken Walls, Restorer of Streets with Dwellings.

(Isaiah 58:12)

By and large, Christians tend to have a rather negative view of the problems in the city. Maybe it stems from the way the Bible describes Babylon as an urban outpost of hell on earth. That's ironic because Isaiah, who prophesies about Babylon, does not tell us that to overcome her we need to dream of rolling fields. He tells us that the answer to Babylon is not *no city*, but *a better city*. To defeat each urban outpost of hell on earth we have to co-operate with God's plan to build an urban outpost of heaven instead. There is a decidedly urban flavour to these final chapters of Isaiah, and never more so than here.

Jesus may well have been thinking back to the final chapters of Isaiah when he announced his strategy to his disciples in Matthew 5:14: *"You are the light of the world. A city built on a hill cannot be hidden."* Have you noticed how little of the book of Acts takes place outside the walls of the major cities of the Roman Empire? The followers of Jesus quickly grasped that he wanted them to become like the Greeks with their Horse of Troy. He wanted them to go to every outpost of Babylon and to build Zion within her walls. The Lord therefore lays down **instruction #3: Zion is to be a countercultural city within the city**.

In 58:1–5, the Lord points out the failure of the Jewish days of fasting in Old Jerusalem. He is not trying to trivialize their abstinence from food, from drink and from sex. Jesus reaffirms the value of these Old Testament commands in Matthew 6.[1] The Lord is simply pointing out that abstinence is only one aspect of fasting. We refuse to dine on what this world has to offer in order to feast on what heaven has to offer us instead. The fact that the Jews were quarrelling with each other and exploiting their workers while they fasted was clear proof that their hearts were still in love with the trappings of this world. If the Church is like the world, no number of days of prayer and fasting will ever change our cities.[2] Babylon will never be changed if the colony of heaven within her midst behaves as much like a colony of hell as she does.

In 58:6–7, the Lord describes what it means to abstain from this earth's food in order to eat the food of heaven. It means believing that all heaven's riches are now ours through the Messiah's sacrifice and therefore feeling no further need to copy the way that Babylon grasps after material things. It means promoting fairness towards our workers. It means gladly sharing with the poor, thinking little of what they can give us in return. It means seeing family demands as an opportunity to imitate the love of the Father and the sacrifice of the Son.

In 58:8–9, the Lord tells us that this is how Zion overcomes Babylon from the inside.[3] Evangelistic missions fail when they treat cities in the same way as merchants – as a useful concentration of a market commodity: money for the merchants and people for the Church. Churches that suck from their community like a leech instead of serving their community

---

[1] Fasting from food and wearing uncomfortable sackcloth were two normal Jewish ways of expressing the humility which God demands in 57:15 and 18. Contrite prayer almost always involves discomfort.

[2] God's warning in 58:4 and 9 that the state of our hearts affects the way he answers our prayers is also echoed in 1:15, Psalm 66:18, 1 Timothy 2:8, Hebrews 5:7, 1 Peter 3:7, and Proverbs 15:8, 15:29, 21:13 and 28:9.

[3] Verse 8 is probably best translated as *"your Righteous One will go before you."* Jesus will go before and behind us.

like Christ are doomed to fail. But churches that become like Jesus – giving, serving, confronting, comforting and healing – discover that their mortar sticks far better than the bitumen of Babylon.[4] Serving a city for Jesus leads to winning over a city for Jesus. The Lord promises churches: *"**Then** your light will break forth like the dawn, and your healing will quickly appear; then your righteousness will go before you, and the glory of the Lord will be your rear guard. Then you will call, and the Lord will answer; you will cry for help, and he will say: here am I."*[5]

In 58:9–12, the Lord describes what will happen if we live by the countercultural values of Zion right at the heart of Babylon. We will not only succeed in our calling to be the light of the world, but we will be like the Middle Eastern sun in all its noonday brilliance. While churches that fail to pass on heaven's blessings to others become stagnant and arid, churches that pass on what God has given them become like a high-pressure spring.

That's the beautiful irony about Zion. If she hoards the riches of heaven to herself, she becomes poor, but if she rises to the calling that God gave Abraham in Genesis 12:2 – *"I will bless you... and you will be a blessing"* – she becomes the envy of the entire world. People in the community turn to her and give her positions of influence that she could never have won for herself by pursuing the self-centred scheming of Babylon. Unbelievers turn to the Bride of Christ and ask her to help make their marriages work. Unbelievers ask the children of God to teach them how to parent. Unbelievers ask those who have renounced this world's riches to advise them on their budgeting. The people of Babylon ask them to extend Zion's

---

[4] Babylonian builders used bitumen as their mortar (Genesis 11:3 and Herodotus *Histories* (1.179)). We can never build Zion using their dark materials.

[5] There are five ifs and five thens in most English translations of 58:8–14. The Lord is determined to build Zion, but he is also determined to give us a meaningful role. How we respond to him genuinely affects the outcome.

streets and walls further into their city. The Lord promises, *"Your people will rebuild the ancient ruins and will raise up the age-old foundations; you will be called Repairer of Broken Walls, Restorer of Streets with Dwellings."*[6]

In 58:13–14, the Lord suddenly starts talking about Sabbath rest again. Those of us who are involved in urban transformation ministry know why. It can be seriously exhausting! It's as if the Lord wants to remind us here that we can never transform a community in our own strength. We can only do it through the same Gospel message by which we were forgiven from sin, freed from our old lives and strengthened in our weakness. Jesus was willing to be rejected by the people of Babylon when he was nailed to a cross outside the walls of Old Jerusalem. As a result, he was able to step out of the tomb and re-enter Jerusalem to transform it into Zion. Our success also rests in the way of death and resurrection, following in the footsteps of Jesus as we trust that all we have to do is be our new selves. All Zion has to do to transform Babylon is to be Zion within Babylon.

Listen to the echo of this chapter in Revelation 22 as the story of the Bible ends, not in the Garden of Eden, but in an urban expression of heaven planted in earth's soil.

> *Then the angel showed me the river of the water of life, as clear as crystal, flowing from the throne of God and of the Lamb down the middle of the great street of the city. On each side of the river stood the tree of life, bearing twelve crops of fruit, yielding its fruit every month. And the leaves of the tree are for the healing of the nations.*

---

[6] All of the promises in 58:8–14 are made to *you singular*. The Lord makes these promises to Zion.

Lousy Suckers (59:1–21)

Surely the arm of the Lord is not too short to save,
nor his ear too dull to hear. But your iniquities have
separated you from your God.

(Isaiah 59:1–2)

You know what it's like. You are hoovering your home when suddenly the hoover stops sucking. You jump to the conclusion that there must be something wrong with the machine. You start wondering what has happened to its motor. Then you suddenly notice that there is a kink in the hose. There is nothing wrong with the sucking of the hoover, but a kink in the hose is preventing any of its power from coming through.

Perhaps you can't identify with that at all. If not, then well done for the fact that you have clearly been successful at persuading someone else to do your hoovering for you. Nevertheless, you must have encountered this principle elsewhere, perhaps with a kink in your hosepipe while watering the garden or filling up a paddling pool.

The people of Judah were experiencing a similar problem with the power of God. The Lord inspires Isaiah to address it here in order to lay down **instruction #4: Zion is to be committed to living righteously**. Although Isaiah is prophesying to the citizens of Old Jerusalem, these words have also been recorded here for the people of the New Mount Zion. We often wonder why we are not seeing the level of breakthrough that God has promised us in terms of miracles, conversions, church planting and so on, so Isaiah gives us a very simple reply. He says that sin makes lousy suckers of us all.[1]

---

[1] The primary speaker in Isaiah 56–58 is the Lord. In 59:1–19 it is Isaiah. The Lord only speaks up in 59:20–21.

In 59:1-2, Isaiah puts his finger on the problem like an experienced hoover repairman. *"Surely the arm of the Lord is not too short to save, nor his ear too dull to hear. But your iniquities have separated you from your God; your sins have hidden his face from you, so that he will not hear."* Isaiah says that there is no mechanical problem. The arm of the Lord has not grown tired over time. The Messiah's ability to save is still just as strong as ever.[2] Nor has the Lord become as deaf as his people. We are looking in the wrong place for the problem if we start to doubt the sucking power of the hoover. The problem is a kink in the hose at our end. Our continued sinfulness blocks the power of God. The Lord only wants to empower us to serve him. He will not empower us to rebel against him![3]

In 59:3-15, Isaiah knows the people of Judah will try to resist this diagnosis, like a customer doubting the advice of a hoover repairman because it all sounds too simple. He quickly anticipates their rejoinder by listing some of their evil actions in 59:3-8: lies, blasphemy, lack of integrity, reliance on their own strength, injustice, violence and even murder.[4] There is not just one kink in their hoover hose. There are more knots in it than in a sailor's hanky.[5] Therefore he shows them in 59:9-11 what their sin is producing.[6] It is robbing them of the guidance and deliverance that ought to be the daily experience of Zion. Instead of the bright noonday sun which he promised them at midnight in 58:10, they are experiencing midnight darkness in

---

[2] The Hebrew word in 59:1 is actually *hand* rather than *arm*. It is translated this way to echo God's question to Moses in Numbers 11:23: literally, *"Has the arm of the Lord grown shorter?"*

[3] 58:4 and 9 warn us not to underestimate how important our own submission to God's authority is to our ability to wield his authority in the world.

[4] In the context of God commanding us in 40:29-31 to repent of wearing the clothing of our own weakness, it is very fitting that Isaiah should accuse us in 59:6 of trying to dress ourselves in cobwebs.

[5] Paul quotes from 59:7-8 in Romans 3:15-17 to demonstrate the universality of human sin.

[6] The Devil tries to dupe us into thinking that sinning has no further consequence for us as Christians. Isaiah points out that this is as foolish as thinking we can hatch a viper's eggs without being bitten.

the middle of the day.[7] Try as they like to deny it, they know he is right. The hoover is not working. In 59:12-15, Isaiah therefore leads them in a prayer of repentance which confesses that the result of their persistent sin is that *"justice is driven back, and righteousness stands at a distance."*[8]

Now for the good news in 59:15-19. Isaiah tells the people of Judah that the Gospel sanctifies (makes us righteous) as well as justifies (declares us righteous). *"The Lord looked and was displeased that there was no justice. He saw that there was no one, he was appalled that there was no one to intervene; so his own arm achieved salvation for him."* The Messiah does not just save us from our sins. He also saves us from ourselves. He justifies us when we believe he died and rose again instead of us, and he sanctifies us when we believe that we died and rose again with him. Jesus was not unique as a carpenter. Many people could fix furniture in Nazareth. But Jesus is totally unique as the Sanctifier. Only he could take our old nature to the cross and to the tomb and leave it there when he rose again. Therefore only he can teach us to say no to sin and yes to righteousness.[9] Only he can deal with the kink in the hose which prevents us from ministering to the full extent of heaven's power. He is the one who justifies us, sanctifies us, strengthens us and makes us fruitful. He saves us by faith from the very start to the very finish.[10]

If you know the writings of Paul, you will know that he explores this theme in quite some detail. He refers back to 59:17 in Romans 13:12 and 1 Thessalonians 5:8, promising that, if we put our trust in Jesus to sanctify us through his death and resurrection, he will enable us to put on his breastplate of righteousness and his helmet of salvation too. He refers

---

[7] 59:11 tells us that they feel the pain of this, yet they do not repent until Isaiah actually leads them in prayer.

[8] The word *tsedeq* and its associated words are used five times in this chapter.

[9] Romans 6:1-14; Galatians 2:19-20; Colossians 2:20-3:14; Titus 2:11-14.

[10] Romans 1:16-17. Paul explains all of this in much more detail. Romans 1-5 tells us how to be justified (59:1-15) and Romans 6-8 tells us how to be sanctified (59:15-21).

back to 59:17 again in Ephesians 6:13–18, expanding on the metaphor to describe our sanctification in terms of the armour of a Roman legionary. Paul tells us that there is a war on. The Devil wants to put a kink in the hose of our hoover by tempting us into persistent sin which prevents the power of heaven from working fully through us.

But Paul also tells us that we have a powerful ally. It's why the Lord takes over from Isaiah and finishes the chapter in 59:20–21.[11] The Lord promises that Jesus the Redeemer will come alongside the people of Zion and empower them by filling them with his Holy Spirit.[12] In words that are echoed later by Ezekiel 36:26–27, the Lord promises that the Holy Spirit will (I know it sounds obvious) make us holy. The Holy Spirit has the word "holy" written on his calling card. Making God's people holy is what he does. He comes and changes believers from the inside out so that they can work with God in power, as part of Zion, to change their cities from the inside out too.

So don't let the Devil turn you into a lousy sucker. Don't fall into pride, thinking you can achieve something on your own, but don't slip into despair either, thinking that God's power is for somebody other than you. There is nothing wrong with God's power. The arm of the Lord has not grown tired. He is simply waiting for you to submit to his authority so that he can use you fully to assert his authority throughout the world.

---

[11] Isaiah also mentions the Holy Spirit in 59:19, saying that *"the Spirit of the Lord"* puts our enemies to flight.

[12] Paul quotes 59:20–21 in Romans 11:26–27 as part of his confidence that God will save large numbers of Jews towards the end. In realizing that Zion means *more* than the Jews, don't assume it means *less* than the Jews.

Three Billion Cubic Miles
(60:1–22)

The least of you will become a thousand, the smallest a mighty nation.

(Isaiah 60:22)

There is a brilliant scene in the movie *Casino Royale*. James Bond is trying to bankrupt a terrorist financier named Le Chiffre in order to force him to play ball with the British government, so he goes head to head with him in a high-stakes poker game. Eventually, the two men have laid down over $100 million on the table in front of them – enough to bankrupt whichever man loses. Le Chiffre smirks arrogantly as he reveals that he has a full house. James Bond turns over his own hand to reveal a straight flush. James Bond has won. Le Chiffre gulps hard and looks very pale as he staggers from the table.[1]

That picture is a poor shadow of what happened when the Messiah fulfilled the fourth Servant Song. It was a high-stakes contest. The entire human race was on the table. The Devil looked at the weak and disfigured man from Nazareth and started crowing that he had won. He had finally succeeded where he failed in Isaiah 14:12–15. As Jesus gave up his spirit and was buried, all hell broke loose and started shouting.

But then the Devil heard a sudden stirring. The stone rolled away from the mouth of the tomb. God revealed his arm and played it as the mightiest trump card in history. The winner took it all and Satan was sent out of the room with nothing.

---

[1] *Casino Royale* (Metro-Goldwyn-Mayer, 2006).

That's what the Lord wants us to grasp in this chapter. He is excited about **instruction #5: Zion is to advance constantly and aggressively**.

Churches don't have a great track record of doing this. We are less like William Carey and more like the older man who tried to discourage him. We have forgotten that selfish ambition is sinful because it is selfish, not because it is ambition. We have not grasped what made Paul quote the fourth Servant Song in Romans 15:20–21 as the driving force behind his *"ambition to preach the gospel where Christ was not known"*. If Jesus has truly won as big a victory over Satan through his death and resurrection as Isaiah claims, it would be a sin for us not to be ambitious for his Kingdom. If General Patton could look at the German frontlines and tell his men that *"I don't want to get any messages saying, 'I am holding my position.' We are not holding anything! Let the Germans do that. We are advancing constantly and we're not interested in holding onto anything except the enemy,"* then how can the followers of Jesus settle for anything less?[2]

First, Isaiah points out in this chapter that Zion is more than a conqueror. She has not had to pay any of the price of victory, yet it is undoubtedly hers: *"Arise, shine, for your light has come, and the glory of the Lord rises upon you."*[3] Isaiah rattles off the names of some of the nations that now belong to her – people from Midian, Yemen, Arabia, Lebanon and distant islands such as Britain and Japan.[4] The Church's advance will

---

[2] Patton gave this speech several times from March to June 1944 in the run-up to D-day.

[3] The word for *you* throughout this chapter is a "feminine singular". God addresses these promises to Zion and to all those who are granted a share in her.

[4] *Ephah* was the oldest son of Midian (Genesis 25:4). Those who once chased Israel on camelback will now bring their camels as a tribute gift to Zion (9:4 and Judges 6:1–6). *Sheba* is modern-day Yemen. *Kedar* and *Nebaioth* were both sons of Ishmael in Arabia (42:11 and Genesis 25:13). Even Islam has been conquered.

be unstoppable because the manpower and money needed will come from each new nation that she conquers: *"Foreigners will rebuild your walls... Your gates will always stand open, they will never be shut, day or night, so that people may bring you the wealth of the nations."* Nobody who truly grasps the scope and scale of the Messiah's victory can ever lack ambition for Zion's progress. It is ignorance that keeps our plans small, not faith. Let's leave retrenchment to the Devil.

Second, Isaiah points out in this chapter that the forces of Satan are utterly defeated. Provided we learn the lesson of the hoover in the previous chapter, they stand no chance against us, *"for the nation or kingdom that will not serve you will perish; it will be utterly ruined."*[5] Twice Isaiah names God as *"the Holy One of Israel"*, so in the context of this chapter it is worth noting that the demons seem to particularly fear this name. When one demon saw Jesus it cried out *"Have you come to destroy us? I know who you are – the Holy One of God!"* An entire legion of demons cried out to him in panic, *"Have you come here to torture us before the appointed time?"* Those demons weren't being defeatist. They know full well that they have lost.[6] Their only hope is for us merely to skim read this chapter.

Third, Isaiah tells us that the population of Zion is going to be exceedingly huge. He ends the chapter with a promise that *"The least of you will become a thousand, the smallest a mighty nation."* Think about that carefully for a moment. He is saying that the person in your church with the scantiest understanding of the Gospel ought to expect to lead a thousand people to salvation, and that a very run-of-the-mill believer ought to see enough converts to fill a soccer stadium. We cannot downsize these promises because of our own weaknesses, because the

---

[5] Verse 21 says every citizen of Zion is *tsaddiq*, or *righteous*. None of us need fall for the old kinked-hoover trick.

[6] Matthew 8:29; Mark 1:24; Luke 4:34; 8:31; Revelation 12:12.

Lord says that their fulfilment rests primarily with him.[7] *"I am the Lord; in its time **I will do this** swiftly."*[8]

Isaiah does not tell us precisely how many people will be saved, so John Calvin concludes that *"Christ is much more powerful to save than Adam was to destroy... As the sin of Adam has destroyed many... the righteousness of Christ will be no less efficacious to save many."*[9] Charles Hodge speculates that *"The number of the saved shall doubtless greatly exceed the number of the lost... We have reason to believe that the lost shall bear to the saved no greater proportion than the inmates of a prison do to the mass of the community."*[10]

We don't have to speculate. Not only do we have the Lord's promise in this chapter that the nations will flock to *"the City of the Lord"* and that her very walls and gates will be named "Salvation" and "Praise", but we also have God-given commentary on this chapter in Revelation 21. John sees an angel with a measuring rod. *"He measured the city with the rod and found it to be 1,400 miles in length, and as wide and high as it is long."* Come again?! John tells us that Zion's size will be just shy of three billion cubic miles!

So let me ask you a question. What are you attempting for God, as an individual and as a church? Is it God-sized? Is it worthy of his victory over Satan when he revealed his mighty messianic trump card on the first Easter Sunday? Because it turns out that Isaiah wasn't even telling us the half of it when he said that we are going to need a bigger boat.

---

[7] God emphasizes the miraculous nature of our victory by saying literally in 60:16, *"You will drink milk from the breasts of kings"*!

[8] The Lord uses the same Hebrew word to describe Zion as a *shoot* in 60:21 that he used to describe the Messiah in 11:1. He also tells us that it is *"a shoot of my planting"*. Any church we plant is his church plant.

[9] John Calvin in his *Commentary on Romans* (1540).

[10] Charles Hodge in his *Commentary on Romans* (1835).

Wind of Change (61:1–11)

*The Spirit of the Sovereign Lord is on me, because
the Lord has anointed me to proclaim good news to
the poor.*

(Isaiah 61:1).

The first film in *The Matrix* trilogy was one of the greatest
science-fiction movies ever made. The second and third films in
the trilogy – well, the less said about either of them the better.
There are probably many reasons why the first film became an
instant cult classic and the other two films were panned by the
critics, but here is at least one of them: in the first film, Zion
was portrayed as something glorious, but in the second film we
finally see what it's like and it is a colossal disappointment.

The people of Zion are smiling, just as we were promised,
but it turns out that their smiles are drug-induced. Zion has
peddled them escapism instead of real escape. As we watch
them raving together in an underground cavern, hoping to
forget the fact that evil machines are attacking their city, we are
left wondering whether Zion is really worth saving after all. It
has cheated its people into fleeting fun instead of lasting joy.

Many people's experience of church can be like that,
smiling like a Cheshire cat but with all the power of a mouse.
That's why the Lord lays down **instruction #6: Zion is to be a
place where the Holy Spirit transforms lives**.

Jesus quoted the first few verses of Isaiah 61 in the
synagogue in Nazareth at the start of his ministry: *"The Spirit of
the Sovereign Lord is on me, because the Lord has anointed me to*

proclaim good news to the poor."[1] Jesus informed his startled neighbours that he was about to demonstrate what God can do through any weak human who is completely surrendered to him. He told the crowds that *"It is by the Spirit of God that I drive out demons."* Luke explains his ministry very simply: *"The power of the Lord was with Jesus to heal those who were ill."*[2] The Messiah's song in this chapter tells us that he is more than Zion's Saviour. He is also a flesh-and-blood demonstration of what he wants Zion to be.

In 61:1–3, the Messiah tells us that the Holy Spirit works an amazing turnaround in people's lives.[3] The Church is not to be a place of vacant smiles like the cavern in *The Matrix*. It is to be a place where deep and lasting transformation leads to deep and lasting joy. The Holy Spirit makes the poor rich because he empowers humble hearts to lay hold of the riches of heaven. He makes the broken-hearted joyful because the Spirit of God chases away a spirit of despair. He leads Satan's prisoners out of their dark dungeons and into the glorious light of the Gospel. He causes people to weep in the dust over their sin and then lifts them up to reign with Jesus forever.[4] When the Messiah declares that the whole of AD history is *"the year of the Lord's favour"* before the moment when he returns for *"the day of vengeance of our God"*, he is saying that the Holy Spirit will lead people into the freedom that was prophesied by the Jewish Year of Jubilee.[5]

---

[1] Luke 4:16–21. Since the Messiah speaks in 61:1–6, followed by two encores in 61:7–9 and 6:10–11, many regard this as the fifth Servant Song. However, unlike those four Songs, the word "servant" is not used here.

[2] Matthew 12:28; Luke 5:17. Luke 4:1 and 14 also emphasize that Jesus ministered as the perfect Spirit-filled man: *"Jesus, full of the Holy Spirit… was led by the Spirit… in the power of the Spirit."*

[3] The verb *māsach* in 61:1, meaning *to anoint*, is the root of the noun *Messiah*, meaning *Anointed One*.

[4] The Hebrew word *p'ēr* is used to refer to the bridegroom's headdress in 61:10 and to our headdresses in 61:3. Through the Gospel, we become as beautiful and honoured as the Church's Bridegroom, the Messiah.

[5] See Leviticus 25. The Hebrew phrase for *"proclaim freedom"* in 61:1 is fairly uncommon, but it is the same phrase that is used in Leviticus 25:10.

We should find this pretty challenging. Jesus is saying that he wants our churches to be known for their freedom in the Holy Spirit. We must not reduce our corporate experience of God's Spirit to the Christian equivalent of the empty raving in *The Matrix*. Lively worship is important, but Jesus warns us that he is less interested in the volume of our singing than he is in the volume of lives that are being changed.[6] It is not wrong for us to create mission statements for our churches, but they must fit into the one that Jesus has already given us: joy through pain, freedom through humility and power through weakness.[7]

In 61:4–6, the Messiah challenges us still further. He reminds us that it is not God's plan to bless believers who have no intention of blessing others. One of the biggest reasons why our churches fail to see the true power of the Gospel is that our hoover hose is kinked through our self-centredness. As soon as we gain the Messiah's perspective, we also gain the Messiah's power. God wants to fill churches with his Spirit so that they can *"rebuild the ancient ruins"* and *"renew the ruined cities"*. The Spirit of God wants to empower believers to transform communities ruined by the spirit of Babylon.[8]

In 61:7–9, God the Father sings an encore over his Son.[9] He promises to respond to the shame and disgrace of the cross by granting the Messiah a vast inheritance of believers all around the world. He promises to ensure that the New Covenant that the Messiah brokers between God and humankind through

---

[6] In reality, this produces much livelier worship anyway. Isaiah says literally in 61:10 that *"I am utterly overjoyed in the Lord; my soul shakes with excitement over my God."*

[7] The reference to *"oaks of righteousness"* in 61:3 links back to 60:22. Even the weakest are made strong.

[8] Verse 6 says these promises are given to all believers. See Romans 15:16; 1 Peter 2:9; Revelation 1:6.

[9] The Father phrases his encore as a clear endorsement of his Messiah's song. His first word in Hebrew is *tahat*, meaning *instead of*, which is the same word that the Messiah used three glorious times in 61:3.

his blood will be an everlasting covenant, which brings them everlasting joy.[10]

In 61:10–11, Isaiah sings his own encore. He bursts out in praise on behalf of all those Christ has redeemed. He celebrates the fact that, since the Messiah came in weakness and was stripped naked for us on the cross, we can now be clothed with the same clothes which the Messiah wore. We can wear his *"garments of salvation"* and his *"robe of righteousness"*.[11] In other words, we can stand sinless before God and ask him to give us everything: the joy that was in his heart when he declared the unfallen universe to be *"very good"*, and the power that he gave Jesus throughout his earthly ministry.

We get to do more than sing an encore to the Messiah's song at the end of this chapter. We get to live it out every day. Luke's gospel does not simply tell us that Jesus embodied the words of this chapter by ministering as a weak human filled with divine power. It also closes with Jesus' promise in Luke 24:49: *"I am going to send you what my Father has promised; but stay in the city until you have been clothed with power from on high."*[12]

Jesus sent his initial 120 followers into Old Jerusalem until the Holy Spirit fell on the Day of Pentecost and transformed them into Zion. If your church feels too much like Old Jerusalem, plead with God to do the same thing for you. He is waiting patiently because he longs to answer your prayer.

---

[10] The Jewish Law gave twice as much inheritance to the firstborn son as to his younger brothers (Deuteronomy 21:17). The Father promises to mark the Messiah out to the world as the object of his love.

[11] The Hebrew word for *righteousness* in 61:3 is *tsedeq*. In 61:10 and 11 it is *tsedāqāh*. See Zechariah 3:1–5.

[12] Jesus is very clear in John 7:37–39 and 20:21–22 that, like him, we are to be channels of God's Holy Spirit.

Make Some Noise
(62:1–12)

*For Zion's sake I will not keep silent, for Jerusalem's
sake I will not remain quiet.*

(Isaiah 62:1)

The nineteenth-century American evangelist D. L. Moody used
to claim that *"Every move of God can be traced back to a kneeling
figure."* Strictly speaking, that's not entirely true. Every move
of God begins with the figure of Jesus hanging on a cross. But
whenever people lay hold of that figure in prayer, what D. L.
Moody says is absolutely true.

Isaiah sang a song of praise at the end of the last chapter,
but celebration is no substitute for supplication. He begins this
chapter by making some noise. He says he cannot remain silent
while God's people fail to live in the fullness of all his promises.
Through Isaiah's noisy praying, the Lord lays down **instruction
#7: Zion is to pray big prayers**.

In 62:1, Isaiah teaches us how to see all of these promises
fulfilled in our churches: *"For Zion's sake I will not keep silent, for
Jerusalem's sake I will not remain quiet, till her vindication shines
out like the dawn, her salvation like a blazing torch."* This is why
the apostles refuse to get caught up in ministry programmes
in Acts 6:2–4. They grasp that the greatest gift any leader can
give their church is to pray for these promises to be fulfilled.
Church leaders ought to be those who see Zion more clearly
than those they lead, and those who lead the charge in prayer
for the eternal promises of Isaiah to be fulfilled in their own day.

In 62:2–5, Isaiah stirs us to pray by giving us a clear vision of what Zion ought to be. The reality is that most of us have grown used to the Church looking weak and feeble. That's why one of the first steps towards revival is studying these chapters until a great vision of Zion grips our souls. That's what happened when Augustine wrote *The City of God* after the fall of Rome to the Visigoths in 410 AD. He convinced a generation of believers that the Church ought to be far more glorious than Rome had ever been in its prime, and that they ought to pray and serve until she actually was. It's also what happened when Charles Spurgeon confronted the intelligentsia of Victorian England, warning them not to hark back to the pomp of medieval Roman Catholicism. He cried out, *"Rome stands on her seven hills and has never lacked a poet's tongue to sing her glories, but more glorious by far art thou, O Zion, among the eternal mountains of God!"*[1]

Isaiah therefore addresses Zion in these four verses and tries to stir our passion by prophesying over her.[2] He promises that God will give our churches a new name that carries power and authority.[3] He promises that God will turn the Church into his crowning glory, the object of his great delight and his beautiful Bride.[4]

In 62:6-7, Isaiah shows us that it is not enough for us to make noise like this on our own. He says that his prophecies aim to raise up many others like himself, and that together they play a vital role in Zion's warfare. They are like the watchmen who used to stand and guard the walls of Old Jerusalem. He therefore

---

[1] Charles Spurgeon commenting on Psalm 87, a great song about Zion, in his *Treasury of David* (1885).

[2] For grammar lovers, Isaiah addresses Zion with "feminine second person singular pronouns" throughout.

[3] Note the way that Revelation echoes many of these promises (2:17; 19:12; 21:2, 9–10). Hephzibah is Hebrew for *My Delight Is In Her*. Beulah is Hebrew for *Married*. Since King Manasseh's mother was named Hephzibah (2 Kings 21:1), 62:4 also offered him a very personal invitation back to faith in God.

[4] The Lord promised in 28:5 that he would be Zion's *crown*. Now he promises that she will also be his.

gives them their orders as the guardians of Zion: *"You who call on the Lord, give yourselves no rest, and give him no rest till he establishes Jerusalem and makes her the praise of the earth."*

The great church leaders of history have always called believers to the task of making noise together on the walls of Zion. The eighteenth-century hymn writer John Newton, who played a major role in galvanizing British Christians to fight for the abolition of the transatlantic slave trade, did more than simply point out from 61:1 that the Gospel ought to spell freedom on the plantations. He also taught them to sing a famous hymn:

> *Glorious things of thee are spoken, Zion, city of our God!*
> *He whose Word cannot be broken formed thee for His*
> *   own abode;*
> *On the Rock of Ages founded, what can shake thy sure*
> *   repose?*
> *With salvation's walls surrounded, thou mayst smile at*
> *   all thy foes.*
>
> *Saviour, if of Zion's city I through grace a member am,*
> *Let the world deride or pity, I will glory in Thy name;*
> *Fading is the worldling's pleasure, all his boasted pomp*
> *   and show;*
> *Solid joys and lasting treasure none but Zion's children*
> *   know.*[5]

In 62:8–12, Isaiah gives us a prayer list so that we can make some noise too. He does not assume that any of the marvellous prophecies he has spoken over Zion are automatic. He expects us to pray his words of prophecy back to God in the same way that Daniel prayed the words of Jeremiah concerning Zion in Daniel 9:1–3. Isaiah encourages us to pray for Gospel fruitfulness, for

---

[5] John Newton, "Glorious Things of Thee Are Spoken" (1779). Note the references to Isaiah 26:1, 26:4, 60:11–12 and 60:18, as well as to Psalm 87:3.

the nations to stream to salvation along God's holy highway[6] and for the imminent return of the Lord Jesus in power.[7] He urges us to pray until Zion's names become the daily experience of our churches: the *Holy People*, the *Redeemed of the Lord*, the *Ones Sought After* and the *City No Longer Deserted*.[8]

I live in the land of Charles Spurgeon and John Newton. Frankly, things are not going very well for Zion. In the four decades since I was born, church attendance has almost halved in Britain. By the time I can expect to die, the newspapers seem to agree that British Christianity will be all but wiped out entirely. Perhaps it is similar where you live. So how should we respond when the Church does not look very much like glorious Zion?

First, we should repent of our sin. Isaiah warns us in 62:4 that there will be times when the Church deserves to be named *Deserted* and *Desolate*. He wants us to recognize that 62:8–9 attributes this to the curse which God placed upon his disobedient people in the Jewish Law.[9] He encourages us to believe that the Messiah is able to fulfil these promises if we repent and believe. As John Newton puts it in his hymn, Isaiah calls us to believe that the Word of God cannot be broken. Then Isaiah tells us that we need to make some noise. For Zion's sake we must not keep silent. For the sake of the New Jerusalem we

---

[6] This is the final mention of both the "holy highway" and the "banner" motifs which we encountered in 11:10, 11:12, 11:16, 19:23, 35:8, 40:3–4, 49:22 and 57:14. We are to make it easy for people to see and come to Christ.

[7] Jesus strongly echoes the words of 62:11 in Revelation 22:12. The Final Judgment presents each one of us with a choice. We can either receive the reward of his perfect life or the recompense of our own sinful lives.

[8] The Hebrew word for *sanctuary* in 62:9 and *holy* in 62:12 is *qōdesh*. The one who is holy, holy, holy promises to make us holy and to admit us into his Holy Place. All we have to do is repent and believe.

[9] See Leviticus 26:16; Deuteronomy 28:33. Galatians 3:13–14 says that Jesus became this curse for us in order that we might be restored to fruitfulness when we repent.

must not keep quiet. Isaiah deputizes us as watchmen for our own day when he tells us:

> *You who call on the Lord, give yourselves no rest, and give him no rest till he establishes Jerusalem and makes her the praise of the earth.*

Far Sterner (63:1–6)

*I trampled the nations in my anger; in my wrath I made
them drunk and poured their blood on the ground.*

(Isaiah 63:6)

A year is a long time. It lasts for 365 days or 8,760 hours or
525,600 minutes or 31.5 million seconds. But then it comes to
an end. A year does not go on forever. Not even the year of the
Lord's favour.

Isaiah makes a sudden, crunching gear change in these six
verses. He stops describing the glories of Zion throughout AD
history (*"the year of the Lord's favour"* in 61:2), and he starts
describing the moment when the Messiah will suddenly return
to judge those who have chosen to side with Babylon instead of
Zion (*"the day of vengeance of our God"* in 61:2). You may find the
prophet's sudden change of tone jarring, but this is intentional. It
is meant to demonstrate that no one knows when the Messiah will
suddenly return. Even though Isaiah spoke very frankly about the
Messiah's Second Coming in 62:11, we are still surprised when
it happens only two verses later. These verses therefore mark
a turning point in the book of Isaiah. The prophet has begun to
move towards his grand finale. History will not go on forever.
He wants to use these final four chapters to remind us of his
message and to help us choose how we are going to respond.

These six verses warn us not to misunderstand the
Messiah. Isaiah begins with a startled question: *"Who is this
coming from Edom, from Bozrah, with his garments stained
crimson?"* This guessing game is anything but child's play. The
first-century Jews reaped disaster because they had a false view

of the Messiah and therefore rejected Jesus when he came. We do the same thing in our churches whenever we depict God the Father as the stern judge and Jesus as the loving Son who protects us from his angry Dad. It's no wonder that Steve Chalke responds to this misrepresentation of the Christian Gospel by labelling it *"a form of cosmic child abuse – a vengeful Father, punishing his Son for an offence he has not even committed"*.[1] But Steve Chalke has misunderstood the Gospel. Isaiah has already told us several times that God the Father is as much our Saviour as Jesus the Son. In these six verses he also tells us that Jesus is just as much our Judge as God the Father.[2] The Triune God is completely indivisible in his burning hatred towards human sin.

Except for the prophet's two startled questions, these six verses are spoken entirely by the Messiah. Isaiah 61:1–9 and 63:1–6 would be labelled the fifth and sixth Servant Songs were it not for the fact that the Hebrew word for "servant" is absent from both. They are as truly a description of the Messiah, so Isaiah warns us that we have misunderstood him unless we grasp that the Messiah's work of salvation involves judgment as well as forgiveness. John echoes this message when he describes Jesus in Revelation 19:11–16:

> *I saw heaven standing open and there before me was a white horse, whose rider is called Faithful and True. With justice he judges and wages war... He is dressed in a robe dipped in blood, and his name is the Word of God... He treads the winepress of the fury of the wrath of God Almighty. On his robe and on his thigh he has this name written: King of kings and Lord of lords.*

Jesus did not simply die to save us for the glorious things that Isaiah describes. He also died to save us *from* the terrible alternative. When we summarize the Gospel by quoting from

---

[1] Steve Chalke and Alan Mann in *The Lost Message of Jesus* (2003).
[2] 17:10; 43:3, 11; 45:15, 21; 49:26; 60:16. Paul also insists that Jesus is the Judge in Romans 2:16.

John 3:16, we tend to place the emphasis on the first half of the verse: *"God so loved the world that he gave his one and only Son,"* but this makes no sense without the second half of the verse: *"that whoever believes in him **shall not perish** but have eternal life".* We do not fully understand what the Messiah means by "salvation" until we grasp that he is both Saviour and Judge, both the orchestrator of the year of God's favour and the executioner of the day of God's judgment. Unless we accept the blood that he shed on the cross to deliver us from our sins, he will stain his clothing with our own blood when he comes to root out sin from the earth once and for all. That's a pretty sobering thought.

To help us grasp this, the Messiah returns to the same image he used in chapter 34. Edom was the inveterate enemy of Israel, so the Messiah uses it to represent everyone who refuses to become part of Zion.[3] The name Edom means *Red*, so the Messiah appears in clothing stained red with the blood of those who have rejected his blood sacrifice for their sin at Calvary.[4] The name of its capital city Bozrah means *Grape Harvest* and it was famous for its wine, so the Messiah declares he is the one who treads the winepress of God's judgment against sinful human rebels.[5] It is no use fooling ourselves that Jesus is too powerless to judge, since he tells us he is strong enough to judge the world single-handedly (note the echo of 59:16 in 63:5).[6] It is no use fooling ourselves that he is too compassionate to judge,

FAR STERNER (63:1–6)

245

[3] No nation was more persistently hostile towards ancient Israel than Edom. See Numbers 20:18; 1 Samuel 14:47; 1 Kings 11:14; Psalm 137:7; Lamentations 4:21–22; Malachi 1:2–4.

[4] In Hebrew, Isaiah asks the Messiah in 63:1–2 why his clothes are *'ādōm* on the way back from *'edōm*. Another pun is that the Hebrew words for *staining* and *redeeming* are the same in 63:3 and 63:4.

[5] The Old Testament often uses drunkenness from wine as a metaphor for God's judgment (29:9; 51:17; Psalm 60:3; 75:8; Jeremiah 25:15–16; Lamentations 4:21; Ezekiel 23:32–34; Habakkuk 2:16; Zechariah 12:2). Jesus also uses it to refer to his own willingness to bear this judgment for us on the cross (John 18:11).

[6] Jesus does not really need our help to judge sin in 63:5. He is simply looking for us to support him by praising him rather than criticizing him for his fierce hostility towards human sin.

since his resoluteness in the face of human sin is motivated by compassion![7] There can be no paradise on earth unless he first eradicates all trace of hell from the earth. The Messiah cannot be our Saviour unless he is resolute about acting as Judge. These six verses describe the Saviour of the world in all his glory.

Frankly, this is very good news. N. T. Wright reminds us that

> We have judged apartheid and found it wanting. We judge child-abusers and find them guilty. We judge genocide and find it outrageous. We have rediscovered what the Psalmists knew: that for God to "judge" the world meant that he would, in the end, put it all to rights, straighten it out, producing not just a sigh of relief all round but shouting for joy from the trees and the fields, the seas and the floods.[8]

The Messiah therefore expects us to worship him for his blood-stained clothing in these verses. He expects us to start singing this song of judgment with him.[9]

The year of God's favour has lasted a very long time, but don't let that fool you into thinking that the day of God's vengeance isn't fast approaching. Don't miss the sudden change of tone as we move into the final chapters of Isaiah, and don't delay in making your response to this book of prophecies. Isaiah warns us to make the right decision. God is far sterner than we think.

---

[7] 1 Thessalonians 1:10 says that Jesus will rescue us from God's righteous anger against sin if we receive him during this long period of God's favour. Isaiah 63:5 says that if we refuse to receive him, the Messiah's own righteous anger will stop him shrinking back from judging us on the Final Day.

[8] Tom Wright in *Surprised by Hope* (2007).

[9] Verse 1 actually says the Messiah is *"robed in splendour"* because his clothes are bloodstained. The Bible calls us to see God's judgment as a reason to worship him. See Psalm 97:8 and 119:119, and Revelation 18:20.

Far Holier (63:7–64:12)

*All of us have become like one who is unclean, and
all our righteous acts are like filthy rags.*

(Isaiah 64:6)

The English theologian A. W. Pink reflected in 1930 that

> *The wrath of God is as much a Divine perfection as is
> His faithfulness, power, or mercy... Indifference to sin
> is a moral blemish, and he who hates it not is a moral
> leper... How could He, who delights only in that which is
> pure and lovely, not loathe and hate that which is impure
> and vile? The very nature of God makes Hell as real a
> necessity, as imperatively and eternally requisite, as
> Heaven is... The wrath of God is His eternal detestation of
> all unrighteousness. It is the displeasure and indignation
> of Divine equity against evil. It is the holiness of God
> stirred into activity against sin.*[1]

Isaiah wants us to understand this. The great theme of his book
of prophecies is that God is *qādōsh*, holy, out-of-our-league, far
bigger than we think. Having echoed the message of chapters
13–35 in 63:1–6, Isaiah therefore echoes the message of chapters
1–12 in 63:7–64:12. He warns us that we must not think that
the coming of the Messiah will tone down God's fierce hatred
towards sin. If anything, it will make the vision that Isaiah had
of God's holiness in the Temple courtyard even more important
than ever.

---

[1] A. W. Pink in *The Attributes of God* (1930).

Most people read these verses so quickly that they miss what Isaiah is saying. Since the third Person of the Trinity is called *"the Holy Spirit"* over ninety times in the New Testament, they fail to spot that he is only given that name three times in the entire Old Testament – once in Psalm 51:11 and twice here, in 63:10 and 11. The Old Testament tends to call him *"the Spirit of God"* or *"the Spirit of the Lord"*, so Isaiah's double reference to him as *"the Holy Spirit"* is of enormous significance.[2] The more we grasp of God's greatness, the more we grasp that everything about him is holy. The more we experience his Spirit, the more he expects us to become holy ourselves.

The New Testament writers understood this. They warn us that the Messiah has not made God more tolerant towards our sin. He has saved us by taking our sin away from us and initiating us into the holiness of God. Paul rejoices over this by quoting at least twenty times from Isaiah in his letter to the Romans, warning us: *"Consider therefore the kindness and sternness of God: sternness to those who fell, but kindness to you, provided that you continue in his kindness. Otherwise, you also will be cut off."* The writer of Hebrews also explains in great detail how the Messiah has removed our sin, warning us that *"Anyone who rejected the law of Moses died without mercy on the testimony of two or three witnesses. How much more severely do you think someone deserves to be punished who has trampled the Son of God underfoot, who has treated as an unholy thing the blood of the covenant that sanctified them, and who has insulted the Spirit of grace?"*[3] We therefore need to read these verses slowly. Isaiah is warning us that God is far holier than we think and that we need to respond to him.

---

[2] By the time Jesus was born, the Jews had spotted this and had begun to talk about *"the Holy Spirit"*. Note the way that Paul deliberately echoes the words of 63:10 in Ephesians 4:30.

[3] Romans 11:22; Hebrews 10:28–29. These verses are not saying that we can lose our salvation. They are warning us that anyone who is truly saved will embrace God's holiness.

Isaiah uses the history of Israel to warn us of just how sinful we are. The Lord chose the Israelites to be his holy people and his true children (63:8). He became their Saviour and Redeemer, freeing them from slavery in Egypt (63:8–9). They responded by rebelling against him in the desert and turning their dearest Friend into their direst Foe (63:10).[4] Nevertheless, he forgave them and created an earthly extension to his heavenly throne room in the city of Jerusalem (63:15 and 18). He made Zion his holy mountain, Jerusalem his holy city and the other towns of Israel his sacred cities too (64:10). The Israelites responded by rebelling against him yet again, provoking him to demolish the extension to his holy throne room (64:11). The Temple was still standing in Jerusalem when Isaiah prophesied these words, but he spoke them for you and for me. He wants us to understand that the Messiah did not come to tell us that we no longer need to be holy. He came to reveal just how unholy we are.

Isaiah's book of prophecies is full of vivid metaphors, but none of them is as deliberately repulsive as the one he uses in 64:6. Egyptian women used tampons made of soft papyrus to absorb the blood flow during their periods. Jewish women used folded rags as sanitary towels. Isaiah has these in mind when he tells us literally that *"All of us have become like an unclean thing, and all our righteous acts are like menstrual rags."* If you find this picture disgusting, it shows you understand it. It is how God feels about human self-righteousness. The Jewish Law barred menstruating woman from God's presence, let alone their dirty menstrual rags.[5] God is far holier than we think.

Isaiah wants us to see that we can only become holy when we confess that our attempts at holiness are doomed to failure.

---

[4] Contrast this with God's amazing promise to Israel in 41:8–14. He is a wonderful friend but a terrible foe.

[5] Zechariah 3:3–4 uses another grotesque metaphor to describe our sinfulness. It homes in on one of the best behaved men in Israel and tells us that he is dressed in clothes that are covered in *excrement*.

The true benchmark of holiness is the Messiah that Luke 1:35 describes as *"the Holy One"*. A. W. Tozer reminds us that

> *We cannot grasp the true meaning of the divine holiness by thinking of someone or something very pure and then raising the concept to the highest degree we are capable of. God's holiness is not simply the best we know infinitely bettered. We know nothing like the divine holiness. It stands apart, unique, unapproachable, incomprehensible and unattainable. The natural man is blind to it. He may fear God's power and admire His wisdom, but His holiness he cannot even imagine.*[6]

We become holy when we look at Jesus and confess we need God's help to become like him.[7]

Isaiah reveals that the third Person of the Trinity is called the Holy Spirit because he is the answer to our prayer. Gritting our teeth and trying really hard will never sanctify us. We can only become holy by opening up our hearts to the Spirit of Holiness and inviting God to come and change us from the inside out. If we ask him, he will initiate us into his own holiness by making us the new earthly extension to his heavenly throne room. He will come and live inside us through his Holy Spirit every day.

The Holy Spirit helps us believe that we have died with Jesus, been buried with Jesus, been raised to life with Jesus and been taken up to heaven with Jesus to sit at God's right hand. Whenever the old nature that we inherited from Adam attempts to climb out of its coffin, like a zombie in a low-budget horror movie, the Holy Spirit reminds us that it is dead and that we now live by God's resurrection power. What the bloodied

---

[6] A. W. Tozer in *The Knowledge of the Holy* (1961).

[7] 64:5 tells us that God only helps those who remember the holy lifestyle of Jesus and who gladly embrace it themselves. The New Testament calls this *repentance*. It cannot be a reluctant decision, only a joyful one.

menstrual rags of our own effort could never achieve becomes ours through faith in the bloodied cross of Calvary. Do you want this? Then lay hold of it in prayer: *"You are in Christ Jesus, who has become for us wisdom from God – that is, our righteousness, holiness and redemption."*[8]

---

[8] 1 Corinthians 1:30. Paul is not simply saying that Jesus has become our justification (the one who *declares* us holy despite our sin), but that he has also become our sanctification (the one who *makes* us holy).

Far Stronger (63:7–64:12)

*No eye has seen any God besides you, who acts on
behalf of those who wait for him.*

(Isaiah 64:4)

Isaiah was a Jew. I know that's pretty obvious, but it's easy to
forget it when he starts to prophesy about a new and multiracial
Mount Zion. Isaiah never forgot it. He is the go-to prophet when
Paul wants to argue from the Old Testament in Romans 9–11
that God has not finished with his plans for Israel. As Isaiah
prophesies about the Day of Judgment in 63:1–6, he therefore
bursts out in anguished prayer for his countrymen in 63:7–
64:12. He pleads with God to spare the Jews from becoming
part of spiritual Edom. He asks God to use the Jewish nation to
show the world that he is far stronger than they think.

In 63:7–10, Isaiah reminds the Lord of his purposes for
Israel.[1] They didn't choose him. He chose them to be his people
and his children. He chose to become their Saviour and to take
their side against those who wanted to destroy them.[2] All they
brought to the relationship was their rebellion and sin, yet God
chose to intertwine the glory of his name with the fate and
fortunes of the Jewish nation. Isaiah reminds the Lord that
he has been glorified in the past by showing love towards the

---

[1] The Hebrew word *zākar* in 63:7 means *I will remember* or *I will make
memory of.* Isaiah teaches us to remind the Lord of his plans and purposes in
our prayers. This means understanding the Bible's overarching story.

[2] God chose to save the world even before he created it (Ephesians 1:4; 1
Peter 1:20; Revelation 13:8), but 63:8 tells us that he also chooses to *become*
Saviour to specific people at specific points in time.

undeserving people of Israel. He must not forget the Jews as he pours out his love on the Gentiles.

You don't have to be a believer to recognize that Isaiah's prayer has been answered. Mark Twain believed that the Bible contained *"upwards of a thousand lies,"* yet even he was forced to marvel that *"Properly, the Jew ought hardly to be heard of, but he is heard of, has always been heard of... His importance is extravagantly out of proportion to the smallness of his bulk... All things are mortal but the Jew; all other forces pass, but he remains. What is the secret of his immortality?"*[3] Isaiah tells us the secret. God still cares very deeply for the Jewish nation. *"In all their distress he too was distressed, and the angel of his presence saved them."*[4]

In 63:11–14, Isaiah tells the Lord that he and the other faithful Jews are wondering where he is for them.[5] They are on the brink of exile and are about to spend seventy long years in Babylon. Why did the Lord prophesy about his *"glorious arm of power"* if he doesn't plan to use it for his people? Why did he talk about his zeal for the glory of his name if he doesn't plan to glorify his name through them as at the Exodus?[6] Isaiah prophesies that, even after their return from exile, the Jewish people will have to wait a long time for the Messiah to come and

---

[3] These two quotes come from his essays *Letters from the Earth* (c.1909) and "Concerning the Jews" (1897).

[4] Isaiah is talking about Jewish history, but this is also a wonderful general promise. If we grieve for others in the body of Christ (1 Corinthians 12:26; Romans 12:15), we can be sure that Christ grieves even more (Colossians 2:19)! 63:9 can be translated as, *"It was no envoy or angel but his own presence that saved them."*

[5] Isaiah uses the same Hebrew word *zākar* in 63:11 that he used in 63:7. It can either be translated as a statement that *his people recalled* their history, or as a prayer – *may God recall* their history.

[6] Isaiah argues in 63:14 that God is far more glorified by reviving his people than he is by disciplining them. We are to make this the basis for our own confident prayers for revival today.

for the age of the Holy Spirit to begin.[7] If you are struggling with unanswered prayer right now, Isaiah says he knows exactly how you feel.

In 63:15–18, Isaiah reminds the Lord of *his character*: his jealousy, his strength, his tenderness and his compassion (63:15).[8] He reminds the Lord of *his name*: even if Abraham and Jacob were to disown the Jews as their children, the Lord would not cease to be their Father (63:16). He reminds the Lord of *his purposes*: he chose the Jewish nation and not the other way around, so it is time for him to reclaim his sovereign inheritance (63:17). He reminds the Lord of *his history* with Israel: the ruins of Jerusalem are still the place of his former sanctuary (63:18). He reminds the Lord of *his passion to make his name known*: the triumph of the pagans over Jerusalem makes the whole world assume that the God of Israel must be weak and worthless (63:18–19).[9] Isaiah models for us how we are to pray. God is far more eager to respond to our prayers than we can ever imagine.

In 64:1–7, Isaiah therefore begs the Lord to tear open heaven and come down to earth to save his people.[10] He echoes the message of chapters 40–55 when he says that *"Since ancient times no one has heard, no ear has perceived, no eye has seen any God besides you, who acts on behalf of those who wait for him."*[11]

---

[7] The Exodus saw a glorious combination of God's anointed leader (Moses), God's active presence (the pillar of cloud) and God's mighty arm (miracles). We need to ask for all three of these things in the Church today.

[8] Although Isaiah is praying for the entire Jewish nation, he tells the Lord literally in 63:15 that the Lord's character has been withheld *"from **me**"*. Our personal pleas can stir God to save an entire nation.

[9] This is such a powerful argument that it is also used in similar prayers in 64:11–12 and Psalm 74:3–11.

[10] In 63:15, Isaiah merely asked for God to *"look down"*. As he prays he grows in passion and pleads in 64:1 for God to *"come down"*. If you feel no passion to pray, start praying. Then passion will come.

[11] Although the Hebrew word for *waiting* is not the same in 40:31 and 64:4, Isaiah is clearly attempting to cash in the promise which God gave us regarding supernatural strength in 40:29–31.

When Paul quotes this verse in 1 Corinthians 2:9, he equates *waiting for* God with *loving* God, because this is an amazing statement about our relationship with him. Idols attempt to gain glory for themselves by attracting an army of cringing slaves, but the real God is so strong he has no need of any help from us. He is looking for an army of weak worshippers who are humble enough to wait for him to act on their behalf by strengthening them with his power. God is never more glorified than when he displays his glorious divine strength in our inglorious human weakness. Jesus echoes this when he tells us in Mark 10:45 that *"the Son of Man did not come to be served, but to serve."* Only the God of Israel is strong enough to be glorified by taking the role of the lowliest servant to demonstrate that he is the greatest King.

In 64:8–12, Isaiah therefore ends his prayer in abject humility. The first two sections of his prayer began with a reminder; the third and fourth sections began with a request to look down or come down; this fifth section simply begins with surrender: *"Yet you, Lord, are our Father."* Isaiah confesses that the Lord is the Creator and that the Israelites are mere creatures (64:8).[12] He confesses that the Lord is the Judge and that the Israelites are sinners (64:9). He confesses that everything Israel once treasured – even Mount Zion and Jerusalem and the Temple which was their crowning glory – is merely a charred heap of ruins (64:10–12). He has given up entirely on impressing God with Israel's virtues. He confesses Israel's weakness and rests his hope on God's strength alone.

Isaiah's prayer was answered. The Jewish exiles were sent home by Cyrus after seventy years in Babylon. Five hundred years after that, the promised Messiah was born to Israel. Although the Jewish leaders rejected Jesus, such a large number of Jews were saved during the first century that the leader of the

---

[12] This is the third time Isaiah has used this metaphor of a potter and his clay. See 29:16 and 45:9.

church in Jerusalem exclaimed excitedly to Paul in Acts 21:20: *"You see, brother, how many thousands of Jews have believed."*

Even today, we can still expect Isaiah's prayer to be answered. Even though G. K. Chesterton marvelled, *"How odd of God to choose the Jews"*, these verses give us faith to tell our Jewish friends that Jesus is their Messiah. They make us reword Leo Rosten's famous reply: *"But not so odd as those who choose a Jewish God yet have no hope for the Jews."*

Far Closer (65:1–25)

Before they call I will answer; while they are still speaking I will hear.

(Isaiah 65:24)

Some people misunderstand what Isaiah says as he prays for the Jewish nation. Since he tells us in 64:4 that God *"acts on behalf of those who wait for him"*, some people assume that he is saying God does nothing in the world except in response to our prayers. Thankfully, that isn't true. If it were, then prayer would become a righteous act of our own, and all our righteous acts are like bloodied menstrual rags. Isaiah clarified in 64:3 that God always loves to do the unexpected. Now, as the Lord responds to Isaiah's prayer in chapter 65, he clarifies still further that he is always the prime mover and never us as we pray. Salvation never depends upon us. God is far closer than we think.

In 65:1, the Lord responds to Isaiah's prayer by telling him that he is going to save many Gentiles from every nation of the world.[1] It does not matter that most unchurched people are neither seeking God nor even vaguely interested in Christianity. The Lord did not need any help from our end to create us and neither does he need help from our end to save us. We tend to imagine that it is very difficult to see an out-and-out unbeliever saved, but Watchman Nee reminds us why it is very easy:

---

[1] If you find the opening two verses of Isaiah 65 confusing, read their God-given commentary in Romans 10:20–21. Paul quotes both verses, explaining that 65:1 refers to the Gentiles and 65:2 to the Jews.

*I always believe that the Holy Spirit is **upon** a man when I preach to him. I do not mean to say that the Spirit is **within** the hearts of unbelievers, but that He is outside. What is He doing? He is waiting, waiting to bring Christ into their hearts. The Holy Spirit is waiting to enter the heart of the hearer of the Gospel. He is like the light. Open the window-shutters even a little, and it will flood in and illumine the interior. Let there be but a cry from the heart to God, and **at that moment** the Spirit will enter and begin His transforming work of conviction and repentance and faith – the miracle of new birth... Perhaps the biggest condition of success in bringing men to Christ is to remember that the same Holy Spirit, who came to our help in the hour of darkness, is at hand waiting to enter and illumine their hearts also, and to make good the work of salvation to which, in crying to God, they have opened the door.*[2]

Since Isaiah 49:6 tells us that God has made his Messiah *"a light for the Gentiles"*, we should not imagine that seeing non-Jews saved is a difficult task. We don't have to drag salvation down reluctantly from heaven. The light of salvation is waiting to flood through any slight movement in the window-shutters. God is far closer than we think.

In 65:2–16, the Lord responds to Isaiah's prayer by telling him that he is also going to save a remnant of believing Jews. Yes, many of them will prove too obstinate to allow any movement in their window-shutters.[3] Yes, many Jews will use their synagogue devotion as a mask for inward impurity and

---

[2] Watchman Nee in *What Shall This Man Do?* (1961).

[3] In 64:12, Isaiah accused the Lord of giving the Jews the silent treatment. In 65:2, the Lord replies that he was never silent. The Jews had simply stopped listening. The same is often true of us today.

rebellion against the Lord.[4] Yes, many Jews will talk much about Zionism while caring little for God's New Mount Zion.[5] Yes, many Jews will become part of spiritual Edom and will be caught up in the slaughter of God's judgment.[6] But no, this does not mean that God has finished with the Jewish nation. The Lord will answer Isaiah's prayer by saving many Jews. He will make beautiful wine out of the discarded grapes of the vineyard of Israel (65:8). The God who chose Jacob and Judah will choose many of their descendants to become part of the New Mount Zion (65:9).[7] In the Valley of Achor, where an Israelite chose Babylon instead of Yahweh and was cut off from God's people, many Israelites will seek Yahweh instead of Babylon (65:10).[8] God's judgment on the Jewish nation does not mean that he is finished with them. It will result in the final salvation of many Jews (65:16).[9]

That's why, in 65:17–25, the Lord is able to prophesy that he will answer Isaiah's prayer beyond his wildest imaginings. He will not merely bring the Jewish exiles back to the Promised Land. When the Messiah comes a second time to judge the world, he will turn the entire earth into a new and better Promised

[4] In 65:2, God describes their religious devotion as *"their own imaginations"*. They are like the worshippers at the high places of Judah, pious outwardly but thoroughly unkosher inwardly. The King James Version translates 65:5 as *"I am holier than thou"*, which has become proverbial for smug religious hypocrisy.

[5] *"The mountains"* and *"the hills"* in 65:7 are meant to stand in contrast to *"my holy mountain"* in 65:11.

[6] The words used for *Fortune* and *Destiny* in 65:11 are *Gad* and *Menī*, the Babylonian gods of Chance and Fate. The Lord therefore makes a pun in 65:12 when he says *mānīthī*, meaning *I have made your fate* the sword.

[7] *"My mountains"* in 65:9 is meant to hint that the New Mount Zion is far greater than a single geographical mountain. Verse 9 tells us literally that God will raise up *"a seed"* from Jacob and *"an heir"* from Judah, who will enable *"my chosen ones"* and *"my servants"* to inherit the land. These Jews will be saved through Jesus.

[8] Achor was another name for Achan. See Joshua 7:24–26; Hosea 2:15.

[9] Twice in 65:16 the Lord calls himself the *'elōhēy 'āmēn*, meaning the *God of Truth* or the *God of Amen*. There is no doubt that he will fulfil these promises. This verse is echoed in 2 Corinthians 1:20 and Revelation 3:14.

Land (65:17). The Gospel is not the promise of an airlift to heaven. It is the promise that heaven will come down to earth and that God will fuse the two together to become our eternal home.[10] Revelation 21–22 describes this new heaven and new earth as the New Jerusalem. It will be infinitely greater than its predecessor, since it will know no sadness, loss or fruitlessness (65:18–23).[11] It will be a place where God dwells with his people so intimately that their prayers are answered before they can even pray them (65:24). The enemies whose names crowd the pages of Isaiah will be no more (65:25).[12]

So don't imagine that prayer is laying hold of a reluctant God. If Isaiah's prayer for the rubble of the Old Mount Zion was answered with promises about *"my holy mountain"*, what better answers ought we to expect to our own prayers for the Church to flourish in every nation of the world? Paul models for us at the end of Ephesians 3 how this chapter teaches us to pray to the God who is far closer than we think:

> *I pray that you may have power, together with all the Lord's holy people, to grasp how wide and long and high and deep is the love of Christ... Now to him who is able to do **immeasurably more than all we ask or imagine**, according to his power that is at work within us, to him be glory in the church and in Christ Jesus throughout all generations, for ever and ever! Amen.*

---

[10] Verses 16–17 are not telling us that we will forget world history when it ends, but that its pain will be swallowed up by the joys of the new world. That's the tragedy when Christians obsess about 8,000 square miles of land in the Middle East. God has something far better in mind for his people.

[11] This has to be talking about the New Jerusalem rather than the Old Jerusalem after the exile. Verse 17 is quoted in Revelation 21:1 and verse 19 is echoed in Revelation 21:4. The new heavens and new earth are also described in Matthew 19:28, Romans 8:19–22 and 2 Peter 3:10–13.

[12] Verse 24 is a deliberate reply to Isaiah's plea in 64:12. See Daniel 9:20–23 and 10:12. The snake in 65:25 represents Satan. He will have no share in the new creation. He will be destroyed (Revelation 20:2, 10).

Final Decision (66:1–24)

These are the ones I look on with favour: those who are humble and contrite in spirit, and who tremble at my word.

(Isaiah 66:2)

Isaiah has given us plenty of warning throughout these final chapters that we have an urgent decision to make before we are ready to put down his book of prophecies. He has warned us that we are still in *"the year of the Lord's favour"* and that *"the day of vengeance"* is fast approaching. We do not have an eternity to decide how we are going to spend eternity. Isaiah has warned us that many Jews will be counted as "Edom" and that many Gentiles will be counted as "Israel" when the Messiah suddenly returns. He put the choice starkly in chapter 65: *"**My servants** will eat, **but you** will go hungry; **my servants** will drink, **but you** will go thirsty; **my servants** will rejoice, **but you** will be put to shame. **My servants** will sing out of the joy of their hearts, **but you** will cry out from anguish of heart."* As we reach the last page of his book, Isaiah pleads with us to make the right final decision.

In 66:1–4, the Lord warns that the return of the Jewish exiles from Babylon was a mere sideshow compared to the eternal decision that is taking place in your own heart right now. Stephen quotes these words while standing on trial for his life in Acts 7:48–50, warning the chief priests in Jerusalem that God is far bigger than they think. The man-made Temple that was completed on Mount Zion after the return from exile was merely a picture of the true and better Temple that Jesus embodied throughout his earthly ministry and that he now wants to embody in his Church.[1] The sacrificial blood of bulls and lambs in the Temple courtyard was simply a pointer to the cross of Jesus, which enables us to become the dwelling-place of God.[2] The Lord invited us to make a choice back in 57:15: *"I live in a high and holy place, but also with the one who is contrite and lowly in spirit."* Now he repeats the same invitation in 66:2: *"These are the ones I look on with favour: those who are humble and contrite in spirit, and who tremble at my word."*[3]

This decision is momentous. The Lord is offering to come and fill us with his Holy Spirit, turning our weak bodies into a far better Temple than the one which the returning Jewish exiles built on Old Mount Zion. If we reject this offer, the Lord is also warning us that we will reap far greater judgment than the Temple when it fell to the Babylonians.

In 66:5–6, the Lord presses home our need to make the right decision. Will we tremble at Isaiah's prophecies as the Word of God or will we simply treat them as a matter of opinion? Christian leaders talk little today about fearing God and trembling at his Word. We are far more inclined to sit in judgment over the Scriptures than we are to allow them to sit in judgment over us. Nevertheless, A. W. Tozer warns us that *"The greatness of God rouses fear within us, but His goodness encourages us not to be afraid of Him. To fear and not be afraid*

---

[1] See John 2:19–22; 1 Corinthians 3:16–17; 6:19; 2 Corinthians 6:16; Ephesians 2:19–22; 1 Peter 2:4–10. Ancient thrones had footstools (2 Chronicles 9:18) and the Jews viewed their Temple as the earthly footstool of God's heavenly throne (Psalm 132:7). The Lord corrects them in 66:1. The entire earth is now his footstool.

[2] There is a beautiful symmetry to the book of Isaiah. Verse 3 mirrors the Lord's strong words in 1:11–14. Unless Temple sacrifices were offered with humble and contrite hearts, they did not please God. They insulted him.

[3] Isaiah pleaded with the Lord in 64:9–11 to *nābat*, or *look upon*, his ruined Temple in Jerusalem. The Lord promises in 66:2 that he will *nābat*, or *look upon*, a far better New Covenant Temple.

– *that is the paradox of faith.*"[4] To emphasize the importance of this final decision, the Lord says something shocking. If the Jews do not respond to this book of prophecies after their return from exile, their Temple will be destroyed once again.[5]

In 66:7–11, the Lord becomes more positive. Instead of emphasizing all the bad things that will befall us if we make the wrong final decision, he begins to emphasize all the good things that will be given us if we make the right one. The fall of the Old Mount Zion was swift and unexpected in 586 BC and 70 AD, but so too is the establishment of the New Mount Zion. Like the day when King Cyrus arose to signal the return of the Jewish exiles in 539 BC, King Jesus will return swiftly and unexpectedly on the clouds of heaven to end world history. The birth of a child takes nine months from conception to delivery, but the New Jerusalem will come down from heaven in a single day.

When people truly believe the promises in the bo(k of Isaiah, they also find that spiritual revival suddenly con   to the Church. God wants us to grieve like Isaiah over the r   of the Church today so that he can cause us to rejoice over her restoration tomorrow. The New Jerusalem was pictured suckling milk from the nations in 60:16, and now that prophecy is fulfilled. She suckles converts from every nation in 66:11. Whatever is stopping you from surrendering your life completely to Jesus as you end the book of Isaiah, the Lord wants you to know that it is nothing compared to what you will lose if you say no to his glorious plans for the people of the New Mount Zion.

In 66:12–24, the Lord therefore lays out your choice in the starkest of terms. If you express your humility and contrition by trembling over the fact that God speaks these prophecies over you, he will come and dwell inside you through his Holy Spirit. He will grant you peace like a river, power like a stream

---

[4] A. W. Tozer in *The Knowledge of the Holy* (1961).

[5] The Romans destroyed the Second Temple in 70 AD. It is possible that the Lord is talking about the destruction of the First Temple in 66:6, but it is more likely a threat of further destruction yet to come.

in flood, comfort like a child,[6] growth like grass and a personal experience of his mighty hand. However, if you express your pride by sitting in judgment over God's Word, the Lord will come and judge you.[7] You have almost reached the end of this book. The Lord says it is time for your final decision.

God has given us a sign that these prophecies are real by judging the Jewish nation (66:17 echoes 65:3–5) and by saving people from every Gentile nation (66:18). He has given us a sign by using a scattered band of Jews to preach to the world that Jesus is the Messiah, and by using their testimony to make many Gentiles part of his New Mount Zion (66:19–21).[8] He has given us a sign by preventing the Jewish nation from being destroyed (66:22) and by bringing together people from every part of the human race to worship the God of Israel (66:23).[9] These signs should inform your final decision. The Messiah is about to return to throw those who reject him into hell (66:24) so that the new heavens and the new earth can be established for God's people (66:22).[10]

Jesus quotes from the final verse of Isaiah to describe hell as *Gehenna*, the valley outside Jerusalem where the Jews

---

[6] The Lord has revealed himself to us as God the Father, but he emphasizes his compassion several times in Isaiah by likening his love to that of a mother with her child (42:14; 49:15; 66:13).

[7] Verse 16 insists that God's judgment will come on *all flesh*. Don't fool yourself that you are exempt. It will either be borne by Jesus in your place or you will have to bear it yourself.

[8] The places listed represent the entire earth for an ancient Jew. *Tarshish* in Spain and the *distant islands* were the far west. *Tubal* on the Black Sea was the far north. *Libya*, *Lydia* and *Greece* were the lands in between.

[9] Paul echoes 66:20 when he tells us in Romans 15:16 that God has given him *"the priestly duty of proclaiming the gospel of God, so that the Gentiles might become an offering acceptable to God"*. 66:21 tells us that many of these Gentile converts will become church leaders too. Some will have a similar ministry towards the Jews.

[10] Note again the symmetry of the book of Isaiah. It began with the Old Jerusalem and the old heavens and earth (1:1–2). It ends with the New Jerusalem and the new heavens and earth (66:20–24).

slaughtered by the Babylonians were left to burn or to be eaten by maggots.[11] Isaiah's book of prophecies ends with the horrors of hell, because this will be the fate of anyone who makes the wrong final decision.

Isaiah has offered you heaven or hell, salvation or damnation, the glories of God's new creation or the destruction of the old. So don't make the wrong choice. Tremble at the Lord's words throughout Isaiah. God is waiting for your final decision.

---

[11] Mark 9:44, 46, 48. Part of this valley was named Topheth, which Isaiah used as a picture of hell in 30:33. For a description of what happened there, see Jeremiah 7:32–33 and 19:1–15. *Fire* is also used to describe God's judgment in 1:31, 9:19, 10:17, 26:11, 33:11–14, 34:9–10 and 66:15–16.

Conclusion: God is Bigger Than You Think

I… am about to come and gather the people of all nations and languages, and they will come and see my glory.

(Isaiah 66:18)

In 5 BC it finally happened. Isaiah's prophecies about the Messiah started coming true.[1]

At the start of the year, an angel suddenly appeared to a young virgin named Mary to fulfil the prophecy in Isaiah 7:14. The angel told her that she would conceive a son by the power of the Holy Spirit and give birth while still a virgin. Her child would be the second Person of the Trinity – *Immanuel*, meaning *God With Us* – but he would also have another name. Like the name *Isaiah*, he would be given a name which meant *The Lord Saves*.[2] The long-awaited Messiah was conceived, as prophesied, in a virgin's womb.

Mary was descended from the royal line of David, fulfilling the prophecy in Isaiah 11:1. This meant that she was forced to travel south to register for a Roman census in David's town of Bethlehem. The sudden birth of her baby while she was there

---

[1] Confusingly, there was no year 0 AD. 1 BC led straight into 1 AD. Even more confusingly, the people who built the modern calendar around the year of Jesus' birth misjudged it by four years.

[2] Although they look very different in English, the Hebrew names *Isaiah* and *Yeshua* are similar. They are both a combination of the two words *yāsha'* (to save) and *Yāh* (the Lord).

fulfilled the prophecy in Isaiah 66:7.[1] When she travelled back north to her own hometown of Nazareth, she fulfilled the prophecy in Isaiah 9:1–7 that the Messiah would be a Galilean. While she brought him up as the supposed son of a carpenter in nowheresville, she fulfilled the prophecy about his apprenticeship in obscurity in Isaiah 49:1–2.

Finally the day arrived in 27 AD. The Lord took his thirty-year-old Messiah out of his quiver and fired him into the bull's-eye of the Jewish nation. The rugged prophet John the Baptist had been fulfilling the words of Isaiah 40:3–5 by baptizing crowds of Jews in order to prepare them for the arrival of their Messiah. Jesus went to him, fulfilling the prophecy in Isaiah 50:5 by ignoring John's attempts to talk him out of being baptized alongside them. As he came up out of the water, the prophecies in Isaiah 42:1 and 61:1–3 were fulfilled. God the Father anointed Jesus with his Holy Spirit and with power.

This marked the beginning of the three most important years in the history of the Jewish nation. Jesus fulfilled the prophecies in Isaiah 40:29–31 and 57:15 by choosing to share his life with a dozen weak and lowly disciples. He fulfilled the prophecy in Isaiah 42:3 by extending love to the damaged and the hurting. He fulfilled the prophecy in Isaiah 35:5–6 by healing the blind, the deaf, the mute and the lame. He fulfilled the prophecies in Isaiah 11:10 and 49:6 by attracting many converts among the Gentiles, but he also embodied the message of the second section of Isaiah by the way in which he confronted the Jews. Whenever Jesus came into contact with the chief priests and rabbis, he revealed that God was holier and sterner and stronger than they thought.

When eventually this led to his arrest and crucifixion during the Passover of 30 AD, a host of Isaiah's prophecies were fulfilled. Jesus refused to argue his way out of trouble (53:7),

---

[1] 66:7 does not simply predict the birth of a baby to Judah. It predicts the sudden birth of *zākār*, or *man-child*.

willingly offering his back to those who whipped him and his cheeks to those who beat and spat on him (50:6). He was pierced through his hands and feet when he was crucified between two robbers (53:5 and 12). His cruel torture disfigured him beyond human likeness (52:14) and he was so thoroughly deserted by his friends that his death appeared to be in vain and all for nothing (49:4). After he died, he was laid in a rich man's tomb and his body was left to rot (53:9).

The message of Isaiah was being fulfilled, but still the Devil must have thought that he had won. He hadn't read the prophecies thoroughly enough. Three days after the crucifixion, God fulfilled the words of Isaiah 53:10–12 by breathing life into the corpse of Jesus. The strength of God in human weakness proved more than a match for the demon armies of hell. The cross proved that God is far holier and sterner than we think, and the resurrection proved that he is also far stronger. Ten days after Jesus ascended to heaven, on the Day of Pentecost, God proved that he is far closer than we think by pouring out the promised Holy Spirit on all his people. He turned his ragged followers into his new Temple and his new Mount Zion. The Devil has never recovered. Everything Isaiah prophesied from chapter 54 onwards about the glory of the New Jerusalem is being fulfilled.

So as we end our journey through the book of Isaiah, let's surrender our lives completely to Jesus as our Lord and Master. Paul warns us in Acts 17:30–31 that *"He commands all people everywhere to repent. For he has set a day when he will judge the world with justice by the man he has appointed. He has given proof of this to everyone by raising him from the dead."* Let's also be humble and contrite and thirsty for the Holy Spirit to come and live inside us. Let's pray the promises of 40:29–31, 57:15 and 66:1–2 back to God by asking him to turn us into his new and better Temple. Let's get ready to play our part in God's great plan to save multitudes of people from every nation of the world.

Let's express our love for God by pouring out our lives to pray for Zion, to build up Zion and to announce to the world that Zion is a foretaste of the age to come. Let's express our love for him by rejecting the individualism of our culture and devoting ourselves to being living stones together in God's new city. Let's respond to the wake-up call of 52:1: *"Awake, awake, Zion, clothe yourself with strength! Put on your garments of splendour, Jerusalem, the holy city."*

Let's step into Isaiah's shoes. Let's be transformed by what we have seen in this book of prophecies with regard to God's holiness, God's severity, God's strength and God's closeness. Let's respond to God like the prophet in the Temple courtyard in Isaiah 6: *"Woe to me! I am ruined! For I am a man of unclean lips, and I live among a people of unclean lips, and my eyes have seen the King, the Lord Almighty."* Let's surrender our lives to his agenda for the world: *"Here am I. Send me."* Let's proclaim to a world that has largely forgotten God that he is far bigger than they think. Let's put down our books and let's start fulfilling Isaiah 52:7 together every day:

> *How beautiful on the mountains are the feet of those who bring good news, who proclaim peace, who bring good tidings, who proclaim salvation, who say to Zion, "Your God reigns!"*

STRAIGHT TO THE HEART SERIES

TITLES AVAILABLE: OLD TESTAMENT

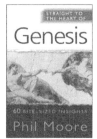

ISBN 978 0 85721 001 2

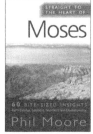

ISBN 978 0 85721 056 2

ISBN 978 0 85721 252 8

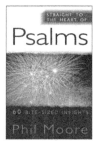

ISBN 978 0 85721 428 7

ISBN 978 0 85721 426 3

ISBN 978 0 85721 754 7

STRAIGHT TO THE HEART SERIES

TITLES AVAILABLE: NEW TESTAMENT

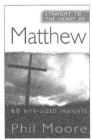

ISBN 978 1 85424 988 3

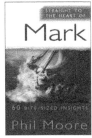

ISBN 978 0 85721 642 7

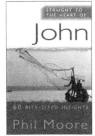

ISBN 978 0 85721 253 5

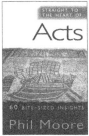

ISBN 978 1 85424 989 0

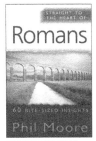

ISBN 978 0 85721 057 9

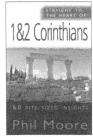

ISBN 978 0 85721 002 9

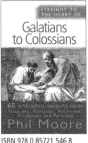

ISBN 978 0 85721 546 8

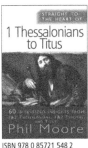

ISBN 978 0 85721 548 2

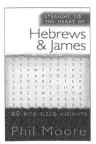

ISBN 978 0 85721 668 7

ISBN 978 0 85721 756 1

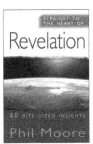

ISBN 978 1 85424 990 6

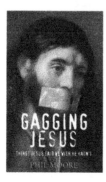

GAGGING JESUS
Things Jesus Said We Wish He Hadn't
Phil Moore

If you ever suspected that Jesus wasn't crucified for acting like a polite vicar in a pair of socks and sandals, then this book is for you. Fasten your seatbelt and get ready to discover the real Jesus in all his outrageous, ungagged glory.

ISBN 978 0 85721 453 9

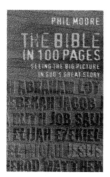

THE BIBLE IN 100 PAGES
Seeing the Big Picture in God's Great Story
Phil Moore

Most people want to discover the message of the Bible but they find it hard to see the wood for the trees. That's why this book is so helpful. It will help you to see the big picture in God's great story. It will help you to read the entire Bible with fresh eyes.

ISBN 978 0 85721 551 2

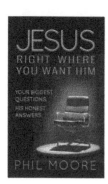

JESUS, RIGHT WHERE YOU WANT HIM
Your biggest questions. His honest answers
Phil Moore

Written in a punchy and easy-to-read style, this is a starting point for those who want to address key issues and get answers to the big questions, such as: Hasn't religion been the cause of appalling violence? Aren't Christians a bunch of hypocrites? And isn't the Bible full of myths and contradictions?

ISBN 978 0 85721 677 9

Printed and bound by CPI Group (UK) Ltd, Croydon, CR0 4YY

25/03/2025

14647347-0001